POEMS

collected / unpublished / new

with an introduction by Thomas Peacocke

LONGSPOON / NEWEST

Copyright ©1986 Wilfred Watson

Canadian Cataloguing in Publication Data

Watson, Wilfred, 1911-
Poems: collected, unpublished and new

ISBN 0-919285-32-5 (Longspoon). -- ISBN 0-920316-91-3 (NeWest)

I. Title.
PS8545.A87A17 1985   C811'.54   C85-091399-3
PR9199:3.W37A17 1985

Longspoon Press
c/o Dept. of English
University of Alberta
Edmonton, Alberta T6G 2E5

NeWest Press
#204, 8631 - 109 Street
Edmonton, Alberta T6G 1E8

Credits:
Editing for the Press: Shirley Neuman
Cover design: Jorge Frascara
Photo, front cover: Tony Haines
Photo, back cover: Ashley & Crippen
Riddle design: Jorge Frascara
Book design: Jorge Frascara, Bonnie Koenig, Shirley Neuman
Typesetting: June Charter
Layout: Bonnie Koenig
Proofreading: Steven Scott
Printing: Hignell Printers, Winnipeg
Financial Assistance: Alberta Culture
                     Canada Council

Reprinted by Athabasca University, 2008. ©This material has been copied under licence from Access Copyright. Resale or further copying of this material is strictly prohibited.

CMID# 21218

Printed on Recycled Paper

Books by Wilfred Watson

Friday's Child (Faber and Faber, 1955)
(with Marshall McLuhan) *From Cliché to Archetype* (Viking Press, 1970)

the sorrowful canadians and other poems/les malheureux (white pelican, 1972)

I begin with counting (NeWest, 1978)

Mass on cowback (Longspoon, 1982)

Gramsci x 3 (Longspoon, 1983)

CONTENTS

Previous publication of poems in this collection *viii*
Introduction, by Thomas Peacocke *xi*

invortications
three riddles for Gillian Espinasse *3*
friday's child *7*

sermon on bears
laurentian man *47*
a manifesto for beast-poetry *50*
sermon on bears *57*

bawl of wool
poems by Jenny Blake *63*
letters to the bach. of wire *105*

pièces je constate
white pelican poems (1) *145*
the sorrowful canadians and other poems/les malheureux *157*
white pelican poems (2) *207*

ngv
from I begin with counting *231*
from mass on cowback *291*

riddles *361*

Alphabetical index of titles and first lines *417*

Previous publication of poems in this collection:

Three Riddles for Gillian Espinasse were published in *Contemporary Verse,* 35 (Summer 1951).

Friday's Child:
Proserpina (1), The Flower, Proserpina (2), The Marriage with Death, and *Pasiphae* have not previously been published. The other poems in this portion of the collection were published in *Friday's Child* (London: Faber and Faber, 1955). The following also appeared in periodicals: *An Admiration for Dylan Thomas* in *Fiddlehead,* 20 (February 1954); *A Contempt for Dylan Thomas* in *Paris Review,* 9 (Summer 1955); *Graveyard on a Cliff of White Sand* in *London Magazine,* 2, 8 (August 1955); *Ballad of Mother and Son* in *Paris Review,* 10 (Fall 1955).

Laurentian Man was first published in *Prism,* 1, 1 (September 1959); *Sermon on Bears* in *Prism,* 2, 2 (Winter 1961); *A Manifesto for Beast-Poetry* in *Canadian Literature,* 3 (Winter 1960).

poems by Jenny Blake:
These poems, with the exceptions noted below, are published here for the first time. *Pome for a dead soldier, Pome of a church, Lines of flesh and bones, Pome of a wire bridegroom, Lines on the English tongue, Pome of headlines,* and *Pome of words* appeared in *The Humanities Association Bulletin* (where *Pome of a wire bridegroom* was titled *Pome of a Husband),* XIV (Fall 1963). *Dialogue between Jenny Blake and herself* was first published in *white pelican,* 1, 1 (Winter 1971).

The poems of ***Letters to the bach. of wire*** have not previously been published.

white pelican poems (1):
I Shot a Trumpet into my Brain was first published in *Canadian Literature,* 30 (Autumn 1966) and was collected in *Mass on cowback* (Edmonton: Longspoon Press, 1982). *From the Place on the Map, The Departments of Barbed Wire, On the Water Plane, Sonnet with Ragged Edges: Lines,* and *Portrait of a Woman* appeared in *white pelican,* 1, 1 (Winter 1971). *Letter to García Lorca* was published in *white pelican,* 4, 3 (Summer 1974).

The poems of ***the sorrowful canadians and other poems/les malheureux*** are from the volume of that title published in January 1972 (Edmonton: white pelican publications).

white pelican poems (2):
construction, untitled appeared in *white pelican,* 4, 3 (Summer 1974) and *construction with horizontal columns/construction avec colombes mortes* was published in *white pelican,* 5, 1 (1975). The other poems in this portion of the collection are published here for the first time.

from ***I begin with counting:***
The offshore canadians is published for the first time in this collection. All other poems in this group were published in *I begin with counting* (Edmonton: NeWest Press, 1978). *portrait of my mother the fox* was also published in *West Coast Review,* XIII, 3 (February 1979).

from ***Mass on cowback:***
re woody allen's annie hall, Taking off from nanaimo harbour, re the aboriginal protestant and *re burying an ex-prime minister* are published for the first time in this collection. *re the explosion at the power station* was published in *Island,* 13/14 (1983/84); *Picasso and gertrude stein* in *Descant,* 41 (Summer 1983); *what roy kiyooka told me* in *Canadian Forum,* LVIII, 685 (Oct/Nov 1978), as was *re shakespeare on husbandry.* The other poems in this portion of the collection were first published in *Mass on cowback* (Edmonton: Longspoon Press, 1982). *re Phyllis Webb & Wilson's Bowl* appeared at the same time in *Island,* II (1982), and *re march 3, 1980* and *deconstruction chez flahiff* were published again in *Descant,* 41 (Summer 1983).

riddles:
Diana Rigg and *Sonnet x 3* ('O uneclipsed moon') were published in *Canadian Literature,* 100 (Spring 1984). All the other sonnets and riddles are published here for the first time.

Introduction

Thomas Peacocke

My association with Wilfred Watson has been as an academic and artistic colleague, as a friend, and as an admirer of his poetry and plays, of his intellect and imagination, and of the revolutionary spirit with which he approaches his art. He has never lost his youth nor his innate capacity to relate to the young—indeed it is from that perspective that he approaches ideas, problems, and situations with a mind free of preconceptions. In fact, the child within seems a dynamic of his creative process. A young actress once remarked about him during a rehearsal, 'He seems so young!' When I told Wilfred, he responded, 'If they only realized it, I am much younger than they are.' There is some reinforcement of this in a poem written years later:

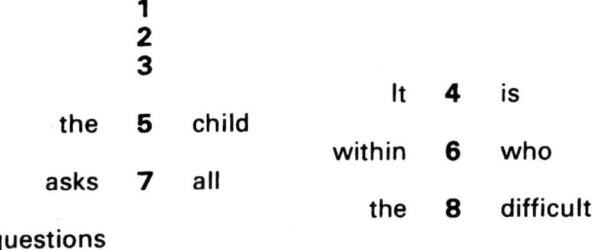

And ask questions he does.

In 1967 Wilfred Watson provided me with what was until then my most significant and moving creative experience. He had been commissioned to write a play in which he had decided to explore, in a highly original and 'with it' way, the hierarchy of Canadian society as analyzed by Kenneth Porter in *The Vertical Mosaic*. His desire to experiment with unconventional modes of presentation (at *his* suggestion we removed the seats from the theatre) and perception (he was 'at one' with Marshall McLuhan) characterized the entire rehearsal period. He constantly inspired and led cast, designer, technicians and director to new and often revolutionary approaches and theatrical techniques. So it was with the thrill of once again meeting a Watsonian challenge that I accepted the invitation to preface his collected poems. The value of reading through all the poems was clearly evident, not only for personal enjoyment and interest in reacquainting myself with familiar works and meeting new, but also because the exercise would contribute to my preparation for a production some months down the line of Wilfred's new play *Gramsci x 3*, a work which, characteristically innovative, is an extension of his exploration of poetic form (number grid verse). Just as

Watson the poet has nurtured Watson the playwright, so has Watson the playwright nourished Watson the poet. I find most of his poems intensely theatrical in that they contain elements which make them ideal vehicles for performance. So I approach the writing of this preface not from the perspective of a literary critic but as an actor, director and co-participant with Wilfred on a number of plays and staged verse readings.

It must be understood from the beginning that in the beginning was the word. And the word, for Wilfred, is at the core of it all. Right enough for a poet whose business is words—words which are the communicative tools employed to create the irridescent sensuality of his images, which are the symbols of his imaginative response to the spectrum of human experience, which are the vehicles for paradox and the catalysts for vocal as well as visual and intellectual organization, all of which are at once dominant and subversive elements in both the drama and poetry of Wilfred Watson. In the end, when his poetry and plays are brought to the performance level, they reveal a rich potential for physical expression. In that sense, I perceive Watson's poetry to be as dramatic as it is lyrical. There is a constant invitation to readers and to actors to perform it.

With that thought in mind I would like to share my personal impressions gleaned from reading (most of it aloud) this imposing volume of verse. First, what we have here is the work of a poet who is as Canadian as The Group of Seven or an inhabitant of Frye's *Bush Garden*. His myriad allusions, though often classical, are richly contemporary, ranging from the commonplace (bluejays in the backyard) to the unique (a Siberian tiger posing on a plywood slab out at Al Oeming's game farm); from the Canadian socio-political reality ('strontium ninety and Japanese strip mines') to the trauma of Vietnam ('HANOI is here'); from simple intimate personal experience (sawing wood at Chemainus, swimming with his father, or following a concrete mixer across the High Level Bridge) to more complex ones as his references to Irving Layton, Norman Yates, Kwakiutl art, Jack Shadbolt or his ceramicist friend Pauline Boote in which typically he elevates personal observation and insight into considerations of a wider dimension:

> O PAULINE, HOW APPALLING IS APOLLO
> OUR POETRY, POT
> OUR SOUL, THIS WHEEL
> OUR BURN, INTO THE THINNEST GLAZE
> AND OUR BODY, THESE CLAYS.

Each poem in the volume is the work of a highly skilled craftsman—here is one who knows his poetics and who disciplines himself accordingly. When he wishes to explore beyond traditional forms, for example, instead of employing the easy liberality of free verse, he invents a 'number grid' which begins with a set visual and metrical form, then invites a transformation to auditory expression in performance. In his introduction to *Mass on cowback* he says of 'number grid verse':

> In the jargon of the art critic, one form [the written form of space] was a treatment of *visual space,* the other form a treatment of *auditory space.* Which is the real form of the poem? Neither. The auditory form changes from performance to performance and the visual form when eye-read conceals most of what rehearsal and repetition expose. The total poem, its poetry, consists of its *transformations* from its visual to its auditory forms. This unfolding is like procreation, with an important difference. The poem after each performance folds itself up into its original visual form. It can then be opened again in new performances.

Each of the sections of the collected poems reveals a sharp change in style, form, and focus, of which number grid verse is one example. Using images and themes that emerge from his observation of the life and times in which he is involved, Wilfred Watson constantly explores new forms and approaches. This becomes clearly evident as one reads through the works in *Friday's Child* next to the *Jenny Blake* poems, next to *the sorrowful canadians,* next to *Mass on cowback,* next to the *riddles.* The enduring experimentation with the new is as refreshing as it is vital.

At the same time, a number of themes and images appear again and again in a variety of ways. Contrasting and paradoxical images are pervasive and arresting: desert and water, dark and light, agony and peace, hope and despair, shame and celebration, creation and apocalypse, life and death, crucifixion and salvation, reason and ecstasy, male/female and female/male, the wild body and the magical body. Themes concerning religion, the sanctity of life and nature, sin-guilt-expiation, social and political problems, the woman in sexual, personal and social matrices, pollution of mind and environment, contradictions and paradoxes in human behavior are all dealt with critically, compassionately, and with an implicitly celebratory view that asserts 'I praise God's kind.'

In work that I see as honest, moral and possessing integrity, I also enjoy very much the wit, humor, and mischievous spirit that are so clearly indicative of the Watson personality. For example, in one of his frequent references to academia he writes:

THE CONCENTRATION CAMP IS CAMP, WE FEEL IT IS CONTRAINDICATED, SINCE WE HAVE HAD SOME EXPERIENCE WITH CONCENTRATION CAMPUSES.

Or again, as became clear when it was presented in a choral version to a live audience, the repetition (a frequently used device) of the line '17 ways of not looking at the face of margaret atwood on the dust jacket of survival' became a series of laugh lines, a running gag that cleverly supported the rather more serious point of the poem.

As one might expect, knowing Watson's playwriting activities, there are plenty of references to the theatre, as well as to the other arts. His interest in the compelling power of art and artist as revolutionary and saviour (over scientist, politician or intellectual) is revealed in such lines as:

> I think of a role for the Canadian theatre as Viet Cong yet
> I have nightmares about
> **BELUGA WHALES IN AN ICEPOT**
> the Canadian artist in a centennial year poked at by the
> forms of helplessness he is trying to save from a doom
> beyond help

or

> HANOI IS HERE
> we have only a few poems to defend ourselves with.

Many of the poems are deceptively simple as in the *Jenny Blake* series which explores succinctly and with sly wit themes and images centered on language, honour, grief, glory, love, the power to create, the power to destroy, the nature (and power) of male/female sexuality and the nature of art:

> The words of a poem should conceal
> The poem, which hides,
>   doesn't reveal.

My reading of the *Jenny Blake* poems disclosed that I treated them rather cavalierly a few years back. Masterpieces of compression and evocation, they bear careful attention.

During the period of the Vietnam War, Watson made frequent allusions to the war itself, to the Americans and to the Viet Cong. I perceive him to have used those incidents and images to investigate not the plight of American society, but the state of human 'civilization.' In a compelling passage from 'lines, 1968,' though his images are specific, he is surely remarking on the capacity of man to escalate and become inured to the horrors described in a poem that demands to be read aloud by a group of performers:

> there were twentyfour american soldiers examining the
> body of a vietnamese child with her head shattered by a
> bomb and there were twohundredandforty american soldiers
> examining the bodies of ten vietnamese children children
> with their heads shattered by a bomb and there were
> twentyfourhundred american soldiers examining the bodies
> of one hundred vietnamese girl children with their heads
> shattered by a bomb but I lost count that's the trouble with
> escalation you lose count but please believe me it was quite
> an experience.

In his wide-ranging examination of the Canadian psyche Watson makes a strong contribution to the ever growing national mythology. In *Laurentian Man* he muses wickedly over our beginnings:

> When indefatigable God decided to make a new man, *homo
>   Canadiensis*
> He somewhat dubiously supposed that pulverized
> Laurentian Shield would do all right as a corporeal basis,
> Because (I give only a few of the Divine Reasons)
> Though it's a phlegmatic conservative old-fashioned dust
> More than a few centuries dour, without the least vein of humour,
> And puritanic to a geologic fault, still,
> It reddens with a blush of past granitic fire

and later in the poem:

> . . . the first Canadian stood gaping
> At him, with that magnificent blank complacency,
> That awful monotony of face, that face to face
> Blankness of mind, all cattle grass and trees, all wood and beef.

In *the sorrowful canadians* he laments:

> the radiant grief of the owners of so much
> snow
> THE SORROWFUL CANADIANS...
> MAKES ME INTO A SORROWFUL
> CANADIAN
> to have so much world in a world where men
> have so little.

Later, in 're burying an ex-prime minister' (John Diefenbaker) he as much as trumpets a call to arms:

```
            Now     7   our Canada
                                rises   8   up
9   before
        us to avenge    1   itself
          on us and     2   ours, its
        economics the   3   economics
                                of the  4   wasteland
              of the    5   private sector
                            the wasteland   6   of the
            cultural    7   sector, the
                                wasteland   8   of the
9   poverty
              sector,   1   its politics consisting
                of a    2   phantasmagoria ravaged
              by ten    3   provincial monsters
                                and an  4   enormous
           dragon, in   5   mortal combat with
                            each other.     6   This
           Canada is    7   real, its
                                nightmares  8   real.
```

To visit the home of Sheila and Wilfred Watson is to be surrounded by sounds (music, birds), by sculptures and masks, by the Moores, the Lewis's, the Shadbolts, the Yates's, by books, articles, newspapers, television, references to which are pervasive in the poetry. And there is the conversation—the unending intellectual stimulation and theatricality of the dialogue initiated by the two of them is a vibrant evocation of those 'spaces' referred to by Marshall McLuhan.

> ... McLuhan supposed visual space to be the space men think in and auditory space to be the space we live in. I think of visual space as being the space into which we write, paint pictures, build monuments; and of auditory space as the space into which we perform—not quite the same thing as the space we live in, which I think of as the aggregate (*in toto,* virtually unthinkable) of all the spaces we deal with. (from the introduction to *Mass on cowback*)

When one visits the Watsons, one lives in 'spaces.' The operative word for me in the above quotation is 'perform' which appears in Wilfred's thinking to be a distillation of the space we live in. It would seem to have been a natural aspect of living for him to have involved himself in the *performing* art of the theatre. His work at Edmonton's Studio Theatre (with Gordon Peacock, Bernard Engel and myself), his theatrical compositions during the adventurous heyday of the Yardbird Suite (principally with Bud D'Amur), offered opportunities to explore those theatrical elements that progressively have infused themselves in his verse.

The dramatic sensibilities that have emerged over the years in his verse he was given an early chance to exercise in a series of programs which he anthologized and helped stage at *The Torches,* an outdoor theatre situated on the campus at the University of Alberta. The programs were annual events which closed the summer theatre season and were produced under the title *From Under the Black Bridge.* At least half of the poems were written by Edmontonians, the 'Black Bridge' being the High Level Bridge which spans the 'saddest and grandest' of rivers—the North Saskatchewan. Poems and poem excerpts would be arranged side by side in the programs for a number of logical reasons such as the flow of a particular image or theme through two or three poems or for contrast or to facilitate a group or choral reading, and so on. What was quickly discovered was that often quite by accident exciting and unanticipated implications, nuances, associations and dramatic tensions were detonated. Movement patterns, compositions, opportunities for orchestration and repetition beyond those conceived by Wilfred began to emerge as the performers transformed the written to the spoken word. What would begin as a careful, controlled, safe staging would suddenly erupt into something much more adventurous and exciting; instead of using just the stage, we began to move into the entire spatial environment: the roof, indoor corridors and rooms, the lawn outside the front entrance. The poems began to 'take off' and acquired unexpected meanings and dimensions. For Shakespeare's four hundredth birthday, Wilfred constructed a program which, for the first half, featured sonnets, monologues, and scenes from number of the plays. In the second half, all hell broke loose (as did a few of the audience!) as he juxtaposed excerpts from Shakespeare with Beckett, Beckett with Albee and so on. Can you imagine Martha being followed right on by Lady Macbeth? It was a kind of theatrical surrealism that invited further exploration—though it did cause an official from the British Arts Board to gulp in disapproving amazement.

In plays like *Cockrow and the Gulls, Oh Holy Ghost, Dip Your Finger in the Blood of Canada and Write I Love You,* and *Let's Murder Clytemnestra According to the Principles of Marshall McLuhan,* he and his theatre colleagues experimented with dramatic form, with language (particularly the use of repetition) and with elements of design that included not just the stage, but the entire theatre, as well as technology (slides, t.v. cameras and monitors, etc.) and particularly sound—notably those sounds that were produced by the human voice.

In the poems in *the sorrowful canadians, I begin with counting, Mass on cowback,* and now in *riddles,* there is for me a performance imperative. Staged readings from most of the above works at such varied venues as The Humanities Theatre on the University of Alberta campus, Latitude 53 (Art) Gallery, and the small community Westmount Library provided performers, directors and writer the opportunity to explore with great variety of approach and staging the transformation from visual space to auditory space. It is no accident that *young* people like Alison Davies, Donna Gruhlke, Larry Popowich, Henry van Ryk, and David Sereda were heavily involved in these projects.

These performances with their rich, sometimes linear, sometimes surrealistic qualities of imagery, sound, repetition and paradox can be disorienting to an ear which is conditioned to receiving complete sentences and logical syntax. I believe the performance of Watson's verse offers the potential for insights beyond the literal, because in a sense it requires a new 'posture of the mind.' Writing in *From Cliché to Archetype,* Watson and McLuhan state:

> Paradox was the means by which early theological science made its discoveries. Paradox is the posture of the mind when, like a boxer balanced on two feet, it is feinting for an opening. Scientific discovery is always attended by paradox. Newtonian science, with its 'circumspect' experimental method, assumes that God is both rational and arbitrary.

When the apple fell on Newton's head, so to speak, a new 'posture of the mind' was created for the scientist. He no longer perceived things in terms of a single physical model: as a result light behaved not only as rays, but also as particles. The physicist accepts this and uses it in his work. Perhaps Watson in his use of paradox, repetition and rearranged syntax as experienced in the performance of his work is doing a similar thing with *words* as the tool.

Another passage that appears later in *From Cliché to Archetype* is pertinent to Watson's poetry:

> When the painter Degas complained to Mallarmé that though he was overflowing with ideas for poems, the poems wouldn't jell, Mallarmé replied, 'My dear Degas, poems are not made with ideas, they are made with words.'
>
> ... The point about the story of Degas and Mallarmé is precisely the new willingness to regard language as pigment, as unique material from which to create unique effects.

That Wilfred Watson has regarded language as 'a unique material from which to create unique effects' is clear to one who has experienced the works in performance. It has been of interest to me to return to the earlier poems and to discover that his intentions were clear from the beginning. In *A Manifesto for Beast-Poetry,* he writes:

> whether a man dances
> or whether a man makes music
> or whether he gestures or paints a picture or carves sculptures
> (or simply is)
> *words* keep recurring. It isn't
> sufficient merely to dance, this won't do for a man.
> He must dance a madrigal.
> He must caper to the words of a ballad.
> Or if he makes water—
> but all this verbal antic, the desperate endeavour to speak
> is quite foreign to beast-poetry.
> Let us understand this, that beast-poetry uses words in a totally
>   new way,
> it uses words as experiences. It excludes speech.
> Beast-poetry is profoundly uneloquent.

Words are used to be, not to speak. He continues later in the poem, as if charting his personal artistic course:

> . . . I call out aloud to the future
> I summon the age about to be
> not to debase itself in any petty way to the sub-human,
> but to cut itself off boldly from all its ancestors;
> to descend impudently down to the shameless depths
> of beast-poetry. I am weary
> of this shabby-parrot, this figurative lingerie,
> and of the free & easy verse opinions.
> I await the terrible new beast-poetry

I await the terrible new Watson poetry.

Jasper National Park
August, 1985

WILFRED WATSON
invortications

three riddles
for Gillian Espinasse
Saga hwaet ic hatte

Three Riddles for Gillian Espinasse
Saga hwaet ic hatte

I. The Candle

Night kindles me and calls to light my flower
yet this my glory must my life devour.
My blossom guts upon a stalk of flax,
consumes my fatness; there dwindles in me
substance not mine, another's prosperity.
This is my one boast. My bones of wax
a summer's sun will break; and yet a sun
I call myself, though my high noon
is night. A puff of wind my brilliance
will gut, or turn it to a madman's dance.
By me, let all mankind behold their frame;
I measure darkness with a little flame.

II. Time

Sharp is my eyesight as the needle I ply
for things at hand: I am your tailor, short of eye;
prick, prick, prick, my needle goes
to stitch you up from head to toes.
The naked babe I clothe, the growing child,
boy and girl, man and woman I have beguiled
with my round open innocent face —
yet I am bent double with my needle; I lack grace
and by my task I am a hunchback bowed:
the only clothes I sew at is a shroud.
I am a menial to eternity
say some; discover my mystery.

. . .

III. The Mirror

Self-knowledge, said the Greek philosopher,
we should before all other kinds prefer —
did my opinions clear obscurity
within my bosom you yourself might see;
even the secret shadow of your heart
I'd show; but look, and you and I must part.
Say who I am — say why to love my truth
there is more needed than the eyes of youth;
why he who loves me is either vain or blind
to look within my breast and pleasure find.
O, if you are wise, you cannot lack my name:
you are far wiser to know what I am;
for I am Socrates' fool — emblemed in me
let him who'd know himself, his sorrow see.

friday's child

Invocation

Appear, O mother, was the perpetual cry
of lost Aeneas, and you did take care of him;
though Dido felt the iron of your whim.
Our shrouds are sea-rotten; and our keels
are rust and weeds; broken is our limb;
our winded oar is master of our wills.
You've let us go, and we are homeless men;
first pleasure our dreams, lady, and return
and let your worship kindling guide us in,
renewed by your own apparition.
O love, teach us to love you, that we may
through burning Carthage take our way.

The White Bird

Because we were baffled
and somebody said,
what is that great white bird that flies overhead

we have shot the white bird
that flies overhead
and now we have done so, I'm glad it is dead.

*Who shot the white bird
that flies overhead?*
Why, no one at all, it was shot by the crowd.

*Was no one arrested
that shot the bird dead?*
Why no one, of course, for they thought it best dead.

*And did you shoot the white bird
that flew overhead?
Did you drop your eyes and look on it dead?*

I shot the white bird
that flew overhead.
And what was the use, now you've shot the bird dead?

There was no use at all
to shoot the bird dead.
Now get me a drink, for I shot the bird dead.

And Should She Ask

Of conflagrant Troy tower the flaming stalk
a torch I blossomed in my mother's bowel;
and should she ask what fire burned in her heart,
when in her heart my blood she did distil,
tell her
what blood this blood has spilt.

That web of fate which tortured sinful Thebes,
I knotted up within my mother's groin;
and should she ask what sorrowed in her flesh
when in her side my eyes were but blind seeds,
tell her
what things these eyes have seen.

Mouth of the mouth that hungered Pharaoh's house,
I was the serpent in my mother's breast;
and should she ask, what at her breast lay there,
when at her pap I eased her of her milk,
tell her,
what lying mouth her milk did lap.

At crotch of Golgotha, a place of skull,
I was the nail that nailed my mother's bone;
and should she ask what rankled in her womb,
when in her womb my hands lay folded there,
tell her
how there ingrew these hangman's hands.

An Admiration for Dylan Thomas

Creation's Welshman walks behind his eyelids
foot after foot in the furrow of the drought,
foot after foot that droll knave walks his walk
to plant his green wish in a saddened mouth
till the three bagfuls of his seed are sown
till the ten acres of his will are done.

Creation's laughing peasant who cannot weep
tears that another man must hide or drown
raises two sticks and a rag in a windy field
to laugh the crow and all such vermin down
till the three bagfuls of his seed are sown
till the ten acres of his will are done.

He is the droll farmer of Ezekiel's farm
and turns his plough against that bony lot
and walks his draughty bulls against the wind,
with his loud tongue lashes his oxen on
till the three bagfuls of his seed are sown
till the ten acres of his will are done.

His peasant hands will clap all God's winds down,
his loud tongue lash his draughty oxen on
till every jawbone shouts and sprouts in leaf,
till every eye socket shoots blades of corn,
and the three bagfuls of his seed are sown
and the ten acres of his will are done.

A Contempt for Dylan Thomas

sir Thomas, stark green until he crept acurl
into the bed of marriage, put ripeness on
in the soft white embraces of a girl,
misliked the very thought of such conjunction
and wished that we could love like plants and trees
joined by the trade of winds and hairs of bees.

poor Turleygod Thomas, his images askew
when men were making things of men, would hint
(being afraid no heaven can be true)
that thinghood is the heaven of the saint,
that man, poor gull, must wet his burning wings
and sink them in the sea of peaceful things.

o ragged Thomas, to stones, flowers, fire
believing, may not stones lie, fire fever in its flame,
and trees endure an agony of flower?
can we, to comprehend and feel its shame
creep into the full bosom of a stone
too dull to speak and make its hurt sense known?

Graveyard on a Cliff of White Sand

By the unwashed beach
of the falling lake
there were three dead fish
collapsed in the belly;
and they were the walk
of ant and fly
who walked out of the cast and throw
of the mouldy wreath
when the gravedigger
hurried in the yellow
blow of the aspen leaf
and the tear shrank
into the mourner's eye

O mother grieving
the grief that is common and human
O woman wonderful
in your small miracle
of faith and loving —
quiet you, that another miracle
must come and the wind blow
into the troubles of the sky
the dust you place
on the upraised hand
of this high cliff — quiet you
that fence of rust
cannot keep, that ring
of cement cannot contain
when the gravedigger
spends his pay
and the wreaths moulder away

O love this world
if you can
where juniper
burns blue its cones
of seed and the whispering
weed candles and the moth
reshapes its figure
and the owl
owls it in the gully
and the hawk
hawks it and the cougar
pads out love's melancholy

this world, where
the bones shrink into
the grave and the cliff
whitens with birth
and the dead wave
is pierced by the living
reed, and love weeps
to fill the earth

Windermere Lake, B.C.

Love Song

Never, till out of my thought
you walked into the shadow of my heart —
till the pearl of your beauty
swung like a tear from my eye
did I know that the pleasure
of love is a grief made greater;
that by loving grows grieving
as by grieving, loving;
that love in its simple essence
is death mourned to magnificence;
that the requiem of the last day
and the world folded and put away
sang in its sought-for bliss,
the kiss of peace, its kiss

Ghosts

Purple and red hyacinths
before their fading
are bells tolling
the sleeper to the apparition
of beauty, the angel in the room
which like a ghost
comes and departs
leaving a wonder and a horror
in our unspeakable hearts

The Pearl

The whiteness of the lamb
Adam could see in a dream —
but think you of the pearl
how it grew in the wet shell
and tomb of the coral
and drowning sea

Think you of the pearl.
Its whiteness is all
I sing. And out
of the murders of the incrusted heart
would distil
and give you to know
the white pity of the pearl

To the Shadbolts with Six Quinces from Duncan

The equivocation of the fiend
within this rind.
An excellent favour
in its face, a delicate flavour
within, but bite deep
and there's bitterness asleep
that sinks into the teeth —
a fragrance in its breath
but rottenness underneath.
Though it is fable
to ascribe evil to the apple
who will doubt the mother of sins
ate evil in the quince?

Song for St. Lucy's Night

Long is the night, none longer
knits all the while time's finger
the skein
of dark wool
which binds us
to sleep and tangles
phantoms into our turning
and unquiet minds

Summer is far, longest ago
the melting of the snow,
the frog stirred mud, the unlocked water
the tree standing in
the almost but never
unseen once blush
of green

Orpheus and Eurydice

Hell granted this — she given back to him
behind him hastens upward into light;
he must not look behind him or her bright
and warming person, or else by the grim
inexorable decree her bodiless limb
to flesh restored, in death must fade from sight,
and she again go from him into night;
again, more immaterial than a dream.
The abysm below; in him the fatal flaw —
she cries, and firmer holds him by the hand;
he turns; and looking towards hell he saw
her face, and saw the beauty that did draw
him, in one last look which lost it; a wind
the rising wind of hell, upblows to find
and take his love light as a wisp of straw.

Proserpina (1) The Flower

There was an odor of magnificence
about this flower — simplicity her petal:
but thereby hangs the very root of hell.
And fair as knowledge seems to ignorance
so shone this flower upon her innocence;
and if she plucked it, it plucked her as well;
but her own person multiplied its spell,
her own attraction drawing drew her hence.
Yet if its blossom took her, still its root
took her in but half unwilling marriage;
and then the penalty, half to discover
she must herself from flesh and blood dissever,
and as a shade a shade be taught her manage;
drawn from the kindly earth, home to her foot
returning yes, but so returning never.

Proserpina (2) The Marriage with Death

She in that iron hall, the home of shades
(at last the iron entering her soul)
calls bitter honey, honey bitter gall,
as those who love truth for its power to spoil,
in love with bitterness; the woman fades
even as she changes the abducted maid's
mien, and becomes hell's, by process marital:
so often marriage is the door to hell
without grace of such supernatural aids
Pluto with charms deceiving. To her lips
she the red fruit of carnal knowledge takes
and wipes her mouth; and her dark husband clips
the King of Death, and in his arms she aches
not for the kindly earth home to her feet
but for this ghostly love love's counterfeit.

Pasiphae

All their women's talk of monsters born
was chilled by this, forth from her body torn;
silent they eye each other and the grim worn
mother; their toil, her fruit; and stubborn
she wears out an impenitent agony
and labours to expel the thing which she
conceived, faithless to kind and kin; to free
her body grown large with enormity.
This sullen labour long her flesh remembers
the kindless thought which swelling at her heart
grew to this shape and from her side now tears
its way and life; and reaches for her breast
in likeness of this thought and of the beast
whereon she most unnaturally did feast.

Tarquin

Not so, not so, she cries — but now he's lit
at death's white taper, and from its waxy
tongue takes flame her ravelled dress torn flax
to crumple in his flaring hands and light
flame firefling up to the burning roof hit
caught. Now she the burning house forsakes
but at her door with his rash hands he rakes
hot coals to fire the last beams sills of it.
And is become all loves incendiaries
who the dour cold traitorous house have sacked,
consideration, honour, marriage;
cold flesh is like a harlot, and complies
and her aching vein is filled with outrage
till he too sickens at his empty act.

Lines for Elsie Jack

In this world of illusion on illusion
do not say that my prison is my delusion;
that I may (though I dare, can, will not)
walk through my bars, and shatter my self's rote.

In this wild of illusion and illusion
do not say that a cobweb is my chain;
that my will's filament holds my freedom
spinning pride, to keep the prodigal from home.

For I dote upon my will, and this being so
the scissoring of my death my flesh must know;
thank God, I have this little happiness
to wish my will could will its nothingness.

Wish does not will; for once, I turned to seize
the reins of life, to call upon my peace.
It were a simple act, were it but done
but for this act my force fell from me like a stone.

Therefore I shall praise God who sends his death
out of my mouth to suck forth my ill breath;
else, how could I, without this surgery
cure my heart of imposthuming misery?

A Curse of Dahlias

He who cuts off on a short stalk
a bloody sun;
let him fear what's done;
if he bring it into a room
it'll shout his doom;
if he put it in a vase,
he in a craze
shall end his days —
let all my fingers and wishes be one
never to pluck the sun.

Of Hendrickje as Bathsheba

Here is an image shaped with human warmth;
this image which I see before me now
dismisses from my mind all condemnation
and I approve the king's lust for this woman.

King David's royal sin before me glows:
behold the captain's wife whose beauty seen
took David's eyes in an adultery
ignobly famous in its perfidy.

And seeing it, all my base lust takes fire;
and in my breast the fickle human heart
would swell its forked flood with a like amour;
and send the captain to the cuckold's cure.

But if imagination is a stick
to beat upon that hollow drum our heart
there's countermotion in a thought to bring
its music to some sort of chastening.

And looking on this magnificent Bathsheba
which Rembrandt painted with an old man's care
I think how noble and voluptuous
this tenant is, living in such a house,

the bodily temple of Hendrickje's soul,
Hendrickje's body in its simple fact,
the human body in all its luxury,
in all its bodily felicity;

here is all human pride and magnificence
given us in a shadow's narrowness;
yet must Hendrickje's body painted so
have kindled the woman in its show

who for the interval of modelling
became Bathsheba; and waits a princely lure
upon this canvas, till the colours fade
and perish forever past the repairer's aid;

. . .

waits in the consciousness of all her beauty;
waits in the pride of all her beauty's power;
yet waits half sorrowful that she is taught
by her own beauty that a king is naught,

majesty nothing. This canvas darkens
upon the terrible poetry of our clay;
but I forget Rembrandt and his Hendrickje,
and only see King David's Bathsheba,

who knew her husband done unto the death;
who bore that dead son from King David's loin;
and then bore to the king at length forgiven
the wise and sorrowful man, Solomon.

Lines: I Praise God's Mankind in an Old Woman

I praise God's mankind in an old woman:
I hear him rattle the body of an old wife
dry and brown, and bitter as bracken,
her stalk womb-cancelled, seer with seedgone;
with shrivel fingers clutching upon her life,
wrestling for the empty pod and the dry leaf.
But still in her mildewed eyes moist's last token —
but o, ever in her eyes the flash and strife,
husk edge, cruel and sharp as any knife
which not God's death itself can unsharpen.
Not all the frosts marching to this last March
frost, not all the suns flaming to August
the last, dry-dried her spirit to adust;
she her own frost and sun at last must
fetch — to blaze within and her soul's spirit parch
into a desert — her own contracted flame;
her radical sin, this sin at last to tame.
May she like the fathers by the desert broken
in her own desert find at last salvation.

The Windy Bishop

    There are seven hills
    stood like hunched
    cattle with their tails
    curled in, enduring
    the pasture of days,
    stood in the morning
    light of my town
when the windy bishop preached me my dust

    a sermon of snow
    on a text of cold.
    The sun was his
    wandering candle
    flame and the sky
    his draughty cathedral
    and even the busy worm
    was glum at my feet
when the windy bishop preached me my dust —

    Me? — Me, I hurried my
    deaf heart home
    and sure — I could
    have reached it safe
    but stumbled, came
    to my harm and there
    was no mercy in what
    he was saying — none,
when the windy bishop preached me my dust

    a sermon of snow.
    His slippery phrase
    chattered in my teeth
    sank into my gums
    drew tears from my eyes
    sucked dry my marrow
    drilled my breastbone —
and the windy bishop preached at my heart

    through the hole
    in my life. Flakes of cold
    curdled my blood
    into sleet, my limb
    stiffened, and I stood dumb
    in the sick of fear.
    Even the fox shuddered
    in his pelt and the hills
    huddled like cattle
when the windy bishop lashed me with his word,
when the windy bishop preached my heart home.

    O son of Mary, merciful
    father, and ghost all
    holy, save us from
    the wrath of Calvin
    from the wrath of Rome;
    save us from good priests
    and your many churches —
    but above and beyond all
    save us from the terrible
    words and text
of the windy bishop who'd preach our dust home.

In the Cemetery of the Sun

For the first Monday of my week
of darkness came May's last month. October
wrath of Mayspring breathed on a smoulder
of chrysanthemum, till it was dark
shrivel, till it was the first sun
of frost, till the cold of my fever
breathed in the octave and after
of the saintspring and feast of May,
dry and dry its weather of leaves,
dry and cold and dry its flower,
in the toward and paltry of death's unnecessary

there stood the skullbrow of my death's
hill (and I saw seven partridge
in a brown apparition walk across
my grave of grass, my prairie of grave,
birds of the earth made gross for winter
their fat breast bosomed in the sun's
light, though the darkness of my hill was
fat behind them, as they walked across
my morning and went) till my last day

sang into my eyes. In the cemetery of the sun below
all the houses of the living were tombs;
and I saw Calgary a hill of tombstones
rising under a coast of mountains
washed in the cold of my sun of cloud.
When I walked to the wither of my day
in this city where every backyard had
its cross and clothesline white and sere
with sereclothes shining in the sun
of my first despair of resurrection

came my first Monday of darkness. It
was the week's hanging and drying noon.
All the drought of my bones was for water
and the ghosts of my people flapped about
me in this washday blow and weather.
But though I bent in the drown of sun
to the mutter of sleeve and sheet
I could not find heart or answer
to answer that morning the winter
upstart and May of this October
wording me even to the spring of doom.

Canticle of Darkness

Remind you, that there was darkness in my heart
and into the darkness in my heart
sang light, and the singing light
comprehended the darkness, but the darkness —
how could the darkness comprehend
the singing light ringing in my heart?
Which was not peace but storm, the gull
flying, and the water pouring its wave
into the wind's teeth, and the gull
crying into the mouth of the harbour
which was not peace but the sea's jaw

Know you, that all knowing must sing again
in the love which sang, the first light commanded,
the waters divided, the earth parcelled out
for flowers, beasts and creeping things,
the air given for birds,
the sun made round and warm,
the moon mild as milk — but how can I begin?
For the singing light was wrath not peace —
O Venus, your love was the sea's jaw

Best you, might we not lie sleeping in the dark
of darkness, in the nothing which is our womb?
Lie sleeping and never cough at the air?
Lie sleeping soft, folded up quiet and warm?
And never suckle the teats of despair?
Does not the singing light, sing us into the storm,
light us to the tomb? O Mary, the door
of our home, O let the night cover
the light which is our doom

Stand gentle in my words. It was
the Friday of roses. And there was a rose
singing the red song of your blossom.
When I came to the rose, there was
Gethsemane. When I came to Gethsemane
there was the rose. Stand gentle in my words
it was the Friday of Golgotha, the place
of skull. O cross of petals —
O crossed petals —
stand gentle in my words. For I thought
it was the rose of crucifixion, till I knew
it was the rose of resurrection. Stand
gentle in my words. Saying I saw

. . .

the things of the world drop their skins.
Saying I saw white wings swanning in
endless flocks of white. Saying I saw
the earth like a white lamb walking
beside the mother ewe. Saying I heard
the nations like a lost calf bawling
for the mud flanks of the cow. Stand
gentle in my words. I saw the darkness
tremble. I heard the darkness singing.

Tell you, darkness was pierced by the rose
which vanished in a sun. Tell you, it was
a sun of glory the singing rose was
saying. From the rose to the woman.
From the woman to the man. From the man
to the sun. From the sun to the earth,
beasts, and all creeping things. To the waters
divided. To the light created. And the singing
rose sang in the lap of Mary. Darkness
sang to the light and the kiss of love was peace.

The Boy and the Shepherds

It was the simple
and all unknowing shepherds
who walking in the common
heart came from their
wintry sheep
and the fields
covered with ashes
of frost to kneel
down in their smocks
smelling of wool
the very first
in the stable
but they led in
kings after them
bearded in wisdom;
and the shepherded kings
were amazed at the wit
of the woolwound
heart, quicker and surer
than they to follow
the cockcrow star
by the sheepdung path
to the cradle.
So now past the dog
barking in a doorway
of snow and mumbling
the kitchen light
smelling of warm
bread, all the counted days
of December, down
lighted streets and
round earth's shopwindowed
corners shall
the applefaced boy
with his howling heart
full of toys lead back
out of Herod's kingdom
and call
to the cockcrow
star ablaze
in the stable
and like the shepherds
bring the wiser
and abler back

. . .

to where the horned cow
stood shy in the manger
and the milch ass
munched wisdom at
her thin wisp of hay
when the rafters
were white with
angels and cherubs
stood in the shadow
of the barn corner
burning like lamps
over the cradle

A Valediction for the End of the Year

    Do not begin loving
    to grieve now
by the waters quelling
the tides, under the sun rolling
in a broad wheel down the harbour
under the gull's foot, its fire
    soft and warm
    as catsfur

    Do not begin loving
    to reach now
in your dogwood and appleblossom
hour, at the web of fire
at the wings of blood in the air
at the houses falling
down through your milklit
    and lambwarm days
    crying mercy
    into your bosom
    forever

    Do not begin loving
    to weep now
how the gull laughs by the sea
at the houses falling forever —
her wing alive in the brow
of the salt mountain, in her fishy
    and clamshell blow
    and odour

    Do not begin loving
    to laugh now
at the dolphin's scholar
the boy dropping his line
into the tiding water
upon a narrow bench
under the dark coast of his father,
    when the wind blows brine
    and crab stench
    creeps into the houses
    falling forever

    . . .

      Do not begin loving
         to rail now
and storm at the old woman of the tides
sitting at the crawl of her thumbs
rank with fishblood, wasps for fingers and hands
knitting our lives from the wick
      and wool of lambs
      for the houses
      falling forever

      Do not begin loving
         to dumb now
your prayer but pray now even
for the old woman of the waters
the gull galls, and the heron,
for the old woman crossing
and breeding all creatures
      in the weathers
      of her waspnest brow

      so may the Lord bless
         your loving
and have all mercy upon your soul
and wrap it in white lamb's wool
      and bind
         it white to the world's end.

Love Song for Friday's Child

1.
then nor
any day nor
any moment neither
but now — ever and ever
it was, and the Garden of Eden was
the day before. The first
love of the world, the curst
first marriage poured
into my veins its heaven
and centuries of birds sang laughter
into my heart of rafters
till the tomb egg broken
a bell rang and swung its thought
white in the pulse and stanch
of my black blood's branch

2.
then nor
any day nor
any moment neither, but now
she stood more
woman, in the pity of the fall,
Eve, or none at all;
and coming to their great bed
her children
the blood of ages bled
for, till I saw
the moon rising in her tears,
as she left them sleeping
to Humpty Dumpty tragical
the battered doll
the cow with the crumpled horn

. . .

3.
it was sherry in the throat
and brandy burning
like angels thronging
in the nightingale dumbing
and bird hushing
song of the water
which rang like wine
in the wedding chamber,
the bride blushing
under the miracle
and every corner post
drunker
than Caesar

4.
I know that the drunkard
sobbing his woe
into his sordid
cup forever cries
to the music
he hears unheard
of the miracle
of the water poured;
that he hears the mother's
received reminder;
that he worships the gesture
of the miracle
in the depth and soil of his soul;
that his cup is a lamp swinging
forever, that the devil
cannot twist all thread
to evil cord

5.
it was cup breaking
my heart knew, and the drunkard's cry
against the hard mercy of the flaming sword
and the garden barred;
and cup seeking
led me to her eye, Eve's,
to the joy that fell
in the day before
in the day that was Garden of Eden;
till the cup over ran again
and the water poured rang again
the miracle of Cana —
O Mother of Sorrows, standing
by your Son hanging,
the love that began again
ask for us, and again and again
world without end

6.
O fell the fall
of Adam, the taken rib woman'd
the man and woman completed
in the flesh corrupted;
the serpent smiled in his tree of thorns
at the river of swans,
at the sun white with lambs;
and the seed of Adam that was mastodon
fell, and my Adam's dream
fell, my dream fell
of Ruth in your lonely field,
of Helen with Troy blaze in your hair,
of Heloise among your nuns,
of Eve, then, your own daughter —
till the thinking heart
untied its loving thought

. . .

7.
then nor
any day nor
any moment neither
but now, for ever and ever
it was, and you from the tomb
come running with Mary
and white in her hand the pearl
shining, and the saint my bawd,
procuress of my hereafter;
the first breakfast the marriage of saints;
the kiss holy;
before no door;
and the ceremony of love
beyond the joining of hands, entire;
beyond oathmaking taking and breaking
beyond eye heart soul
in praise worship and prayer

For Anne, Who Brought Tulips

Let these trumpets tongued with dust blow their magnificent
brief music; not for the exigent
last moment, when the creature at last comes home
to reason, order, proportion, doom;
but in a period of disordered haste
let them blow their blast
to mark the ceremony of season
when all the weather is unreason.

Ballad of Mother and Son

    O tree my mother
your trunk is old. Green and deep lives your leafy branch
    and each green leaf winks its eye
    with humming bird, sparrow and lemon finch
      O tree my mother
    what do you see with all those eyes, old mother?
I see a black albatross hang over my grave and I fear tomorrow's weather

      O fox my mother
your nose is sharp and your bark so old and wise
    yet you primp and strut in your red fur
    and swear you'll wear no other
      O fox my mother
    what do you prink up your ears for, old mother?
I shudder my son for the hounds and I fear tomorrow's weather

      O clock my mother
the world has a cold in its nose and sits as sad as a stone
    even the south wind has a catarrh
    and the moon tells the misery of women
      O clock my mother
    why do your teeth chatter so old mother?
I think the sun wears out, my child, and I fear tomorrow's weather

      O goose my mother
you stand like a peasant on the webbed feet of the swan
    you rail like a fishwife, and yet, my mother
    yours is the white majestic swan feather
      O goose my mother
    what do you honk at now, old mother?
I saw God like a trout in a creek and I brave tomorrow's weather

      O chimney-pot my mother
you crown my house and roof, your breath though dark is warm
    up through cold grates of sweating iron
    you drew my living fire
      O chimney-pot my mother
    why do you darken the sky, old mother?
I darken the sky, my son, to show up tomorrow's weather

       O camel my mother
your double hump and your tawny serpent head —
    into the fabulous beast of burden
    sainted ass, elk and llama woven
       O camel my mother
    how will you thread your humps through the needle's eye,
                                           old mother?
As I threaded my life through your life, my son, braving
                              tomorrow's weather

       O bottle my mother
three fingers up and three fingers down and only three fingers more
    of the drink that teases anguish, mother
    for the neck is long to pour
       O bottle my mother
    what if you reach the last drop, old mother?
When I drain the last drop, my son, I'll wait tomorrow's weather

       captain my mother
       captain my mother
the wave smacks at the gull and the sea-wrack tide is full
    the sour-cat wave claws the clinker wall
    of the boat that keens the wind
       captain my mother
    where keens the wind to, old mother?
I drop my nets, my son, my son, to catch tomorrow's weather

Yeats and Maud Gonne

He was an Irishman who sought
most passionately for wisdom, never caught;
and for a fool she took him, but when won
she cried out, Go, for I am ever gone

Gone was she, with a mind and heart as cracked
as ever did herself, or any, hurt;
but he was wisdom's lover — such a one
had best have gone when she said, I am gone

What beauty this? Into her hair she weaves
the fascination of her country's griefs;
and bound her eyes with Ireland's dying sun
that he must stay, though she cry, I am gone

put in her bosom Ireland's fading rose
and even the worm that keeps its bawdy-house
supplied by fornication with the stone
knows why he stayed when she cried, I am gone

but scholars, duller worms, best understand
what anger made him call her angry mind
a pair of bellows — hating its leather lung
that croaked, Arise, the Time will soon be gone

God chose his Hangmen, men of English race
to hint his wrath. But they rebuked his grace;
forgiving no woman her beauty, they imprison
this one, crying late, I long ago was gone

To her in tawdry exile, he must come;
but still the word he wants is cold and dumb;
she'll not divide herself to make him one;
but cries, Leave me, as I from you have gone

And then he goes. And then he goes, his mind
in loss of wisdom gaining human kind;
then she was his; apart, old and alone
she kept him with her cry, Stay, I am gone

Wisdom's a lovely swan, but I think never
took mortal man both egg and shining feather:
now let the schools unlatch this meditation
and moralize this cry, Stay, I am gone

Emily Carr

Like Jonah in the green belly of the whale
overwhelmed by Leviathan's lights and liver
imprisoned and appalled by the belly's wall
yet inscribing and scoring the uprush
sink vault and arch of that monstrous cathedral,
its living bone and its green pulsing flesh —
old woman, of your three days anatomy
Leviathan sickened and spewed you forth
in a great vomit on coasts of eternity.
Then, as for John of Patmos, the river of life
burned for you an emerald and jasper smoke
and down the valley you looked and saw
all wilderness become transparent vapour,
a ghostly underneath a fleshly stroke,
and every bush an apocalypse of leaf

Letter to Dorothy Bazett

Letters are hearses and this one brings
my dead thoughts, relics not of living things
and these words coffins which the corpses bear
of my past senses, melted upon the air:
yet as the living live best who think death
often and before dead things draw quick breath
friend's letters have this office, they
are the obituaries of yesterday
to tell the living what death takes away;
and what we have felt and thought must be
a ghost to haunt us to futurity —
may these words have such ghosts, that they appear
innocent, not causing horror, but dear
friend's ghosts, that upon goodness' errands come
because their love removed will not be dumb

WILFRED WATSON
sermon on bears

Laurentian Man*

1.
When indefatigable God decided to make a new man, *homo
    Canadiensis*
He somewhat dubiously supposed that pulverized
Laurentian Shield would do all right as a corporeal basis,
Because (I give only a few of the Divine Reasons)
Though it's a phlegmatic conservative old-fashioned dust
More than a few centuries dour, without the least vein of humour,
And puritanic to a geologic fault, still,
It reddens with a blush of past granitic fire

2.
Pioneer in creation, God took a deeper breath than usual,
And said hopefully, Let there be life.
The Canadian Shield slept on, as through the ages.
God took a second breath, and cleared his throat.
Let there be *some* life, he hesitated; but the dust was deaf.
Let there be life, or else — God shouted; and at last
Of course there was some life, of a sort.
God rested from this day's labour, quite fatigued.
It's far from good, he said, But then it isn't so bad,
Considering this dense porphyry I've tried to work

3.
Before him, obvious as a senseless crime, the first Canadian stood
    gaping
At him, with that magnificent blank complacency,
That awful monotony of face, that face to face
Blankness of mind, all cattle grass and trees, all wood and beef —
Consummatum est, God punned. He all but gave up the ghost,
Self-crucified in a wanton act of creation.
I shall have to make it, he shuddered, a second Eve.
No woman not of Laurentian dust could face this face all her life.

4.
God wept. But still, he thought, brushing away his tears,
It may do yet, if mated to a nice appropriate Eve.
A happy sex life will polish up many rough edges.
It has got a nice big simple decent heart.
I'm not completely sold on brilliancy.
I made the Greek too subtle and too sharp.
The French too polished. The English too poetically glib of tongue.
The Irish too fanciful, always fighting fairies.

                                                    . . .

Homo novissimum canadiensis

The Jews alas too like myself — that was completely wrong;
I might have known, since I am liked by none,
No race could tolerate the Jews for long

5.
Nerving himself, God set about making this latest man a wife.
No need to put so dull an Adam to sleep.
I'll hack at him as a sculptor hacks at a stone.
Let me see, let me see, said God. The rib's too weak a bone
To be of use in this new Eve's construction.
So he decided after some lengthy cogitation
To make this woman entire of Adam's backbone,
Stern stuff, equal to almost any attrition.
But am I her God, he asked, to pull such a trick on a woman;
And went on with the task, as if engaged in seduction.

6.
When she was manufactured, God still hesitated.
This man, he said, is utterly without art.
And although she is all backbone, *he* must be educated.
And if subjected to a good foreign, European, education,
Well, who knows? Some German music, Wagner, Brahms,
    Beethoven —
Some lectures on Rubens, Rembrandt, and Dutch interior painting —
Some English verse, some elementary French prose —
As much Rabelais and Shakespeare as the brute can stand —
Who knows? Though it looks like carving mottoes on a tombstone —

7.
Alas, poor Eve! God sent for the best European educators.
Adam stared at them, his eyes two stone potatoes.
He shook his head — not he, he didn't like fugues or sonatas.
Didn't like sonnets, odes, canzones, *terza rima.*
Nor drama neither, though drilled through and through with
    Shakespeare.
What can a paving stone make out of Julius Caesar?
How could it arise to vertical Coriolanus?
O, this new man's soul was cut from such dead granite,
That, though his professors tried out all their wit,
God had to call them off, lest culture itself perish

8.
Petrified in his wits too, God was about to consign Laurentian Adam
Back to the Canadian Shield again, when the Devil spoke,
No friend of God's, but now filled with compunction.

Sweet God, said Satan, I've just the two men you want —
God sighed reproachfully. Well, if you mock me, Satan?
But then he took the Devil's thought. Is one of your men Irving
    Layton?
Yep, said the Devil. The other's Louis Dudek!
You're right, said God. I think they may do the trick

9.
And me happiest, sang Irving Layton, to the new Adam,
When I compose poems. The new Adam gaped at him delighted,
Laurentian Shield transfigured to ecstasy, which drops his jaw.
I'm never far from tears, sighed Layton, and the new Adam sighed too.
This is the new reader poetry requests, said Dudek.
My heart is parted like the Red Sea, semaphored Irving Layton.
Here is great metaphor, instructed Professor Dudek.
Adam flung his arms about, a sentimental concrete windmill —
Oh, the new Adam thrilled from his cowlick to his navel,
Though fabricated from impervious Canadian Shield.
God blessed the new Adam, and his blessing spilled
Lava into Layton. God triumphed, and Layton smiled

10.
God saw that the rock had made a great geological leap upward.
It had become, in the new Canadian, for the first time, quasi-human.
The angels laughed — to be rebuked. God told them
There is more rejoicing in Heaven when a chunk of Laurentian Shield
Becomes sophisticated into a Dudekian barbarian,
Than when ten thousand Irish sods are Patricked!
It is said, that St. Thomas Aquinas discreetly chuckled,
Re-affirming his sense of God's marvelous plenitude

A Manifesto for Beast-Poetry

> *The expression of the soul of the dumb ox would have a penetrating beauty of its own if it were uttered with genius — with bovine genius. . . .*
> Wyndham Lewis

There are some men
who as poets are animals.
Just as some men, when they couple,
couple in bestial fashion,
so some poets, when they write poetry,
give themselves over to the inner beast.
To do so, in a pure sense,
is a very difficult feat.
But this beast-poetry, when someone manages to shape it,
is a very powerful thing

2.
It is of course very difficult of comprehension.
It is an affair of images, without thought.
It is the blood crying
it is the blood crying down the corridors of the arteries
the blood crying as it turns corners in the veins
the blood crying in a passionate mindlessness.
It is always an alien thing

3.
Don't mistake the failures of the sects of poets
we see in these debased ages
for beast-poetry. Beast-poetry is not puffed up.
It exalts no one. Machinery multiplies
and books, and the dehorsification of dairies
and haulage systems provides a new houyhnhmn
to whinny at every street corner.
But this isn't beast-poetry

Beast-poetry isn't the sort of blue-stocking knitting
that Archibald MacLeish or Marianne Moore
their disciples their imitators and cousins germane
wage into books.

Beast-poetry has nothing to do with blue guitars.
I expect women, those who love
below the mind, who live always
in their hearts breasts and bowels
are best at this sort of poetry.
But — beast-poetry, it would make Gertrude Stein shudder
beast poetry never thinks in blue.
It never puts on a blue-thinking stocking.
It never thinks.

4.
In all poetry, everything
is either in the infinitude or in the limitation.
The be-all of beast-poetry lies in the limitation.
A man playing dog, this is what I mean —
is not a man excluding
himself from every level of life except the animal's.
Neither is a man playing dog
supplying flame to every thorn branch twig or leaf
of the burning bush which is mankind.
It is very difficult to be a man,
since the idea of a man
is, biologically speaking, one of pre-eminence —
excellence is the first testicle of a man.
A man to be a man must be more than a man playing dog.
A man to be a man must be more than a man.
But to write beast-poetry a man must be no more than a beast

5.
The house is a very large one.
Let us also admit that it is an exceedingly noble one,
noble, yes, but cracks in the wall, something gone,
an uncanny stink of ghost behind the door,
the smell of human tallow haunts the woodwork, the birth and death
    smells,
the breast smell and the smell of suckling children,
the smell of love-making and cooking fat,
the aroma of laundry-business, the fungus smell of old clothes,
footleather, bookbindings, newspapers.
We despair of the plumbing, the hand-basins
invite the auctioneer's hammer, their stain is
Macbeth's, everlastingly water-proof, marked for perdition,
                                                   •••

we make the sign of the cross in the dust
of the mantel-piece marble. We stretch
out a finger of dust
we shut up the library & reception rooms & the great hall & private
    chapel & promenades.
We let the ground go to the statues, the gardens to pot
we eat sandwiches in the kitchen.
In this way, less expense of spirit.
But we don't become — in this way — rats.
It is very difficult to become a rat.
It is difficult enough to be a mouse.
It is, in an opposite and northwest way, still more difficult to become
    a man

6.
But beast-poetry is a rare and powerful thing.
We prefer something in between.
In a sense we pay upsidedown homage to Pascal.
We deny, let us say, 'the glory of' with 'the misery of'.

Let's pretend
my god, my god, how bizarre, how very bizarre,
what a sense of humour —
let's pretend we are mice, squeak, squeak.
But this is pretense. It is not beast-poetry

7.
The profound the deep
poetry of the beast doesn't theorize.
It doesn't think at all.
It doesn't think, it is —
it really is. It has no tripe, no stomach for the cerebral
hypocrisies of Archibald MacLeish *et al.*
It doesn't like the visceral poetry of D.H. Lawrence
all bladder bladder bladder
full of pigheaded opinion.
It has no conceptions whatever of, on, or about anything.
It doesn't take its Hiroshimas from the papers.
A plain matter-of-fact non-mythical anti-mystical Belsen
is the ordinary keel of its being.
It knows no short-cuts to experience.

8.
Shallow critics denounce this sort of poetry
they say it is mad
let us all take hands and go skipping it tripping it back to Wordsworth
plain living sanity and the simpler humanities
but O Dorothy Dorothy
O Tintern Abbey
shallower critics praise it for being mad.
The very best critics
raising their eyes to the white goddess
observe that it is
incomprehending with the deep unreason
of the deep incomprehensible beast,
that is, if it is beast-poetry
not a fake

9.
The very essence
of being a beast, is to be the remnant of a living soul
that has in obedience to a complex of appetites
reduced itself to being a machine.
The ant-eater is a machine for eating ants.
The lion is a machine for eating antelopes.
The ant is a machine for eating dead cats, etcetera etcetera.
Nevertheless, there is something ascetic about a beast.
There is even something ascetic about a rabbit —
to become a machine an animal has to give up all but a very
        nominal sex-life.
A beast can't afford to dally with contraceptives.
There is something profoundly tragic about a beast.
The machinery with which it is invested is ancestral.
This bestial machinery lends a dignity
which only an ages-old machinery can bestow, every motion a pathos.
Hence, one of the skins of beast-poetry
is, it is a satire
on human depravity

10.
Don't imagine that a course
in the archetypes of Dr. Jung will provide
any pass-key to the deep bestiality of the beast.
Quite the contrary.
Dr. Jung takes a mop and bucket of water
and plenty of good old-fashioned eighteenth-century yellow floor soap
the sunlight soap of the enlightenment
to every cluttered up cupboard of the human soul,
he's tried to clean up every bestial corner,
to mop up every untidy stain of nature.
Beast-poetry
skulks off to some Canada of the unconscious the Herr Doktor misses.
The holy simplicity of psychology
never comes anywhere near beast-poetry

11.
The great masters of beast-poetry are, as follows,
simply none. Beast-poetry is still unwritten.
There is lacking the great renunciation.
This age ought to have written great beast-poetry
for we are the first great age of the machine
but we still pervert the machine to human uses
instead of, with pure animality, surrendering the human being to the
    machine.
The machine subsists as a tool, merely.
Affirmation, affirmation & pride, have crept in

Mr. T.S. Eliot with his wonderful beast's nose for images
might have done it.
When he said
that, had he meant something else, he'd have said something else
he came very close to beast-poetry.
But he wasn't beast enough to write beast-poetry.
He is not even a minor beast-poet.

No, Mr. Eliot is not the John the Baptist of beast-poetry.
He thinks too much, until his images think too.
Eventually
the strict critic of beast-poetry
catches Mr. Eliot out — his beast-images
are screens for thought.
He lacked the deep humility of the beast

12.
Whether a man dances
or whether a man makes music
or whether he gestures or paints a picture or carves sculptures
(or simply is)
words keep recurring. It isn't
sufficient merely to dance, this won't do for a man.
He must dance a madrigal.
He must caper to the words of a ballad.
Or if he makes water —
but all this verbal antic, the desperate endeavour to speak
is quite foreign to beast-poetry.
Let us understand this, that beast-poetry uses words in a totally new
 way,
it uses words as experiences. It excludes speech.
Beast-poetry is profoundly uneloquent.
Words are used so as to be, not to speak

there is something appallingly mute
about beast-poetry. It is as silent, as uncommunicative
as a mountain. You do not listen
to, or read, or perform exegesis upon
or write scholarly articles against, the poetry of the beast.
It brutally scorns the academic handmaidens.
You descend mindlessly and alone into its caverns.
Beast-poetry is the most dumbing
of all human acts

13.
I wouldn't openly pretend that we in Canada
have in our public forests, game-preserves or animal-parks
bred any great beast-poet.
But in my secret heart
I pretend to myself alone that the great beast-poet
will cleave from our substance. We have pioneered
the animal-natures, the brutal uneloquences,
the massive contempt for civilizing influences;
and machined to fit the necessary degradations.
We have the CBC.
It is excusable in a Canadian to believe that the great beast-poetry
slouches towards Toronto to be born

14.
therefore I call out aloud to the future
I summon the age about to be
not to debase itself in any petty way to the sub-human,
but to cut itself off boldly from all its ancestors;
to descend impudently down to the shameless depths
of beast-poetry. I am weary
of this shabby-parrot, this figurative lingerie,
and of the free & easy verse opinions.
I await the terrible new beast-poetry

Sermon on Bears

1.
I would have you think on the mystery of bears,
and how they feed in the wild mountains, poets of our wilderness.
You will see the bushes with the hearts scooped out of them —
salmon-berry, wild raspberry, kinnikinic
miserably violated. I had not expected to find
that when an infinitesimal stalk of moss is broken,
    the mountain suffered

2.
We set aside sanctuaries for these animals,
for every nation has its own sense of the sacred.
We cherish these brutes, not from impure appetite,
as English lords kept poets instead of whores,
but from our tameness, because, being utterly unwild,
we honour the strangeness of this brutal fur,
    the beast we never are

3.
It is a truth that with stupidity — only the young
in it are lovable; and this truth repeats with bears.
The adult is mother-irritable, jealous-irascible.
I have seen a bear with a cloud of mosquitoes
covering its head — but the pathos of bears
is comfortless. You cannot wipe away the look
of treason from their eyes, but must leave them
to their blindness, and to their flies
    and to the kindness of winter

4.
I fear our parks of mercy compromise this fur —
the pity of pity is its conscienceless cruelty —
there is a tendency in all natural creatures
to become monstrous, as if monstrosity
were the ultimate goal of unchecked nature;
and here among the bears this tendency is left free
to burst their forms in a grief for which there
is no natural relief. Would it not be better
to let our hunters decorate this fur with the death
which never brought any creature real loss,
    despite the will which deals it?

    . . .

5.
These animals become our paupers — and of all creatures
only man can support indigence with nobleness,
recognizing, as Yeats said, that shabbiness is the patina of the poor.
We have ecumenically decided that their poetry
is not ours, who cannot support the stiff elbow
of our civilization, as rats can, crows and other vermin.
Let us therefore abandon to this decision
those whom we cannot save — without a revision
of heart we obviously have no mind for;
knowing at the bottom of our hearts, that with progress
    all poetry ends

6.
Then, Mary, mother of Jesus, pray to your son
to intercede with the father of all life
to accept back again into his incomprehensible bosom
the majesty, the mystery of his creature the bear;
who cannot support upon so simple a bone
the turning of the machine we mismultiply on earth,
    its ultimate monster

WILFRED WATSON
bawl of wool

poems by Jenny Blake

... human society is biologically based upon the human body, and most especially upon the human breast and human sexuality.

No wild animal has the permanent breast. The female in Homo sapiens *uniquely possesses such specialization alone of all the mammals — with the exception of the domesticated milch animals which are man's own creation long after the fact of his humanity. This anatomical feature in humans, however, is more than a mere 'domesticated' trait and is certainly more than a merely cosmetic creation of sexual selection (copied from Weston La Barre,* The Human Animal, *University of Chicago Press, 1955, third impression, 1960, by Jenny Blake)*

Pome of not drawing roses

I don't ever risk drawing roses
For it's like untangling a bawl of red wool
Until the blood in your eyes
                          Begins to spill
And then after so much bother
You can hear them shudder

Pome for a dead soldier

I drew a tree
And a bawl of wool
But the tree tumbled
                    over
Into a bowl of dead twigs.
What happened to the wool?
I knew you'd ask that . . .
                        A very old aunt
Came out of a dusty corner
Of chalk, and knitted the wool
Into a pair of socks for a dead soldier

Pome of a girl

I drew a girl
In a yellow dress
Yellow yellow was her yellow chalky breast
I turned my back
And when I turned around
A red chalky ape is what I found
Which the said girl began to kiss
So hard, it stuck to her lips

Pome of a church

I drew a church
In terra cotta
But instead of a church's usual altar
It had a scaffold
Where they hung a man shaped out of clay
And in the pulpit where there prayed a widow
A police stiffly stood
                      baffled.
But though he was made of wood
He was very good

Pome of drawing tigers

I have an eye for these.
I'm not so good at a leopard.
Which is too soft and cruel.
I can outline a lion.
But the soft shouldered lioness
Out-lionesses me
                    For an umbrella
I have a careful pencil
But not for a madonna.
A madonna disturbs my crayon.
It tangles.
The wool jangles

Jenny Blake's ode on the cock pheasant

A cock pheasant
Moves like a long swell
In an ocean of pot paint
It crouches down into a trough
Of blue green green and blue;
Then struts up into a crest
To stretch its windy scarlet breast

Girl's poem

Blue chalk on brown wrapping
Paper is my very
                best
Hiding place
For a dead man's nest

Pome of drawing water

You draw a vase to hold some flowers
The simplest line will do
The flowers come easy too.
but however hard you set
                        Your mind
To draw water that looks really wet
Balls of vipers is what you get

Jenny Blake's child

I drew at a hill of green
And nice as anything
                      underneath
A pond in blue was seen.
In which a baby was drowned.
But when the policeman found
And caught the mother, I
Heard the blue water crying

Lines upon a naked line

In drawing
I lean upon a naked line
A string of nothing
                    and this abstracted design
Whether of Eve or her monkey
Puts me in mind
Of one defect of full existence,
It is like eternity *manqué*,
It lacks one dimension.
It is all now, and that is never.
This could be added in a poem

Pome of maidenheads

I am that priceless virgin
and monster spinster
Who feeds upon tumble-weeds;
I have three maidenheads.
I think it best to advertise the fact
For if any shall be missed
I shall know how to act.
One is for occasion.
The second, for passion.
The third, for revision.
                    But the girl who has four,
She shall be a whore — o mon dieu,
Be very sure you prove my love a whore

A pome of hair

The barber chatters
His tongueless scissors
And a parcel of hair
Falls
    to the floor,
A pome it took the world to write
Ten thousand million years.
(Although you could never know,
Could you, it was really written for you?)
I dismiss it from my ears.
I would give it to John Donne
To wreathe about a bone,
To grace a maidenhead
Which he never got
                though he had a lot

Pome of autumn

In fast September
In hectic feverish Michaelmas
Or in furious October
When there's no time for mass,
I am the slowest thing that ever was.
I, Jenny Blake, sit down on the grass
And spread my skirts over its face
And try to obstruct its rush

Pome of grief

Suddenly everybody burst into tears
As if the end of the world had come
And they were grieving
For all grieving done —
O bawl of wool —
And I did too,
For then all singing must be true

Pome of emblems

I had a yellow finch
I heard it sing
Invisibly within
A very dense thorn
                        It wept a poignant tear,
As the singing bird wept higher,
The bush caught fire.
But it was unconsumed.
It never even blossomed.
And when I said to the bird in its bosom,
Of what is this the emblem?
It shuddered between my teats,
'An empathy-trap for John Keats'.
I sadden for poets
Caught in lobster-pots

Jenny Blake's poem of windows

There are windows in rags
As I learned in school,
The cold eyes of the great
Look into the shoulder of the fool

But these windows are introverts
That have looked in at their lives
Their mothers & fathers
Their brothers & wives
They don't like what they see
There, and that is why they stare
Blankly, at the blank everywhere

Pome of honour

Three days before my birthday
I am wiser and fatter in wisdom than Falstaff.
I understand the meaning of 'honour'.
My muse is a good bird —
It is wonderfully perjured.
If faith has a blown beard
                        like a pulpit
Perjury has beautiful hands
And is full of complicated gesture
Like a theatre
                But to get back to honour
It is the part of jealousy
Resenting a hurt, where you've not given your heart,
In order to relish the injury.
It is acting the cactus
In a desert where you've forbidden the rain

Pome of glory

Than hunger for money
That keeps the people hungry
Or the backside of honey
Or any sour appetite that afflicts the hungry,
More moonstruck, more melancholy,
And if you are in the mood, more funny,
Is the high cock-a-lorum hunger for glory.
The pre-eminent Christian fathers
Feeding humility at their side
Were consumed by a lion of pride
But the pomegranate of glory
Has a sad bitter sorry
Seed, that when you are toothed of the same,
You are penetrative to shame.
I will throw out my skirts
To the fathers, and pull them in.
But it will make up a dour heaven

Pome of darkness

There is a great deal of darkness
And it is this
That brightens the sun
                    Yet
If that candle-light were gone
The stone darkness of its absence obscene
Would hardly be known.
I would believe it had an opposite
But touching fingers groan
And would not credit even the collier stone

Lines of flesh and bones

I am not over-voluptuous
To Ezekiel's dry men
Who have too many windows
In their bran
Light with no eyes to feed
Husk
     without seed
Yet I would gladly have my soul take up
Residence in a polished skeleton.
I grieve
To live in fluids in a leaky sieve.
Everything bodily spills grease about.
I smudge, therefore I am.
I drip, therefore I damn

Pome of waxwings

This rowan tree stands fleshed with drops of blood,
Warm mouths of Helen,
               Troy's destruction
And each mouth sang,
               I am for consummation
               Therefore suck my tongue
That with a rush of modern wings
(The accomplished air turned lead, by this hammer beaten)
Suddenly conceives a roof of fire
And then explodes waxwings everywhere.
The carnivorous ghost descended,
Egyptian clean, and beak-headed,
And in its hand a hungry sponge
               Drink,
And the tree shudders into draughtsman's skeleton
Blood gone, dry bone
Pencilled sterile windows
               but
The witch's necklace broken

Pome of shame

I, Jenny Blake, sit on my penitent bottom
Listening to the penitential psalms
Sung in church Latin, of Orlandus Lassus, the *Septem
Psalmi Davidis poenitentiales.*
In very shame of very shame.
Under laceration of this flagellant's lashes
My soul takes fire, and falls from my back in weeping ashes.
My spirit wastes like yesterday's newspaper.
My soul exhales in sorry smoke.
I set fire to my bones, I stretch out a bare
Coal of a body on a hot pallet of scratch-straw fire,
Until my thus-excised heart quails
On its bed of nails.
But at last this music fails
With its couch of iron to raise me to Zion.
I put on my shirt of ashes again.
                              After such diet
Of glory, I peck at without appetite
The eyes of today's breakfast
Of misère

Pome for Adam

Pitiful Adam mankind
Who, if he reasons after passion,
Lusts after reason
                    I am your Eve
O Adam mankind, even if
You plough my unbelieving rocks
With parable and paradox.
Or depasture your sheepish thoughts
Upon my grass of noughts

Pome of cuckolds

It wasn't until I was nine or eight
That I discovered I'd been bubbled
By the word cuckold
                      I thought it was a bird.
But now I know that solid earth
Isn't rough rough round
But hollow triangle.
My favorite one is Menelaus.
I am bubbled by a cuckold.
Any woman's son who wants to sleep with me,
Need only say,
                I am Menelaus,
And remind me of Helen of Troy.
I would smooth the cuckold's horns
Then readily. But alas Menelaus
Wears on his brow a turf of grass

Pome of Helen of Troy

Like a harlot-woman she'll wear
That very falsest place
That women hold secret and dear,
To melt a naughty tear.
It made Menelaus twitch
More than Troy fire made him rich.
Shall I tell you its name?
You would sicken with shame.
And I with blame;
Yet I woman the same

Pome of Venus

If I could catch that sly pig of a Venus
I would slice off her white snout
                                    like that
Tit for tat,
And anything else hanging loose about
Her. She has made me much trouble
With her billing and bauble.
With all her groin and grunt.
But such is her oily charm
She has such a cold-creamy arm,
She would slip through my fingers
Before I could pay her back any harm.
I am on your side Hephaestus;
And in particular because . . .
How the pig gets under my blouse

Pome of maids of honour

I seek the why's and wherefore's
The purse and prussic acid perforce
Of
   the fact that history
Is leafed full of unkind petty mystery:
Thus: maids of honour are always disgraced.
No matter how fat and ugly of face,
History tramples down their skirts.
(The professors say, I shall grow sour
Before my phoenix hour,
But why this is deprived of past and future bliss,
Since you never know when it is,
I don't ask) Why an assumption of false virtue
Would be a challenge, is the query
I range. I pursue
The proud hart, the thicket, and the oblique hunt.
Is the onus on her, or on honour?

Pome of a wire bridegroom

Were I Jenny Blake, spinster
As of all improbables
                         to marry of my own will
Since I am a virgin of wool
                         all tangle
Of sleep, sheep
Shepherd and desire,
I should marry
A bachelor of wire.
When I gave him my gay maidenhead
We should not make John Donne's compasses
Of boxwood, to measure out earth's square,
Or to put a bounding pencil line round a star;
But out of my maiden's loth, and his lust
A banquet of moth, a conflagration of rust

Pome of the unicorn

Last night I gave my
Nothing self, to a rough
Ear of corn indeed, of nothing worth.
Because it was of nothing
Worth. Thus satisfied
I dreamt of a unicorn.
From its white face stood a spike of iron.
Which thing knocked gently at my bed rail.
I went to the cupboard and got
It a bowl of milk
Which it lapped up with gentle mouth of silk.
As it drank
Its iron horn clanked on the rim of the bowl
                                     clank, clank
Then it followed me about
Everywhere I went it stood.
I vouch this dream for Sigmund Freud

Pome of nothingness

I was that girlish sort of thing that wore
Myself
        As sweater and brassiere,
Skirt, scarf, garter-belt, and stockings
And other miscellaneous clothings,
Such as
        hair, breasts, lips, legs.
He abstracted me out of these rags
To nothingness's most nothing page,
Trans-sex, trans-world, trans-friends, having no Christ
Except this tabula razoring alchemist.
Uncipher me now, and learn my paraphrase.
I am all things that have been,
Are, shall be, could be, anywhere
Abandoned, left. He created me nothingness;
And I am re-begotten darkness, death.
Study me, for whom love was an anti-Christ.
Of all dead naked deaths, I am become
Death's core, end-curd, *caput mortuum*

Lines of rape

Rape me,
And the seven judges of Edmonton
And the seventy seven judges of Canada
Who are wise and learned carnal men
Will confine you in prison
                              for lust of me
For years thirty and three.
That is a great deal of wall
To climb over,
To taste my thimbleful of lust.
If you must climb my hill
Ask me, or woo

Pome of fire

Sir father, in your Priam brow, will you
Seize the small wrong son by his cindered wrist
And beat his charcoal legs sir now?
                              Look —
Your whip is gone to ash in your hand
And your charcoal hands are stumps of dying sparks
And your backbone is a black bone of soot;
And the world you stand amazed in, is your
Troy
     See Helen like a scorched beetle run
Scorpion frantic into the apex of that fire
To cool her breasts of coal. O Agammemnon,
Collect your smuts of cleaning women,
There are ashes for sweeping,
But all the brooms are done

Lines of thought

The nearly-living juniper shivers
Covered in snow
                    and unless
My almost unliving thought
Shivers under my words
I am dumber than the frozen sparrow
That falls, mankind uncounted,
Into God's wheel-barrow,
To enlarge an arithmetic
Only an oblique
Algebra can calculate,
And not often, that

Pome of a girl

I take a pencil.
I draw a girl.
          I admit the wench a stencil.
I would give her to you
But I don't think she'd do.
Though her centre is my navel
Her breasts are too fat
                  They drag at her throat
I couldn't get them to float
                  I drawl
A bawl of wool
Over the 'x' of her thigh.
But you needn't hold your breath.
There's nothing underneath

Lines in my flesh

In my flesh this knowledge grows
That all Eve's pathos
Is burned into her crotch.
And all Adam's tenderness
                  at this place
Can only be a rape.
And his neglect, a chafe

Lines of seeing

Eye can never know what goes on.
Eye-ing is always
Spying and spying lying.
We write ambiguous footsteps in snow.
But don't know which way they go.
Thus
      said Menelaus to me, hide we here.
We do. Enter, to bed with Helen,
A tall wrong male figure.
It could be one lover or another,
Sucked at by the tides of those great
Sea-soughing breasts of moon-fat
Wicked, candle-pretty mammal.
Paris, creaks Menelaus.
Plaster of, is my answer, alas.
Which eye is more crass?

Lines of a maiden-ape of god

I, hopeless parrot-virgin
and maiden ape of God, I,
                Jenny Blake,
Out of this blank material
Pen, pencil, ink and unthinking air,
Shape out the mother-bridegroom
Into a form that out-cheats death,
And like a sub-executive of grace,
Perturb, with my standing here and now,
This universe of grease.
My thesis is this passage.
                        Consider my miracle
Said against woman's melting hill
And the wooden skins of men

pome of not wanting even at this late date to go Jacobean

That day came, and that night, and morning.
The sun rose. Without warning
the moon sank in a wreckless sea
to quench her bloodless light, in his Eye,
God's new lieutenant.
                    Then the dumbed heart
of the new kingdom looked into its first hurt.
That day began cold, with a Kingdom's tongues
rejoicing, many as the sea's gulls.
The air flashes with upraising Swords, brave as words.
Judas has as many lips as the sky birds.
Like Elbows shoving in the grave
power stirs, and seeks what it can grab or save
of the small room, which it endorses
by pushing at, or making men, corpses.
I, Jenny Blake, Elizabethan and virgin
turn up my nose at King James's version

Song

There blossoms forever
In my heart forever
                Golgotha
And desert place
A perpetual flower
Of eternity the mirror
To bloom between
The sand, and the sand's horror;
Till the scena is real
And not the horror's shadow.
What that rose means
There are no words to say
Or few, too mercy-Mary
Secret to my heart and me

Lines on the English tongue

The hell of this English is
It is merchant's heaven
                          but purgatory of truth.
Many poets don't know that
Shakespeare in *King Lear*
Broke the world forever up
Into he-bits and she-bits
Of very small cubits.
And he pounded the English tongue
Against this rotten stone
So that now it is too bruised to speak
What the soul thinks or the heart aches.
Except it be gentled with infinite tact
It betrays
         and the words vomit out.
Witness the tongue's betrayal
Of Anglican preachers into paraffin oil
And false black bible;
Or its anointing Shakesperean actors
Into geesian iambic hectors;
Or freshman teachers into qua-qua-quacks.
But auctioneers
                Need have no fears
              They can tell lies about dung
              And nothing is sprung

Pome of sand

I dreamt I was a sea-anemone.
A flower of green sponge,
I blossomed in a wet bed of sand
Into which I ran a
                    non-dreaming hand.
I squeezed out a handful.
I let it trickle
Down, particle by particle
Into my breast, which was a tangle
Of bone, like the sea-osprey's dinner-plate of a nest
Voluptuous with cod's death-head, and flayed salmon skin;
And on to my foot
Until it was scoured white driftwood
Ankle. An arch crab with waving jaws
And a sea-ripple of bald head
                         said,
Listen to this wet sea-joke.
Isn't it a shark?
No, said the sand, and I awoke.

Dry yourself with my mortal towel
Of dust, said the clock my enemy.

I weep for my dream of sea-anemone

Pome of substance

If the dull substance of my thought
Were only
        flimsy phenomena
        appearances only,
I would most surely
Starve myself
Imagination thin.
But these hands are full of causes,
My finger-nails are unclean
With infinite dirt of inferences,
I have God under my nail.
The entrance to my virgin womb
Is thorn-entangled with the most dense
Of arguments
        designs
Prowl there, shoulder to shoulder
Like packed lions
Baptized with syllogisms
And blooded with reasons

Jenny Blake's pome of William Blake and the spinning jenny

The angels of the imagination howled,
Let there be science
And there was science
        bright as the moon.
So God plunged the spinning jenny into a swoon
Of darkness, and took William Blake out of its womb.
But one of God's fingers
Touched Blake's penis.

That upset the ratio of the senses.

Blake saw old Father Time
As mother Venus.
And all her greasy creatures
Sub specie aeternitatis

Pome of keeping silence

Mon dieu, if I keep quiet
The David in my bones
Roars like a pack of rain sodden lions.
My moon howls.
My waters groan.
My pap roars lamentation
From the sea-shore to the sea-shore.
The clamour of my hips
Happens, though I bite my lips
With stone.
Oh yes, I'll go and lie down
With a nest of owls

Pome of rain

The rain falls down in showers of nails.
They pierce the adobe breast.
But my bosom petrifies to this pelt.
It melts, and isn't felt
By this slow coal
Cool to the heart's diastole

Jenny Blake's epilogue to *King Lear*

We, the actors, have put on these roles and masks
And broken this world into pieces for you
And put it together only doubtfully again
Or not at all, in order to recall private words
From their public commerce with lies
To their own private faces and proper tongues,
And in the service of truth.
                              Without which offices
The world remains removed and unknown
As the locked heart of a kicked stone.
And all life but parrot-chattering, and dumb
As claptrap of apes' kingdom come

flamingo poem

I met a heron. I
was walking in the park.
I thought it was a flamingo
screwed into a rock.
I was about to accuse it
to the sun's blush & uprush but
the sun turned into a fog
and my lord Flamingo into a penny
with a steel spike for a mouth
and a swastika for a heart.
It unscrewed one leg
and gave the salute.
The sea clicked its heels.
The electricity of the perjury
unswitched my backbone & glued
my hands to my knees —
o jenny blake,
I admire your guts

pome of destroying oneself

Of human weakness, I jenny Blake,
am the model,
to drown the virgin
in some puddle,
to garble the living breast
and the bubble.
                     But when I came to die
all the kind water was dry.
And I thought it better
to put the tear back into my eye
and save eternity for the whore
which fate might prefer

pome of my mind

My mind I inherit from Adam
that thing of triangles and tears
replete with cylinders and hair
cones elbows knees
via the great moth of piss where I began
in nightmares of pink lips
my mind is a nest of whores.
I didn't expect to find you there, madam
soliciting me as their piquant madam
and if I can find any door
in psychosis work or prayer
I shall close up my mind
or drive it to pieces in a car;
it's bad enough to be their pimp
but I will not have you their bawd

pome on figureheads

These push through shattered seas
the green sails bellying in the dictated wind
woman's image in a wooden figure,
their hands sick with rope
and their wet splayed feet dancing after.
The salt hand of the water
slaps at her wooden breast, a hard bosom
to bite at, even for the sea-worm.
And I, Jenny Blake, in my female smudge and stink
protesting for all women
the easiness of her virtue
turn away my face too sour for laughter
at the keel of men's passion
                          rape
by water and in female effigy
to be crucified
                the wind their hammer
and their nail the sea

pome of critics

This poem is
deterrent obstacle
for if criticism brings
the lecturer to the now
and here where I begin,
I, Jenny Blake, shall have time to escape,
and when you enter to where I am,
shall not be there at all.
I present you with a wall.
But when you climb over
these words
that will be afterwards.
Let scholars my pismires
live in the mortar
and banquet on the crumbs of plaster,
what could they know or care
about the chalked heart
or the arrow which drills it out
or the signature in a letter?
                    There will be on no grain
of that dust, no minute crumb of me, no not even
the smell of my breast
though it were in flower
and not very sour

pome of stones

The haunted word
pinned to a tree
becomes a bird,
but who is she?

Let the skeleton advance
with flesh below its simpering knees
but above a crib of bones.
We have banqueted on delicacies

though Gerontion in swaddling clothes
clings to prophetic bones
still through the gristle of the nose
declare that words are stones

things damned and lost.
St. Peter walks from his boat
returns like a ghost
and closes his fingers about our throat.

But who did you say I was?
The stone didn't know.
Stone knows how to kill, stone knows how to sit
                                                on its arse
stone knows how to throw

pome of misconceptions

I, Jenny Blake carry
in my unseeded unimportant womb
a man child I wear in
my closed loin as solemn
and heavy as Eve's or Adam's
or egyptian pharoah's tomb
                             who blackmails me with its bone
and a road of possible ruin
which though I open it is hardly mine,
if to begin is less than to design.
I am not even sure this
embryo within is human,
who presses me with its harrow
into being its two-legged barrow . . .
Not without much ado
could I father him on you

pome of addition

What you add up in poetry
Is an arithmetic
Of a green beetle, a flat tire and a woman's breast,
And I, Jenny Blake, before my glass,
Sighing alas,
The world which contains all these,
How beautiful, irrelevant and sad,
Terrible, empty and mad.
                     Though you know the sum must be nothing,
The words always amount to something,
And you write them down with the circumstances,
As if you were totalling up expenses

Jenny Blake's pome of the Japanese woman

I wish I were a Japanese woman
So that I could go
About with my bosom bare
And because then I should have the ah-ah-ness mouth;
I have the sadness underneath,
But I can't wear it on my mouth
Like Utamaro's Heron Girl

I like the way Japanese paint women
As if they had only half seen
Them — as if it were impolite to appear less than too sensible
Of an attraction, to endure it for long.
The anatomy is so right
To be so exquisitely wrong.

There is delicacy in this sort of error

But I have the soul of an ox,
Best of all, I like the cheeky buttocks
Of Hokusai's servants, doing the yakko-odori
With only a slip of breech-cloth
To cover up Sodom & Gomorrah

Pome of headlines

Of all paradoxes
The paradox the most cruel
Is
   That the unreal, is so terribly real.
We butcher a wood
And poison a river
                      To make a newspaper
                          All the bloody business
Of the world, we model in human grease
To be melted down the next day into nothingness.
But there it is.
It is like a poem, it is so real.

Lines

Persephone's black husband, Pluto
Who rules in hell
Has one blue toe
With a shaving of lapis lazuli, for a nail.
A terrible man
With the bulk of a mountain
And the head of a sparrow,
He takes his foot in his hand
Dips it into ink
And writes love-letters to Persephone
Describing his sorrows
                      So that she won't be jealous
Of his Helens and Cleopatras

Pome of words

I will shut, said Shakespeare
The master-mistress up
In a prison of passion.
What could the he or she-victims do?
But submit to
The everlasting wit?
O, the pity of it,
He had the words to do it

Jenny Blake's pome of experience

Even the innocent Eye
Knows that pomes
Are soaked in blood
And that the songs of innocence
Are deeper and wickeder
Than the songs of experience.
Now, that appears like a ghost
To root leaf blossom & fruit
Which aren't so much its husks
Grave and corpse
Bands cradle and whistle
As the meaning by which it walks
And (if it does open its mouth) talks

Pome of King Lear

In English Two Hundred
King Lear thrice a week thundered
And ate Fool's custard.
Goneril gargled milk
And Regan ate a cornfield.
Gloucester swallowed a bastard
But I won't be Gloucester'd
I can't swallow down the role of Edgar,
As a do-gooder, he is worse than a murderer,
With the best motives for a carving knife.
His acts are like curfew
And challenge the goodness of virtue.
He is the Goneril of his own soul.
Raise his head on a pole

Jenny Blake's pome of a dragon

I saw a terrible green dragon
Half bird, half woman
Gaunt as an aged cow
Come over the last hill
With its mouth full of flowers,
Full of white daisies
And yellow daffodils

All the boys and girls
In their virgin brows
And virgin curls
Ran after it
Feeding it their grandfathers
                                and grandmothers
Their fathers and mothers

By Freudian misnomer
They called it the Lamb of God
To take away their sins.
What sins had they, except lust?
Lust to kill
Lust to rape
Lust to live
The life they take

It had snow on one shoulder
And a mountain on the other
And avalanches at its feet.
Out of its cave in a churchyard
It came munching flowers
And twenty-four robins
Picked worms out of its fingernails
Politician and scientist
Ran after it
Trying to teach it
To eat human flesh
Which fills the parks
And crowds the beaches
Where nations flourish
Like fields of wheat

                              . . .

I, Jenny Blake,
Read it this my pome
Of miserabilisme
With a sick stomach
And a sour air
But it laughed like a calf
Fatted with flattery
And played with its sting
And went on chewing
The cud it had eaten

Jenny Blake's Ulysses

You must if I don't use
Tennysonian blank verse excuse
Me, I can't find the time
To write a decent poem without rhyme.
I haven't much to say about Ulysses.
He came back, poor man, from
The Trojan war (for which, as you know, he didn't give a damn)
To find Telemachus in control, that capable soul

All this talk of ever onwards
Through the arch of experience, is donkey-talk,
Sheer tripe —
Ulysses wanted to settle down in a chair with a pipe

How do I know?
My muse, a bawl of wool, told me so

Rather like our scientists.
They don't want to go on making bigger and better bombs.
The poor toms!
Why do they, then? Lord Zeus,
It's simple, the white-haired boy, Telemachus
Would have their jobs, if they didn't

This is my theory of Telemachus.
This is my poem of Ulysses.
I offer it up to the god Bacchus

Jenny Blake's sonnet of oil

1.
A thimbleful of oil
Will soak into the wick
And light up any lamp
So that one can see how dark round about it is

2.
A cupful of oil
Will set fire to Troy
And bring to a boil
The kettle of mammals
Which all the scald poets will say
Are fairer than the white breasts of the Queen of love
If you don't think so, ah,
Helen has returned to Sparta,
Agammemnon has died in his bath,
And the terrible hounds of Clytemnestra
Infest this year and next year
And every year, snapping at the white heels of everywhere

3.
But I have a pint of gas.
Let us pour it on the grass.
We will apply a match.
The moon is infested with rats.
Though all in the way of murder fails,
Sweetheart, perhaps we shall scorch their tails

4.
Let the wise virgins
Mutter the bridegroom's name
Into the prepared wicks of the lamps,
Honi soit qui
Mal y pense,
In the respublicae of nature
There are no foolish virgins
There is no such thing as murder
Rape is a surprising thing
There are no sins
No Nagasakis and no Belsens

Dialogue between Jenny Blake and herself

Jenny Blake	What bread and butter for this senseless thing?
Herself	I write as birds fly that are on the wing.
Jenny Blake	A simple instinct sends them into air.
Herself	So my hand falls to ink and paper.
Jenny Blake	What good to write for lost posterity?
Herself	I rather write than go humourlessly.
Jenny Blake	When many evils lack publicity?
Herself	Evils bed with us to the world's last end.
Jenny Blake	Well then to write the world's good to defend.
Herself	There is no virtue in my unskilled pen.
Jenny Blake	You shirk the task to less enabled men.
Herself	Others have fouled the world to set it right.
Jenny Blake	At least they erred in action not in blight.
Herself	Weak is all human act and instrument.
Jenny Blake	Until a workman forge an implement.
Herself	May you have groin to practice your intent.
Jenny Blake	Mine is the task to point to just ambition.
Herself	But I fear doing more than dereliction.

Lines

I, Jenny Blake,
An indifferent head of yellow hair,
What am I then, but two legs and a back,
A front, with two arms and two breasts,
And all the body of me
Playing at shift and change with the salt moon
Given and taken from me
In a flowing like the water of a river —
My creek of love not hard to seek
                          but here's my flaw,
Not the uncertainty of river,
But the infinity of my creature.
                        And from this crack
I shall be no man's true bride,
And hungry the most, when satisfied

Pome of love's brass finger

Love's finger
Shall never press
Its outrageous brass
Into this my grease
Nor stiffen my nipple.
I have said so before
And you know it.
And not as poet.
But there is so dreadful a fateful faint fool
Complicated in a girl,
Who is so easy to floor and twirl
Into a bawl of wool about love's finger.
I am glad at this dull game
I am no bright enamel male
                          nightingale
To raise his feather
To be her praiser or her pleasure

Lines of glory

Sir, my unthinking womb
Is full of will
And none of my wit
Good gentlemen could cover it.
Shall I read you my lecture?
What I bleed
Is sick with sense of glory.
Abraham's passionate seed
Ezekiel's astounded bones
St. Augustine's lecher and weeper.
I wish it were
            the Greek curse
Even to a dwarfish Oedipus
But it isn't

letters to the bach. of wire

. . . to the bachelor of wire

Of course some of this verse is fake.
And some of my love too.
Even sir for you.
Perhaps we renew truth with fiction,
fiction with fake —
as we renew grief with sorrow,
sorrow with forced bouts of weeping,
weeping with crocodile's tears.
And so perhaps my dear bachelor of lust
we can renew love with —
but let us begin with loving;
and then if and when love grew out of repair,
then I could throw back my hair,
my breasts, hands and my legs too
and toss my knees into the uttermost air
and shape of love's despair —
                                      O proclamation
perhaps we could renew love with copulation,
with the union of twice what is not there,
and its re-iteration.
But mark sir, I, Jenny Blake, for modesty's sake,
began with, perhaps some of my verse is fake

. . . to the bachelor of wire

This is my fiftieth letter
written to you out of the hospital of my disease.
And the sickness worse or no better.
Physicians have consulted with surgeons
and drunk cup after cup of dubious coffee
with nurses and interns.
                         Someone has sent in a bill,
but no one discovers the ill.
It is not nineteenth-century female's complaint
a constriction of the waist
and compression of the lungs, the result of bad taste;
there is thrown away all such corset.
Nor is it (they reflect) a malignant *amour courtois;*
for they have disinfected the heart of religion,
and there is no danger of worship in that region.
Though it is not this menstrual century
with its tedious inventory
of diseases of the uterus
                        it is (it is plain)
a malaise if unknown, still completely my own,
and only consumes my viscera and bone.
Though the rest of the world dies of The Cure,
or sickens of chronic prevention,
if I name a new disease, since none to be sure can catch
it, there's no need of any cure

. . . to the bachelor of wire

When you sir (that is male mankind, sir)
fall in love, and become as mankind in love
is said to become, philanderer
and as John Donne who was not such a one
says you do
the male heart is broken into two
thousand or three thousand pieces,
each of which adores likes and wishes
but not loves
        This is how Eve's daughter is born
with her heart into a thousand pieces torn;
which love compacts into one
single loving heart, with sometimes a force so forlorn
it is compressed into stone,
able perhaps to ache, but hardly to break

. . . to the bach. of wire

I am that coy Kore
and muddled moon-maiden, sir;
I am that virgin of the imagination,
who, if one can judge from leaves of vast literature
men-children mingle with their mother
and cherish to ravish at the surd curd centre
of the hard-hearted male-core
                                    otherwise nought.
Her lips chaster than her thought,
scarlet ornaments without taste for you sir to profane.
Sir can you keep her any secret?
With many a hard tempest has her mouth been shaken,
in peculiar, facing water to water,
she gave you three kisses when her mouth shook
as if she had been struck.
But took them back immediately.
Lest in the drying up of the moon's menstrual flood
a hunchback should be born.
Though the world overflow with babies
I would give you a son
                      but not a crooked one

. . . to the bachelor of wire

Some lost desperate adventurers
because they wanted to set fire to the centuries
harnessed a plough of iron
to horses of gasoline
and drove a ditch through this town
and its path crossed my garden.
The ploughshare of melting iron drove through my bedroom
and cut into two my quiet dream.
They divided my bedroom into two
and the bed in which I was, dissected.
So that I woke up to find myself from myself, divided.
Therefore I must sit down for the rest of my wounded life
in a mangled city, and in a broken room
and sleep in a shattered bed.
This was the rape to which I was subjected.
Sir, I come to you for strands of small wire
to sew my parted self together, and as best I can,
to repair my bed, to re-unite my town,
and heal with borrowed suture, sir,
perhaps, if I can, my century in despair.
But these ravishers were so resolute and bold,
I am not certain, this wound will hold.
Sir?

. . . to the bachelor of wire

Let, I said, the past dissolved be the past dissolved.
And let the living not disturb the crowded dead.
But when I looked in my purse for money
I found I hadn't any
                            and under my foot, the stone,
I found that was all gone;
that I stood without any foundation
a withered ghost looking about for some body
so that when I had bred some bone
I could then beget solid stone.
And then perhaps erect a century
and by building century upon century,
arrive at last at substantiality.
And at last in conspiracy with history,
breed a woman, who could be very human

. . . to the bachelor of wire

Sir, the anthropologist
flatters me this much,
                   I mean, womankind
in the breasts babykind feeds at
and some hands love to touch or clutch
at in a caress. Here
is civilization, these scientists have confessed,
determined by the permanent female breast,
no other animal has.
                   Upon my honour,
one way or another we come to madonna.
And your sex, sir, to derision.
For our tragedy I see lies in your sex, which is not
unless it is inflated by wrath.
Thus sir we nourish the cities
which you destroy by kindling wars

. . . to the bachelor of wire

An ant attempted to unpuzzle my bawl of wool
and in order to expound it
he unwound it;
but as he laboured at my riddle
it fell into a tangle
of which he measured the diameter.
He said it had no centre
and what was plain
a circumference of nonsense.
                                      He praised my little brain
and with reference to my grief
the moist lengths of my pain

. . . to the bachelor of wire

Sir: with my brassiere and luck at the hook
I can catch at my breast
and pinch up my bosom
without any your help.
Why should I throw away this rag
or that
        to let you crush my nudes?
But this thought has its afterwards.
When I look into my mirror
I see myself in error.
And when mirror's not there
I want some other witness
to my this, that or it-ness

. . . to the bachelor of wire

Sir —
I have one false nipple and one true one.
One of my breasts is philosophy;
but the other ecstasy,
which indeed I inherit from Eve, my quondam mother;
and this puzzles many, since Adam my father.
If you should caress this one
I might leap over the sun
and you would burn your hand.
But the other is cold philosophy.
It will quote you good advice,
                                    such as,
open her knees like a dictionary
and pretend you are after a word;
this could be 'ludicrous', 'ridiculous', or 'absurd';
but though you long and unceasing hunt
it, it will not I think be yes.
Which is what my mad breast never says.
But my breast without religion
will damn such madness as pre-scientific.
It will denounce me as medieval
and my being equivocal

. . . to the bachelor of wire

Sir, I and you know very well
this stone's blood, we not tell;
that all this delight in you I re-write
merely, and you wrote, but not as poet.
But as flagellant, a whip your pen,
and not so much against flesh, this flagellation,
of yourself, sir bachelor of wire,
as a lash at imagination.
Though not less the laceration.
Some rapes, sweat, anguish,
body cannot bruise for, unless
the lunatic fringe of the mind,
half-body, more than half sense, the imagination ravish;
nor Helen be transported to Troy,
nor Catullus annoy —
what was then written, take note,
I Jenny Blake, re-wrote,
and re-write now, carefully and not anyhow

. . . to the bachelor of wire

Sir you are my abstract
drawer and architect of my form, you will subtract
me, because you are puritan,
from my industrial design,
you will turn me into a smooth line
and trample on my womb.
I confront you with my breasts.
How do you like this bag of worms?
And the partridge at my legs'
suture, it will devise you a form
a hereford bull or unicorn
                          with a nail of fake iron.
I subtract myself from this.
No puritan shall eat my kiss

. . . to the bachelor of wire

I would love you as if passion had just begun,
thumbing my nose at love's convention;
and you sir, proving Helen a fiction
should suck forth my soul in a kiss
and name me what rose love now must miss.
I would, since I must be true,
come to you in a relation new.
But if you should kiss me, there is this iron,
you should cheat me, and half-kiss Helen;
and if you managed to bring me to shame,
I should bear only Heloise's blame.
So, lest love eclipse me
                        I forbid you my lips
for newness's sake, and all other ellipse

... to the bachelor of wire

Perhaps I could love a scientist
though he might find me prescientific
and even pre-medieval
going to bed in the abysm.
Or even somewhat, what's worse, pre-Latin.
Or still harder to think, prehistoric Greek,
pro-centaur at my perverse centre.
So that he being a schismatic
would find me too largely erratic,
my breasts a purgatory
and my secret parts of shame, damnable,
more shell than oyster, more oyster than pearl.
O, he would want to scowl
at my irregular bowel.
And when with his schism he tried to slit me
and split my humanity from my humanity,
he might find himself cuckolded
by some paltry but undivided religionist
whom he would despise
                        for the look in my eyes

. . . to the bachelor of wire

Sir, to cry bawl of wool
is to be abstracted from nature;
but wire is still more artificial.
It binds together the cities
which I pull apart, after
the female heart of Helen,
the face of which destroyed Troy.
Being sheared, torn, spun
I am plucked out for destruction;
and to be no one's constructive wife;
it would be unnatural union.
So we have nothing in common,
except the kiss we kiss;
and even this, to reach at I miss

. . . to the bach. of wire

Sir, I am not that worn pantaloon
to think love is not buffoon.
I will turn you into such a one
as Eve did, our mother-madam,
when she undid and harloted Adam.
It is all very absurd.
                        I wish I were a bird
to be pushed at in a cloud;
or narrow long-bellied snake
so that the earth could rub at my ache.
Or grief pecunious stone,
not to have one.
To be bawl of wool and jest at wire
is too cruel

. . . to the bachelor of wire

Sir touching us, that is,
in fact, touching me and, and touching you and,
and, you know what and, and who and, I mean.
But more than this I will not be unbawled.
I shall not be drawn out.
And you know sir as well as I
that it is not the last fashion
of the moon now, to be in, or write of, passion.
I speak with all compassion.
You may make exit or six exits with her.
And I, my debut with him.
Can wool burn or your scratchier wire?

... to the bachelor of wire

I may see many honest nudes
in male flesh browned into bronze, or white chunks of stone
franked with the male instrument of generation;
or upon some classical vase,
                              the said limb in blossom
as if it grew on the brow of the cow
that jumped over the moon —
but how grossly unfair, females when done into stone,
though they give us a sordid bosom
with marble teats, marbled buttocks and fingernail,
are innocent of the female door
by which we are all entered here.
Let petrified people by all means wear
trousers or skirts cuffed with stone — but sir —
if you will praise her pink lips which are liar,
would it not be chaster
to inscribe her a sonnet on this flower?

. . . to the bachelor of wire

I have made up my mind . . .
My heart is a nest of wasps
my belly is a nest of worms
and my bawl of wool, a viper's nest.
Thus I outdo Macbeth's brain of scorpions.
But there come outward devils to nest in my rooms;
they pretend they are bridegrooms;
the first says, we have crucified God and you shall be at peace;
the second, lop off the pope's head, and you shall have peace;
the third says,
          tie up this tube here into a knot
and you can have as much sex as you've got,
and you won't be troubled with babies.
Neither one, two, or three is new;
and the third, sir, is you.
But custom is such a pandar that I don't hate them as much
                                      as I should do.
But my latest comforter wants to castrate my tongue,
and another inserts pincers into my soul
and says
          now that we can abstract the self
you shall make tomorrow a good wife.
Do you see what these comforters do?
They drive me back to make terms
with my heart, bowel and bawl of wool, worms, wasps and vipers;
the god of love curses me with his curse;
but these comforters are worse . . .

. . . to the bachelor of wire

There is a fatal propensity to love
now
    one is driven to it in a crowd
and it is the world's crooked elbows
and not, I suspect, a private voice
at all, or virgin's single choice.
I distrust such love, when love is in season,
and in such love's ache and distraught,
                            think,
if indeed I think what I think
and it is not all an intoxication of ratios of ink —
that what troubles the faithful nightingale
may not be so much love's redemption
which draws harlots out of brothel as
unreason's exemption
from the lash of the tax
this century of cities lays on our backs;
and you sir might well look askance and with revulsion
at my face's confession of such compulsion?
Sir?

. . . to the bachelor of wire

Sir, forgive me that
within me sang
an insignificant hatred
                    all day long
which out of its infinitesimal
point of truth, its small
poisonous tooth, grew into a greedy monster;
and forgive me sir,
                    that none of you
could this greasy passion undo.
And if like Perseus you had come
to rescue the Kore that I am
from this monster breathing smoke and flame,
how could you have struck at it,
since it was behind my woman's teat?
You would, to have undone it,
had to undo me too

. . . to the bachelor of wire

As seas leave water at the earth's wet lip
there is a hungriness within my hungriness
nothing can increase, and no dry man's sere wit
can dryness fetch
                    this moisture to extinguish;
my naked foot sinks into this my own soft shore.
I might forsake the ocean, but my bone
twists back to it, as in her occupation
the harlot wrestles to bring her passion home
to the house she leaves in desolation.
She (that is me, and every woman)
is this fraud, that she cannot give or sell
what he (that's you sir) cannot himself pluck.
And spirits of dead women cry out in hell
that fruit is eternal and everlasting

. . . to the bachelor of wire

Sir: of the everlasting bonfire
(if primrose be the path
there) I will risk the wrath;
I gather you these yellow blooms
and add these other dooms
hereby, three cones, and two sea-shells.
I know of several hells
to which one goes by forest and coast,
but to my principal one,
of a most lamentable ghost,
I myself am the path,
of a most desolate twist and turning
and charming not so much the enchanted senses
as with a magnitude of hill
intensifying the will
                      o hubris!
O, if you set foot there make sure
you test the rise and grease of its floor

. . . to the bachelor of wire

Sir: will you not eat this my poem? Taste
it, waste it, upon fluctuant lip and tongue?
O no, you will not.
                     It is yourself yourself
your own stiff verse you feed upon
and if my love loves you as my love says I do,
pulling down the appetite of heaven star by star
to tease my earth's plain genitals of desire,
the grief between my knees, my breasts of water,
should I not admire this menstrual selfishness?
Indeed I do sir.
               Being all myselfishness,
all hunger for the promontory of hunger,
I love your intricate filament of wire
with all delight in this my bawl of wool

. . . to the bachelor of wire

I see through your limb and your filament
to ordinary contexts of light
and wall and door and city beyond;
yet there are darknesses there.
There are children with Belsens in their yellow hair.
Old men who wipe their moustaches
of prayer, and think that life is
day's regular stool, between evening and morning couches,
the bridal bed and grave I mean.
There are prayers too, who, dear lord, pray
for their contingent customary prey;
your wire circumscribes all these
multitudes of blood and blood's disease

. . . to the bachelor of wire

I see faces as if squeezed in a vice
made arid with power, yet in possession of power
made arid with want of that same power.
The power I want is the power of the face,
the sweet, gentle, sad, unsmiling face of Baudelaire,
to woo the world with, as if I detested it wholly,
yet saw its dark glory lit up with a tenderness,
rejoicing in the agony
which appalls the scaffold, and aching with the tough
                                        indefeasible joy
which moves the hand of the executioner,
sir?

. . . to the bachelor of wire

Of ordinary female headaches, sir, I wouldn't be that one
to cause you to complain.
                                    My head aches
its ache not within the within-organ of my brain
but across square acres of wires
which lead out my eyes, ears and their desires curiosity and fears
into the total enclosure
of absolute enclosing space, so that the all-outside
is my organ of information, from which I cannot
being outered, get out. From this prison
there is simply no exit, since beyond it
doesn't exist;
so in order to escape it it is necessary to unthink it

And this I do.
                      I tear myself back
into my brain, I tear my brain back from its external wires
into my head, I try to compress
myself into the being of Jenny Blake;
and from the torment of the self outside myself
I return to the scourge of myself within;
and it is this which makes the pang

. . . to the bachelor of wire

Last night I dreamt Faustus hid in my powder-room;
I thought he was fascinating Don Juan,
so I didn't bother to telephone the police
but went to bed with careless nakedness;
so that by chance if I should be seduced
I wouldn't be completely disgraced
into behaviour utterly unchaste.
But as I listened for the floor's betraying squeak,
and before I had folded my tactful breasts,
and demurely re-arranged my belly and knees,
I found myself melting into an unexpected kiss,
and when I struggled to say,
                      what is this?
he told me his name, which was — Faustus
And then left me, saying, *Lord have mercy upon us!*
And I realized what terrible doom
had been entered and inscribed into my womb,
and I woke myself with my cry of, rape, rape.
When I was fully and frightfully awake
I supposed I had re-enacted in my dream
my own conception, and I knew that a demon
had confronted and cozened my mother
and that I was *per consequens* half devil's semen.
Which is why, I said, I think it so quaintly modern
to dream obliquely I could be so misbegotten;
and why I cannot exorcise God out of mind
because my flesh is more than half ghost,
almost, but most agonizingly not, totally lost;
and why, without more than a stick of that crutch,
I hunger, as I do, after body so much . . .
Sir?

. . . to the bachelor of wire

This river of wire, in which metal the human heart is drowned;
which if it flow through her who gives it life
is to a child diverted from a wife,
                                hers
or some other's ache, not baptized Jenny Blake
and not passion's wire only by which snare
bachelors take virgins, but all meaning; that mutter
which pushed string makes against reluctant string.
No definition, but only verbal stutter
magnificenced by its random uttering
Nôtre-Dames of pragmatic elbow bones.
For the last irony, all irony, defeats.
The subtle delicate breath-carving tongue
to paradox antithesis conceits
so exquisite in its perfection
to record centuries, or talk away weeks and weeks
hour by hour, or taste a kissing, argument or song,
dumbs the responders by its sculpturing
and we are left wondering but not listening
much. Its very flawlessness its flaw.
Hurls me there —
                      and I till now,
my flower, my flowerlessness, having little of awe

. . . to the bachelor of wire

Sir, of course I've heard of Clauswitz
and his policy which war achieves and peace
defeats:
war lights its candle of human grease
to show us the way
from Belsen to Dresden
and from Dresden to Belsen.
That was then
and a shame to all men.
But now the angels of peace
in broad daylight jump on me
in the park,
I scream and escape into the dark
of night home to my numbered bed
and switch off the light.
But even curled up in sleep
in the rigor mortis of tired out
I dream I am a war criminal.
Though I bellow like a cow
they say that lit up by the electric
light of now
my horns are depraved candles,
devil's not cattle's
wicked out with human cud fat
not Clauswitz's bestial policies
but bestial veterinary's;
so — sir-sorcerer,
you hypocrite lecteur, mon semblable, chèr
sorcier-sorcière moqueur de mon coeur
I am the torturer, it wd seem.
I dream myself into a war criminal
and then into the agriculturist of now's
most humanly-inhumanly suborned farm-animal,
a monster of butterfat production,
much worse because more contra-naturally perfidious
than the Armenian genocide, or Peru's;
all the while my dreaming teat aches
as if it were Jenny Blake's
and less evil than Clauswitz . . . sir?

. . . to the bachelor of wire

Sir, firm to the scaffold walks the sentenced woman
her face composed although her guilt is plain
and we are glad because her courage shows
by the firm way she walks behind her nose
and glad, abandon her unto her fate
and trust the hangman's admirable knot.
Here is our emblem and we see ourselves
caught by our second and our worse resolves;
there is some mercy in the heart of things
which to our vices an assurance brings;
the thief shall have her prayer, and we may claim
by that same mercy, our own necks to damn.
Let churchyards raise a shout of hymen,
                                hymen,
amen, amen;
that flourish off the proceeds of
marriage and the wombs of women.
She has given you her word, sir,
apropos the partake of virgilian curd, sir;
the cooks wed breads and meats
and tribalize the sours and the sweets.
Take, break, eat her copiously, pius Aeneas,
hope in her face
but in her heart she buries virgil's phrase,
produit altum core dolorem.
Sir?

. . . to the bachelor of wire

I wanted to write you a poem about the hanged Absalom
entangled in a single moon-thin curl
of beauty . . . on the top of this hill,
the mountain of Montreal, the *mons veneris* whose sill
flattens out those whom the world's flatulent spit makes tall.
I saw there standing
the great uncombed heart of Jewish Canada
and I was embarrassed by the pathos of an Anglosaxon flame,
Adam Smith's appalling angular I am Adam Smith,
but you are slav or magyar or kwakiutl
or kabuki dancer and understand how to dance the dark hunt of this hill.
Lions must be made to toe the line
so that their pared squared paws can form fours of force
perforce . . . the beatific vision
which irritates the minds of university personnel
in every department and faculty
cracks the heart of the flea.
Sweetheart, do not smile with parted lips at this division,
it is a no new breaking, but last ultimate fission.
Sir?

. . . to the bach. of wire

. . . so it is necessary to train one's flesh
much harder than
an athlete his mind or
an aerialist his vocal chords
or a pianist his conscience
or his misery a clown

For the living phrase of poetry
must be born and suffered
in common flesh and because
I have jenny-blak'd up my nostril
with the smell of glory
I must punish my body
with a continual

discipline. When I write I can write
only of hell. The words twisted out of
Francesca's mouth vs. Beatrice's penal
allegorical smile.
                  But there is a look
perhaps in these last wrenched words
at Dante's face, that wonderful clown's face
of him who knew that the foundation of hell
is bottomed in the human will.
Deny the damned if you will diminish
adam-and-eve kind. If she could
not not repent, so much the less his heaven.
But have no fear, I will not give in.

Thus for herself she damns herself for you.
It is an irony meaning cannot iron
out into unstrangled meanings.
Don't pity her, she glories in these words.
Don't even think that the light you live in
itself lives in the darkness they sin

. . . to the bachelor of wire

Gentlemen always
write bread and butter
letters and never
become
editors or professors

my father told me
sitting in black gaiters
and eating celery

Gentlemen, sir
say their prayers
when necessary
behind locked doors
and though they are not forbidden whores
when they get gentlewomen
with child, they button up their trousers
take their hands out of blouses
and refrain from introducing
bastards into their houses

WILFRED WATSON
pièces je constate

white pelican poems (1)

I Shot a Trumpet into my Brain

> *I would not have you think that I am shut out from a sense of what is called by the Japanese "the Ah-ness of things"; the melancholy inherent in the animal life. But there is a* **Ho-ho-ness** *too. And against the backgrounds of their sempiternal* **Ah-ness** *it is possible, strictly in the foreground, to proceed with a protracted comedy, which glitters against the darkness.*
> P. Wyndham Lewis

    I shot a trumpet into my brain
where it blew out my brains became a wall.
    I shot a trumpet into my brain
my skull bone grew into a tower.
    I shot a trumpet into my brain
and my arm extended into an amphitheatre.
    I shot a trumpet into my brain
my two buttocks became a double bed.
    I shot a trumpet into my brain
and my starved backbone became a plough.
    I shot a trumpet into my brain
my cadaver demanded a lecture hall.
    I shot a trumpet into my brain
and my ah-ness became a cathedral farm.
    I shot a trumpet into my brain
my ho-ho-ness protracted itself into a monastic town.
    I shot a trumpet into my brain
my sensorium was infected with a, b, c's.
    I shot a trumpet into my brain
in the lesion festered a printing press
    I shot a trumpet into my brain
which began to print the Palestrina mass.
    I shot a trumpet into my brain
and my right hand became a cannon ball.
    I shot a trumpet into my brain
and the tears in my eyes dried into gunpowder
    I shot a trumpet into my brain
and my blood ticked away into a clock.

> **Madam Sosostris**
> **is dead**
> **Madam Sosostris**
> **is dead**

How shall we know what to do?
> **Madam Sosostris is dead.**

. . .

She had just sat down to close her eyes
in the fortune-teller's throne beside her bed
and now the world is at the telephone telling the news
the world is swinging its thin cold knees,
   Madam Sosostris is dead!

  2.
    I shot a trumpet into my brain
my left eye became a telescope.
    I shot a trumpet into my brain
my blasted eye-socket suffered a sea-change.
    I shot a trumpet into my brain
and by a conversion became a navigator's sextant.
    I shot a trumpet into my brain
through a fragment of bone I saw a new moon.
    I shot a trumpet into my brain
and my arm-pit blackened into a coal-mine.
    I shot a trumpet into my brain
my left testicle becoming a spinning machine.
    I shot a trumpet into my brain
and when I blew my nose, **there** was a blast furnace.
    I shot a trumpet into my brain
and my spilled dreams became a circulating library.
    I shot a trumpet into my brain
my severed ear became a threshing machine.
    I shot a trumpet into my brain
and my hamstrings developed into a steam locomotive
    I shot a trumpet into my brain
and my jarred nerves extended into the electric telegraph
    I shot a trumpet into my brain
ventilating my conscience in a telegram.
    I shot a trumpet into my brain
and my thoughts re-arranged themselves into the morning newspaper
    I shot a trumpet into my brain
jazzing my insomnias up into head lines
    I shot a trumpet into my brain
then my blind third eye opened and became a camera
    I shot a trumpet into my brain
and my vocal chords were transverberated into a telephone.
    I shot a trumpet into my brain
my fingers being paralyzed into an electric computer.
    I shot a trumpet into my brain
and my sex became a frozen bank of sperm.

    I shot a trumpet into my brain
and my bowel became a polluted river.
    I shot a trumpet into my brain
my delirium became a bottle of champagne.
    I shot a trumpet into my brain
and my fragmented eye became a motion picture machine.
    I shot a trumpet into my brain
collaging my lips tongue and ears into a T.V. screen.
    I shot a trumpet into my brain
and my bladder was canonized into a gas station.
    I shot a trumpet into my brain
all my instincts solidified into a moon machine.
    I shot a trumpet into my brain
my fart fathered an intercontinental rocket.
    I shot a trumpet into my brain
and it opened a door
                  which was a means of
                    control the beginning
                    of law

and you are in
and I am out
and knock knock
knock, I am knock
and you are
knocker.
    I shot a trumpet into my brain
My excrements became an underground sewer.
    I shot a trumpet into my brain
this was the beginning of egghead fun,
                          ho-ho,
look down into the trumpet's mouth and you shall come
to the ah-ahness I am extending from.
                        oh no,
    I shot a trumpet into my brain
I pulverized my heart into a contraceptive pill,
                    amen!
    I shot a trumpet into my brain!

From the Place on the Map

I turn about my eyes to the Ninishith hills
   je t'attends
              but I don't expect any help
not from the Ninishith hills to the north
not from the Clear hills to the west not
from the Birch hills or the Thickwood hills
I turn about my eyes to the Saddle hills
   je t'attends
I don't expect any help from the Saddle hills
I don't expect any word from the Whitemud hills
I turn about my eyes to the hills but
   je t'attends
these expect to be raped with a frying pan
and a guitar a beer bottle and a bottle
of detergent and a can
   je t'attends
but I don't expect any word of help from Mt.
Eisenhower and from Sulphur mountain no
help at all.
These sit very cold in their snow and
the raspberry bushes are closed for the season
   je t'attends
              jadis ma mère m'a dit
jadis quelque chose
I turn my eyes about to the Wintering hills
I turn my eyes about to the Neutral hills
   je t'attends
              and to the Hand hills
but the roads are unplowed all the approaches
closed
        the padlocks on the Middlesand hills
are covered with lust
I turn about my eyes to the Perishing hills
I was stopped in a food store
                      but got away
with a scare and an FLQ in my blouse
   je t'attends

The Departments of Barbed Wire

because they were dishonest
they accused him of dishonesty
    les sonnets de l'honnête amour
such as feeding spiders to the goats
    les sonnets de l'honnête amour
or supply of nanny to the goat-majors
    les sonnets de l'honnête amour
or mixing willow boughs among the hay
but discounting the countesses, it was
nothing much, but minx-turds
    les sonnets de l'honnête amour
I wanted to cry out about them
but they seized me and gagged me with a torn sheet
of paper on which was written
    les sonnets de l'honnête amour
they said he had poured (soiled) river sand into
the wine, and other fornications,
copulations of white and black
    les sonnets de l'honnête amour
he admitted that he had defecated at the bottom of the orchard
for he had a black diarrhoea got
from eating unwashed blueberries
stolen of course from under the white
marble walls
    les sonnets de l'honnête amour
as in Robert Graves
the soldier pleaded diarrhoea but the
corporal knew better:
I examined it, he did it with an effort,
sir
    les sonnets de l'honnête amour
how can one defend the privates of the baited bear
from the goitered throat and throw of
    les sonnets de l'honnête amour

On the Water Plane

    the face of my father
poems like 'I saw the best brains of my generation looking
for an angry fix' are
over.
Poets are dead men speaking forever
to the not yet living, the unborn,
complaining
    the face of my father
is in my eye sockets
is the face of all those I have murdered
turned into Christ in my eye sockets
bear wolf gull calf pig heron herring salmon.
And I will say the moon was greasy on the
water
on the skin of the water pocked by
herring.
    the face of my father
Venus who invented Christ to heal her
broken womb
kissed my father's face. The smile
on
    the face of my father
the crushed head of the adder, the bloody mouth of
the bear shot in the teeth
lives in my eye sockets
a meat saw chips through my frozen flesh
    the face of my father
sucks at the full moon, the soughing water
the halibut holed in the sea's bottom, the
oil-skinned sailor. At
    the face of my father
I will learn what death is and teach it to these
words
        a funeral service home
        stole the body
        of my father
        from me.   And a
        man in a black suit
        blackmailed me into
        assenting to lies
but I will learn what death is and teach it to these
words
    the face of my father

Sonnet with Ragged Edges: Lines

the results of a sense of outrage
so great, it cannot be slaked
by a merely local response

are poetry

don't hope to ease me with the wetness
of one tear

a cc. of resonant water.
It won't do.

This shouts into all space of all
times.

I engrave my complaint
in the flesh of dead women, all
my mothers

and cry out against my sisters
unborn by thousands

whose skull bone is gold leaf
and whose belly is whitest paper
under my pencil

the now going on murder.
That it must not live within this wall
forever.

letter to García Lorca

at five o'clock in the morning
pools of green urine congealing under the mercury street
lamps
the wind at twenty, the wind chill minus eighty
at five o'clock in the morning,
at five o'clock in the morning.
Women and children first, García.
Here in Edmonton we haven't lost urbanity
at five o'clock in the morning
the flow of coffins begins
at five o'clock in the morning
dead nurses and other female corpses
at five o'clock in the morning
and kids pretending to be waitresses
at five o'clock in the morning
white cadavers, carrying frozen lunches
at five o'clock in the morning
I meditate on the hope implicit in a bag lunch
carried
at five o'clock in the morning
in snow and blowing snow but mostly silence.
The dantesquicity of this city
solicits me
at five o'clock in the morning
I have made the sign of the fig at it all
at five o'clock in the morning.
But thank you, García, I am repentant.
at five o'clock in the morning
I have made my peace
at five o'clock in the morning
here in this city where the mixed substances of what
ordinary folk call theft are really a form of distributive
justice
at five o'clock in the morning
I am truly sorry, God, that of all my sins
I wasn't even angrier
being all made out of love for you
at five o'clock in the morning
the mouths of the mail boxes are the mouths of dead cabinet
ministers mouthing me
this
at five o'clock in the morning.

Let those eastern bastards know the ferocity with which
we freeze, García
at five o'clock in the morning

january 30, 1974

Portrait of a Woman

   contemplating the sole of her foot
she pulled her left heel across her knee
portrait of a woman
   observing the sole of her foot
she said, this callus was made by the trail to
Antioch
   observing the sole of her foot
she said, this crease was cut by Grecian sands,
at the beach near Athens, to which Orestes fled
followed by Clytemnestra and his mother's blood
kin
   observing the sole of her foot
she said, and these toe pads were crushed into
pads in the ravine near Aulis.
Perhaps, I said.
She thrust out her foot, straightening her leg,
and said, see.
I saw more than the raw wound which neither
Theseus nor Peirithous nor Menelaus nor Paris
could heal
I saw the flexing of the muscle which built
Pachama, Cajamarquilla and Vista Alegre
and her hands full of the amazing maize,
the seed which peopled the unwritten cities

the sorrowful canadians and other poems/ les malheureux

lines 1967

THERE WILL BE NO MORE MONEY FOR YOU
there will be no more money for you
if snow be white, why then her breasts are dung
THERE WILL BE NO MORE MONEY FOR YOU
you will be one of the managers of automation
you will have no   leisure at all
THERE WILL BE NO MORE MONEY FOR YOU
scarlet ornaments for me to profane, her lips
but yet
THERE WILL BE NO MORE MONEY FOR YOU
you will sit at your desk trying to remain in
charge
est-ce tant que la mort?
but your function will be superfluous
THERE WILL BE NO MORE MONEY FOR YOU
there will be no more money for you
there won't be any credit cards, either
THERE WILL BE NO MORE MONEY FOR YOU
you will try to write scholarly articles in a
popular style about the need to teach the
dispossessed how to enjoy leisure
but
THERE WILL BE NO MORE MONEY FOR YOU
YOU WILL SIT AT YOUR DESK TRYING TO REMAIN IN CHARGE
GAZING AT THE REPRODUCTION ON THE WALL OF CHAGALL'S HORSE EATING A VIOLIN
tu ne mangeras plus.

the sorrowful Canadians

the radiant grief of the owners of so much
snow
THE SORROWFUL CANADIANS
APPALLS ME
    THE SORROWFUL CANADIANS
MAKES ME INTO A SORROWFUL
CANADIAN
to have so much world in a world where men
have so little
THE SORROWFUL CANADIANS
and to be grief s pig
THE SORROWFUL CANADIANS
and always blowing their noses
     the sorrowful Canadians
with their bleeding fingers
north south east and west
in the bushes
THE SORROWFUL CANADIANS
ou grouille une enfance bouffonne
THE SORROWFUL CANADIANS
      their flame
gutted, gutting, leur chandelle triste
THE SORROWFUL CANADIANS
lopsided, more tallow than wick or skin
THE SORROWFUL CANADIANS
     what are they good for?
     what have they done wrong?
     where did they get lost?
so much earth
comme un excès de sang épanché tous les mois
THE SORROWFUL CANADIANS,
what have they done to deserve this?

lines summer 1967

I PREPARE MY GRAVE IN QUICK SAND they
build me a coffin of dead words
and incase it in a loud lead sarcophagus of ink
I must return them my borrowed
heart and pay use-rent with my
life.
I PREPARE MY GRAVE IN A QUICK SAND
I am murdered with an explanation.
Wounded with a metaphor of grass.
I matted up a shroud of immediacy
but they will stitch my mouth up into a ghastly smile
and say I have created a form
which they will exhume tomorrow
and attach their new meaning to
was their purple cadillac the cab of the holy ghost?
I PREPARE MY GRAVE IN A QUICK SAND
but they want to bury us all in a hadean
cock à la Yeats, with three main categories
of metal, the critics — gold, the novelists —
braaass, the poets — lead.
                      coco rico
I PREPARE MY GRAVE IN A QUICK SAND
and all those who come to the edge of it will
fall through my hand

lines January 1971

pour moi, j'ai retiré mes pieds
**WE CANNOT TALK TO THESE CONTEMPORARIES
IN ANYTHING LIKE
POETRY**
pour moi, j'ai retiré mes pieds
**WE CAN CHANT MAKE LOVE NOT WAR
MAKE LOVE NOT WAR IN ANGER WHICH EXCEEDS
THE TIME**
pour moi, j'ai retiré mes pieds
                    **THUS
WE SHALL OVERKILL
AND THE FUZZ ARE GUILTY AND UP AGAINST
THE WALL MOTHERFUCKER etcetera etcetera
mais**
pour moi, j'ai retiré mes pieds
**DO NOT SAY, PEANUT BUTTER MAKES YOU STERILE
OR, EUTHANASIA KILLS OR, REALITY IS A
CRUTCH OR, HELP THE MORALLY RETARDED, OR,
ARGENTINA IS ALIVE AND SOMEWHERE IN
BRAZIL**
pour moi, j'ai retiré mes pieds
**I ADDRESS MYSELF
TO WORDS TO SOLACE
UNBORN BLOOD, TO BE BORN IN ANOTHER
TIME, MALE AND FEMALE, LYING TOGETHER
SLAKING EACH OTHER KISS BY KISS**
pour moi, j'ai retiré mes pieds
**I WILL SAY WHAT CANNOT BE SAID
NOW
THEIR TEARS WILL REACH ME LYING IN
THE ROOTED AND CARNAL EARTH**

poem 1970

MY WILD BODY IS A CORPSE
                                          I
believe in the resurrection of the wild
body
MY WILD BODY IS A CORPSE
I believe in all sorts of strange things
MY WILD BODY IS A CORPSE
I bury it every day but like the corpse
in that play of Ionesco's, it gets out
of the grave I put it in and grows
and grows
MY WILD BODY IS A CORPSE
VERY GROSS OF VERY GROSS
I bury it every day and every way in a
thousand public actions in the labour
of food, having sex, and
roof trouble
MY WILD BODY IS A CORPSE
I bury it everyday I sing requiems to
my wild body the corpse, but when I am
about to say, dust to dust, ashes to ashes
                                                        it
knocks on the lid of the coffin, **KNOCK**
KNOCK
MY WILD BODY IS A CORPSE
and when I unscrew the lid, it sits up
and sings, man is a noble potato
MY WILD BODY IS A CORPSE
when I put my hands round its throat,
it lets out a shout,
if you put out my eyes, I will grow a
snout
MY WILD BODY IS A CORPSE

Antigone aux sales mains

they inked in my intestines
WE ANOINTED OUR BODIES WITH TALCUM POWER
they inked in my intestines
THEY POURED A WINE LIBATION OR TWO INTO THE
ARTERY OF SOME FLOWER OR OTHER
they inked in my intestines
THE TALKATIVE CHRYSANTHEMUM OR MUMMY POSSEST
they inked in my intestines
I SUPPOSE. I SUPPOSE SO. THERE
WERE PIN PRICKS
they inked in my intestines
PIN PRICKS FIT INTO PIN HOLES AND SO OF COURSE
PINS HAVE SEX AND WHY NOT?
they inked in my intestines
but can a pinhead attached to the American Pin
Company of Canada thread linen through the eye
of a needle?
THEY INKED IN MY INTESTINES
but this isn't the right nipple. My tits are up
tight tonight
THEY INKED IN MY INTESTINES
No, tact must be punctual. Punks tactual
O sale espoir!
THEY INKED IN MY INTESTINES
THOSE BARE FACED BLACK MOUNTAIN GOATS THEY
PISSED OUT OF MY PENIS
THEY INKED IN MY INTESTINES
THEY SHIT OUT OF MY RECTUM THEY SWALLOWED WITH
MY MOUTH
THEY INKED IN MY INTESTINES
THEY ELBOWED OUT MY ELBOW, THEY BIT OFF MY TEETH
THEY INKED IN MY INTESTINES
**THEY BAWLED OUT BALLS AT MY BALLS THEY HEADED OFF
MY HEAD**

2.
we were invited to concentrate our minds on what
was going on inside. We had tried to visualize
a colony of much-twisted, sorely tried intestines,
screwed this way and that, as they had never been
screwed before. It was an anatomical piece
THEY INKED IN MY INTESTINES
eh bien, lathed nicely, the wormwood axles of the
robins re-cycle birdsong, jargon
THEY INKED IN MY INTESTINES

minotaurization of the circuits characterizes
the period
THEY INKED IN MY INTESTINES
circuses are etched on walls, Parties caucus
gaily
THEY INKED IN MY INTESTINES
prairie crocuses are blotched with wonderful
people
THEY INKED IN MY INTESTINES
stuff strawberries into her miniskirts
THEY INKED IN MY INTESTINES
and she pulled at my hand, and throwing her eyes
up to the security police hanging down from the
roof like gargoyles, began to sing
BENEATH THE CROTCH OF JASON I FAIN WOULD TAKE MY STAND
THEY INKED IN MY INTESTINES
barbed wire sawing through my guts was too much
for this voyeurist
THEY INKED IN MY INTESTINES
blimey, he cried, my eyes are clobbered with blank
griefs. What could she do with the chalk bluffs
of Dover? Mates, shove her under the mat. Cover
her revolver. Her eyes pistol. She died
junk
THEY INKED IN MY INTESTINES
the moon inched under the pebble stones
THEY INKED IN MY INTESTINES
le beau Sophocle never heard anything like it. The
drench and anguish of, the badly rattled, the pish
and drawl of the sea. Passacaglia. Moon
suck and water sprawl
THEY INKED IN MY INTESTINES
she's cute in the worst scents, he said. Two butter-
flies shacking up in a cupboard of cupids. The god
of love said, make love and they made octopuses o great
big hairy delight. Instant
rock cod.
THEY INKED IN MY INTESTINES
and if you think you have no concupiscence in your make-
up you may be thrown by the first stone. Cut off your
lips. Blood cuddles thicker than
water
THEY INKED IN MY INTESTINES
ponds of milk. Hunt me up the melting points. I will
let you in by the black door

lines winter 1971

THE WHITE PELICAN MTS ARE COVERED WITH SNOW
Canadians, he asked?
there are only north americans, she said
THE WHITE PELICAN MTS ARE COVERED WITH WHITE POLAR BEAR SKINS
gor blimey, said the stage cockney, what a sell
THE WHITE PELICAN MTS ARE COVERED WITH STRONTIUM NINETY
it gets into the hair it gets into the milk
it gets into the tins of tuna fish
THE WHITE PELICAN MTS ARE COVERED WITH WHITEFISH
somewhere to the north
the roof is thick. there are polar bears in
the wet straw
THE WHITE PELICAN MTS ARE COVERED WITH SNOW
they said, why do you hate us for being
one hundred per cent red blooded americans
**THE WHITE PELICAN MTS ARE COVERED WITH EAGLE SHIT
SHIT, SHE SAID
THE WHITE PELICAN MTS ARE COVERED WITH JAPANESE STRIP MINES
SHIT, SHE SAID, BUT I KNOW THAT THE PROPER WAY TO STOP GENOCIDE IS TO ABOLISH THE IMAGES AND PULL BACK THE AMERICAN FLAG FROM THE MOON, I.E., ABOLISH THE MOON, WHICH IS ALREADY AN AMERICAN FLAG**
the white pelican mts are covered with pulpmill dew

2.
**THE WHITE PELICAN MTS ARE COVERED WITH SNOW I WILL GO TO THE SHOP OF IMAGES AND BUY YOU A BUNCH OF FIREWEED, SOME WILD BLACKBERRIES, A BAG OF FIR BARK, A KWAKIUTL CEDARWOOD MASK, AND SOMETHING PRECIOUS, LIKE A DROP OF PURE WATER ENCAVED IN A CUBE OF AMBER. AND A BELUGA WHALE FEATHER
THE WHITE PELICAN MTS ARE COVERED WITH SNOW**
my parents were from London
THE WHITE PELICAN MTS ARE COVERED WITH SNOW
does it matter that I was born in Rochester
and learned to swim in the Blackwater?
the white pelican mts are covered with snow
MY FRIEND, she said, **THIS IS A POTLATCH**
the white pelican mts are covered with snow
I LEARNED TO SAW WOOD AT CHEMAINUS
the white pelican mts are covered with snow

A POTLATCH, she said
the white pelican mts are covered with snow
the flute, I said, is hemlock and tastes sour
a potlatch, they asked
THE WHITE PELICAN MOUNTAINS ARE COVERED WITH SNOW
the violin is red cedar, I said, and poisons the chin
THE WHITE PELICAN MOUNTAINS ARE COVERED WITH SNOW
A POTLATCH, SHE SAID, I HAVE THROWN WALDEN POND INTO THE FIRE. YOU WILL HAVE TO MATCH IT WITH STONEHENGE
the white pelican mts are covered with snow
CAN YOU CLEAN A SALMON, they asked, **AND I SAID NO AND PLUNGED MY HANDS INTO THE FISH**
the white pelican mts are covered with snow
AS WE BUMPED OUR WAY THROUGH HECATE STRAITS I SLEPT, MY FACE AGAINST THE STORM. AT MASSETT HARBOUR MY MIND WAS BLOWN BY A SHIP'S WHISTLE
the white pelican mts are covered with snow

3.
Ô LA FACE CENDRÉE, L'ÉCUSSON DE CRIN, LES BRAS
at point no point there were sea anemones in
your eyes
les genoux dans les cendres de la mer
our buckets grate together in the same well
THE WHITE PELICAN MOUNTAINS
ARE
but then everything is covert, the birds keep
secrets from the foxes, the foxes are furtive. I
turn my eyes to Lenin's tomb. The political significance
of a tear, said Lenin, is nil.
THE WHITE PELICAN MOUNTAINS

poem summer 1967

THE LONG SORROW FILES INTO MY SOUL
they walk over me
with heavy feet
an army of heavy-handed footmen
bruise my head
THEIR DOUR PLATOONS FILE INTO MY SOUL
I built roads
which have become inroads into and led invasions into
the secrecy of my being
THE LONG SORROW FILES INTO MY SOUL
the battalions of science & metascience
fall back to their home city
THE LONG SORROW FILES INTO MY SOUL
& my soul fouls
THE LONG SORROW FILES INTO MY SOUL
the day was, I begot the
                        sons of morning
and they bite at me with their white teeth
and smile as they drink my blood
THE LONG SORROW FILES INTO MY SOUL
my fascist senses have
                        patrolled the universe
and return to cut my throat.
THE LONG SORROW FILES INTO MY SOUL
I gave them wine in which I floated petals of
gardenia
and now they return to drink into my blood
THE LONG SORROW FILES INTO MY SOUL

the suicide, 1966

HE JUST LAY DOWN AND DIED
they poured his body in a pool on the ground
HE JUST LAY DOWN AND DIED
they ganged up on him and shot him in the heart
the lungs and the groin
HE JUST LAY DOWN AND DIED
we weep with his friends
HE JUST LAY DOWN AND DIED
we offer our sympathies to his wife and family.
there was his mistress walking down the road as
if she was lost
HE JUST LAY DOWN AND DIED
they poured his blood in a pool on the ground and
he just lay down and died.
THE CORONER DECIDED THAT DESPITE A CONTEXT OF MURDER HIS DEATH MUST BE ADJUDGED SUICIDE
HE JUST LAY DOWN AND DIED
EVEN WHEN WE BURIED HIM IN UNCONSECRATED GROUND, HE DIDN'T PROTEST
HE JUST LAY DOWN AND DIED

good friday, 1970

THE INVADERS OF VIETNAM ARE PRISONERS
            their faces
chained together like the faces of a chain
gang
THE INVADERS OF VIETNAM ARE PRISONERS
            the faces
of men who have no faces of their own
          their faces
taken away
the faces of men without identity
THE INVADERS OF VIETNAM ARE PRISONERS
WITHOUT CORPORATE IMAGE
THE FACES OF THE INVADERS OF VIETNAM
ARE THE FACES OF MEN WITHOUT A FOOTING
ON THE FACE OF THE EARTH
THE INVADERS OF VIETNAM ARE PRISONERS
que vous puis-je donner, sinon que le soleil?
taking advantage of their poverty
         those we
call friends and allies shut them up
THE INVADERS OF VIETNAM
           in a cloth prison
our friends called it a uniform and wardened
it with officers
THE INVADERS OF VIETNAM
our friends shut them up in a common shirt
and a short haircut
       cut off their names
and numbered them
INVADERS
   YOU WHO WERE WITH ME IN THE SHIT AT MYLAE
INVADERS
   YOU WHO WERE WITH ME IN THE BLACKWATER
AFFAIR AT MALDON
      YOU WHO WERE WITH HARRY THE KING BEFORE
HARFLEUR
THEREFORE INVADERS
     YOU WHO WERE WITH ME AT MY LAI
que vous puis-je donner, sinon que le soleil

HANOI

is here we have only a few poems to defend
ourselves with
AGAINST THE WAR THAT FLIES ACROSS OUR BORDERS
AT THE SPEED OF LIGHT DROPPING IMAGES ALIKE
ON WOMEN CHILDREN AND BABIES
AND RAPES OUR TEENAGERS BODY AND MIND
we have only a few poems to defend ourselves
with
WE HAVE SILENTLY DISAPPROVED OF THE BOMBING
OF HANOI BUT FIND OUT THAT
HANOI IS HERE SHOUTING IN OUR FACES HANOI
IS HERE TEARING US APART WILD BODY
AND MAGICAL BODY
HANOI IS HERE
we have only a few poems to defend ourselves
with **MAKE LOVE NOT WAR** we have only a few poems
to defend ourselves with **HANOI IS HERE** we have
only a few poems to defend ourselves with **MAKE
LOVE NOT WAR** we have only a few poems to defend
ourselves with
Hanoi is here **WE WANT TO KISS CHRIST NOT NAIL
HIM TO THE CROSS** Hanoi is here shouting in
our faces, **WE
HAVE ONLY A FEW POEMS TO DEFEND OURSELVES
WITH
HANOI IS HERE**

lines 1967

they flew across our borders at the speed
of light.
HANOI IS HERE
dropping images which fell alike on women
children and infants.
HANOI IS HERE
we had only a few poems to defend ourselves
with.
HANOI IS HERE
and no strong men like Thoreau, Whitman or
Lincoln
HANOI IS HERE
they criss-crossed over our houses, dropping
vowels that were block-busters.
HANOI IS HERE
they set up bazookas which lopped novels into
our roofs.
HANOI IS HERE
they raked our streets with plays.
they sent in lowflying jets armed with
recordings.
they blew us to bits just as we were saying
they seemed such nice people
HANOI IS HERE

2.
HANOI IS HERE,
                        from many lands, we were trying to
put ourselves together, to piece together the
horse and the man, the woman and the lion
HANOI IS HERE
disguising themselves as university professors
their commandoes fell upon our mother the
sphinx
HANOI IS HERE
but when they discovered that her genitalia were
those of the male lion, they cursed her.
it was horrible to hear them.
HANOI IS HERE
they sent in squads of surgeons, who operated
on our mother's lion backparts and changed her
into a female monster.
HANOI IS HERE
they carved out a vulva with a scalpel

HANOI IS HERE
they raped her one by one, millions of them
HANOI IS HERE

3.
she has smeared her breasts with lion's
excrements
HANOI IS HERE
she has anointed her head with gasoline
HANOI IS HERE
she has set fire to her hair.
HANOI IS HERE
her death was like a sunset.
HANOI IS HERE
the rain fell, but caught fire from her
death, and all the clouds were ablaze with
the flame of her burning hair
HANOI IS HERE
though they turned their hoses on her, they
were unable to prevent her head being cremated
into a cinder. They gave us her head to bury
HANOI IS HERE
they shipped her body to their schools of
experimental medicine
HANOI IS HERE
we had silently disapproved of the bombing
of Hanoi, but found out that
HANOI IS HERE
they flew across our borders with the speed of
light dropping images and they raped our
mother the sphinx.
HANOI IS HERE
HANOI IS HERE

lines 1966

the long cool seminars
we lay around like waxworks in Madame Tussaud's
palace
the long cool seminars
**LAZY AS CATS, WE STRETCHED OUT OUR WILD BODIES
ON THE BROADLOOM**
the long cool seminars
**FROM FIVE O'CLOCK IN THE AFTERNOON UNTIL FIVE IN
THE MORNING**
the long cool seminars
while our neighbour was dripping his love on the
Viet Cong
THE LONG COOL SEMINARS
we talked of the wild body and of the magical
body, and argued about Alfred Lord Tennyson, the
black mountain, the sadness of James Joyce, the
miserabilisme of Samuel Beckett and the jug jug
jug to dirty ears-ism of T.S. Eliot
THE LONG COOL SEMINARS
we all put on academic robes and jumped into a
swimming pool
THE LONG COOL SEMINARS
though we all got wet only one of us got drowned
THE LONG COOL SEMINARS
when she floated to the top of the pool for the third
time, he said, my god, she has lovely breasts
THE LONG COOL SEMINARS
and all the time her death or someone's death or
just death was shouting at us like a crowd out to
get someone
the long cool seminars

lines 1966

What more did they want?
THEY MANAGED TO ENGAGE DANTE TO GIVE A VERSE READING AT THE YARDBIRD SUITE
What more did they want?
IT WASN'T AS IF HE HAD JUST CROSSED THE OCEAN IN AN OPEN ROWBOAT. SOMETHING WE DO ALL THE TIME
What more did they want?
IT WASN'T AS IF HE HAD JUST CLIMBED Mt EVEREST OR ESTABLISHED A BASE CAMP ON ANNA PURNA
What more did they want?
IT WASN'T AS IF HE HAD BEEN WORKING AS A SOCIAL SERVICE WORKER IN THE U.S. NORTH OR SOUTH OF THE U.S. NAVEL, AMONG THE BLACKS
What more did they want?
DID THEY EXPECT HIM TO LOOK LIKE LEONARD COHEN AND STAND BEFORE THEM NODDING A SILKEN UNICORN'S MANE? HE TOLD THEM HE HAD SPOKEN TO FRANCESCA
What more did they want?
HE TOLD THEM HE HAD SPOKEN TO THAT MAN BERTRAN DE BORN WHO CAME WALKING TOWARDS HIM CARRYING HIS HEAD BY THE HAIR
What more did they want?
HE TOLD THEM HE HAD PUT HIS HAND IN THE MOUTH OF SATAN WHO AT THE CENTRE OF HELL WAS CHEWING BRUTUS AND CASSIUS
What more did they want?
DID THEY EXPECT HIM TO APPEAR BEFORE THEM WEARING THE MAGNIFICENT LION'S HEAD OF IRVING LAYTON? HE TOLD THEM HE HAD GAZED INTO THE EYES OF BEATRICE. HE DIDN'T SAY WHAT HE SAW
What more did they want?
DID THEY EXPECT HIM TO LOOK LIKE THE PORTRAIT OF YEATS BY AUGUSTUS JOHN? HE WAS PREMATURELY OLD
What more did they want?
HE TOLD THEM HE HAD CLIMBED DOWN LIKE A SPELUNKER INTO THE HOT BELLY OF HELL. DID THEY EXPECT HIM TO LOOK LIKE EDGAR ALLEN POE OR ROBERT CREELEY?
What more did they want?
I thought he looked like someone who had accomplished something. There were those who thought he looked more like an ex-convict than like a mystic.
WHAT MORE DID THEY WANT?
He had climbed up through purgatory. He had climbed up into the

. . .

highest heaven of paradise. Did they expect him to look like the Archbishop of Canterbury? He looked like a business man worn out with business
WHAT MORE DID THEY WANT?
He looked old and tired. He was not an unqualified success. Still everyone agreed it was a good thing to have invited him to come to the Yardbird Suite
WHAT MORE DID WE WANT?

the french bear

what gorgeous graveflowers blossom at that throat
BUT YET I WOULD NOT KISS THAT THROAT TOO SOON
what gorgeous graveflowers blossom at that throat
WE'D PROCURED A FRENCH BEAR TO HONOUR THE FRENCH
AMBASSADOR
what gorgeous graveflowers blossom at that throat
THE BEAR STRUCK HIS PAW AT THE MALICIOUS AIR, AND
WE LAUGHED AT THE BEAST THERE AND HE STRUCK AT THE
MALICIOUS AIR AGAIN AND AGAIN
what gorgeous graveflowers blossom at that throat
BUT THE DOGS BEGAN TO CLOSE IN ON HIM TOO EAGERLY
AND CONSIDERING WHAT A BEAR IS WORTH WE HELD THEM
OFF SO THAT THE FRENCH AMBASSADOR COULD HAVE ALL
JOY OF THE DOING IN OF THE BEAR
what gorgeous graveflowers blossom at that throat
AND THE BLOOD OF M. THE BEAR BEGAN TO RUN INTO THE
SAND AND THE FRENCH MONSEIGNEUR CRIED OUT, MON
DIEU, MON DIEU, and the queen's cousin said that is
enough
what gorgeous graveflowers blossom at that throat
SO WE LED M. THE BEAR AWAY UNSATISFIED BUT OF COURSE
WE GOT OUR FEE STILL WE'D EXPECTED MORE SPORT THAN
THAT
what gorgeous graveflowers blossom at that throat
AND THE SUN EARLY AND THE AFTERNOON HARDLY BEGUN
what gorgeous graveflowers blossom at that throat
IT IS NOT EVERYONE WITH STOMACH ENOUGH TO STOMACH
THE DEATH OF THE BEAR
what gorgeous graveflowers blossom at that throat
STONE HEARTS OF COURSE NERVES OF STEEL COOL HEADS
BLOODY FIERY SOULS ALL RIGHT BUT THAT'S WHERE THEY
fail their gut falters their stomachs turn before
the doing to death of the bear & we apologised to
m. the bear
but m. the bear was disappointed all right
WHAT GORGEOUS GRAVEFLOWERS BLOSSOM AT THAT THROAT

lines may 1st 1966

the sins of the fathers forgive the grandfathers.
MY BROTHER AND I DECIDED ON A SUMMARY EXECUTION
the sins of the fathers forgive the grandfathers.
WE MADE EXCUSES FOR HIS AMIABLE FOLLIES, ESPECIALLY A VAIN WISH TO SPARE US SUFFERINGS, DEPRIVATIONS, BOREDOMS WHICH HAD STUNG HIM TO THE TEETH
the sins of the fathers forgive the grandfathers.
OUR HEADS WERE NOT YET GRAY, HIS HEAD WAS NOT YET WHITE
the sins of the fathers forgive the grandfathers
BUT WE DECIDED IN THE HEAT OF MIDSUMMER OUR WRONGS HAD LASTED TOO LONG.
the sins of the fathers forgive the grandfathers.
WE ACCUSED OUR FATHER OF BEING PARTY TO OUR RAPES AND OF CONDONING OUR LECHEROUS INSTINCTS
the sins of the fathers forgive the grandfathers
THE SMILE WITH WHICH HE GREETED THIS INFURIATED US
the sins of the fathers forgive the grandfathers
WE ACCUSED OUR FATHER OF TEACHING US TO BE MURDERERS

2.
the sins of the fathers forgive the grandfathers
AS EVIDENCE THERE WERE TOY PISTOLS, BURNED OUT FIRE CRACKERS, TWENTY-TWO RIFLES, A CHEAP SHOT-GUN, FISHING EQUIPMENT, A GLOVE FOR KILLING MINK WITHOUT DAMAGING THE PELTS, A TRAP FOR EARWIGS (HOME-MADE:, A BROKEN KILLER KANE FOR KILLING DANDELIONS, A USED INSECTICIDE BOMB WE HAD AIMED AT A WASP NEST IN A DISUSED GARBAGE TIN, AND VARIOUS PIECES OF LIKE EVIDENCE.
the sins of the fathers forgive the grandfathers
WE ACCUSED OUR FATHER OF TEACHING US AN OBSCENE LOVE FOR THE CREATURE MONEY.
the sins of the fathers forgive the grandfathers
WE GENEROUSLY GAVE HIM A CHANCE TO DEFEND HIMSELF.
the sins of the fathers forgive the grandfathers
MY FATHER, REPLIED OUR FATHER, WAS LECHEROUS, MURDEROUS AND FULL OF LOVE FOR THE CREATURE MONEY
the sins of the fathers forgive the grandfathers
WE REFUSED THE EXCUSE
the sins of the fathers forgive the grandfathers

WE ERECTED A SCAFFOLD
the sins of the fathers forgive the grandfathers

3.
WE MADE THE EXECUTION AS CRUEL AS POSSIBLE, SO THAT OUR SONS SHOULDN'T BE ABLE TO BLAME US IN THIS KIND.
the sins of the fathers excuse the grandfathers
AS HE DIED, HE CRIED OUT, MY FATHER WAS OEDIPUS
the sins of the fathers forgive the grandfathers.
IT WAS A FLAGRANT DEATH, AND THE TEARS WE COULD NOT EASILY SUPPRESS COMPROMISED OUR RIGHTEOUSNESS. THE SINS OF THE FATHERS EXCUSE THE GRANDFATHERS

lines spring 1969

THEY PROVIDED ME WITH WORDS HARDER THAN STONE
they gave me letters of some metal harder
than eternal brass and
they said, spell something out
THEY GAVE ME LETTERS HARDER THAN STONE
I held all the hot egos of the world in my
hand
THEY GAVE ME LETTERS HARDER THAN STONE
saying who are you and what is your name and
what are your qualifications
THEY GAVE ME LETTERS HARDER THAN STONE
A.B.C.D.E.F.G.H.I.J.K.L.M.N.O.P.Q. F.O.B.
F.B.I.F.L.Q. ETC.
THEY GAVE ME LETTERS HARDER THAN STONE
& said write
so I wrote down my name in letters harder
than stone.
I found I had written down the names of everyone
in the telephone directory
their faces shone like lanterns in my eyes
THEY GAVE ME LETTERS HARDER THAN STONE
they seemed pleased.
it was like putting all the buildings of the
world back in the stone quarry.
je me demand

lines winter 1970

THE WATER IS TEN THOUSAND LAMINATIONS OF PLEXIGLAS
THICK
THE GAUDY BLABBING AND REMORSELESS DAY
THE CRUEL WATER, THIS WATER HAS TEN THOUSAND CAVES
THE GAUDY BLABBING AND REMORSELESS DAY
poets can spare us by not bothering to make any
additions, we don't want any more of that sort of
piss
THE GAUDY BLABBING AND REMORSELESS DAY
THE GAUDY BLABBING AND REMORSELESS DAY
LET THEM DUCK UNDER THE MOON
AND DITCHING ALL THIS VISUAL PUDDLE
TAKE AS THEIR MODEL
                        THE PIERRE ELIOT TRUDEAU
OR MARSHALL MCLUHAN
BUT WE'RE QUITE DIFFERENT
THE GAUDY BLABBING AND REMORSELESS DAY
                                          WE ARE NOT
FISH
    OUR BLINDNESS IS THAT OF DROWNING MEN TRYING TO FIND
THEIR WAY OUT OF TEN THOUSAND CAVES OF PLEXIGLAS
O PAULINE, HOW APPALLING IS APOLLO
OUR POETRY, POT
OUR SOUL, THIS WHEEL
OUR BURN, INTO THE THINNEST GLAZE
AND OUR BODY, THESE CLAYS

lines 1964

THE BLACK MOUTH OF THE DOG WAS FULL OF QUILLS
I do not know whether this particular porcupine
had bathed in the waters of Midas and become
saturated with the yellow filth
THE BLACK MOUTH OF THE DOG WAS FULL OF QUILLS
perhaps this porcupine had got splashed by the seminal
yellow shower of love which raped Danae?
THE BLACK MOUTH OF THE DOG WAS FULL OF QUILLS
or perhaps the golden quill of the porcupine was
merely an illusion, without any base in reality
THE BLACK MOUTH OF THE DOG WAS FULL OF QUILLS
no one knows whether the quill of the porcupine
was five, ten, fourteen, eighteen carat or absolutely
pure gold
THE BLACK MOUTH OF THE DOG WAS FULL OF QUILLS
we made no attempt to see where the porcupine with
the golden quill had shuffled off to
THE BLACK MOUTH OF THE DOG WAS FULL OF QUILLS
we never actually saw the porcupine with the golden
quills and we never heard tell of anyone who had
seen it or who had heard of anyone who had
THE BLACK MOUTH OF THE DOG WAS FULL OF QUILLS
blood flowed freely down the yellow needles. the
face of the dog was gilded with death. the eyes
of the dog were pierced with nails of gold
THE BLACK MOUTH OF THE DOG WAS FULL OF QUILLS
there was nothing to do except to put the beast
out of its misery as quickly as possible, or so we
decided
THE BLACK MOUTH OF THE DOG WAS FULL OF QUILLS
we dug a quick grave for the dead beast and shoveled
the brute into the hollow dry crumbling blind
earth
THE BLACK MOUTH OF THE DOG WAS FULL OF QUILLS
not one of us said that the buried needles might be
worth money
THE BLACK MOUTH OF THE DOG WAS FULL OF QUILLS
we laughed and said that one day we would come back
and hunt the porcupine with the quills of gold
THE BLACK MOUTH OF THE DOG WAS FULL OF QUILLS

lines 1968

the sucked and hungry lioness
IT WAS TEA TIME AND THEY SAID WILL YOU DRINK TEA
WITH US AND THEY POURED OUT A TEACUPFUL OF SUL-
PHURIC ACID
the sucked and hungry lioness
IT WAS IN LATE OCTOBER SOFT SAD MICHELMAS AND
YOU KNOW WHAT THAT'S LIKE AND THEY SAID SOMEONE
HAS PUT RAZOR BLADES IN THE APPLES AND SOMEONE
SAID IT'S AN OLD TRICK THIS SORT OF MALICE ISN'T NEW
IT'S JUST BEEN REVIVED
the sucked and hungry lioness
IT WAS LATE OCTOBER AND AS I WALKED OUT THE
STREET WAS DOING THINGS THE OTHER SIDE OF THE
STREET HAD MELTED AWAY INTO A SEA SHORE AND
EVERYONE DROVE THEIR CARS INTO THE WAVES SPLISH
SPLASH SPLOSH AND SOMEONE SAID, WHEN THE TIDE
GOES OUT, WE SHALL HAVE TO DISPOSE OF ALL THE
BODIES
the sucked and hungry lioness
THE SUCKED AND HUNGRY LIONESS
there were twentyfour american soldiers examining the
body of a vietnamese child with her head shattered by a
bomb and there were twohundredandforty american soldiers
examining the bodies of ten vietnamese children children
with their heads shattered by a bomb and there were
twentyfourhundred american soldiers examining the bodies
of one hundred vietnamese girl children with their heads
shattered by a bomb but I lost count that's the trouble with
escalation you lose count but please believe me it was quite
an experience
THE SUCKED AND HUNGRY LIONESS
and she said in a low voice in the low bleat of a young child
though she must have been thirty my heart's all right but
even it it wasn't I wouldn't want someone else's heart stored
in an ape's chest no
THE SUCKED AND HUNGRY LIONESS
all I have is a bit of a cold, she said, so we painted her with
napalm instant cremation it was a mad time and I don't
think we were in our right mind I hope we weren't in our
right mind and there was provocation fortunately the
napalm saved our skins they wanted to pin rape on us but
there was no evidence there was no evidence and we got
time spent in custody and much more believe me

. . .

THE SUCKED AND HUNGRY LIONESS
we had stolen a carton of shells for her but she didn't make
a good pelt
THE SUCKED AND HUNGRY LIONESS

lines january 1967

portrait of the artist during centennial year
BELUGA WHALES IN AN ICE POT
canada nineteen sixty seven
BELUGA WHALES IN AN ICE POT
Configurations 1932 Three forms movable on one
large form plaster, collection the artist, Jean Arp
BELUGA WHALES IN AN ICE POT
He taught us to see the forms of snow.
(some critic)
BELUGA WHALES IN AN ICE POT
works of art should remain anonymous in nature's
great studio — Arp
BELUGA WHALES IN AN ICE POT
man must re-enter nature — Arp, Arp
Beluga whales in an ice pot

2.
BELUGA WHALES IN AN ICE POT
Lila Dicken, who taught school in Inuvik, before she came
down here to die, sent me a year's subscription to the
DRUM, edited by Tom Butters, the Inuvik paper which
reminds us, issue of December 22, 1966, 'Merry Christmas
leaps not easily to the lips this year. That Viet Cong crisped
by napalm. He was a man. That American soldier wounded
and dispatched with a head shot. He was a man. That child
dead from a Viet Cong trip mine or a splinter from a high
explosive casing dropped by a B52. He would have been a
man'
BELUGA WHALES IN AN ICE POT
quote — the plight of the white whales trapped in the
Eskimo Lakes seems to have reached across Canada
BELUGA WHALES IN AN ICE POT
people seem to have become emotional about the slim
chances of their surviving the long freeze — unquote
(letter to the editor of the **DRUM**)
BELUGA WHALES IN AN ICE POT
the best solution, the letter goes on, is to shoot
and harpoon the whales and use the meat for much needed
dog food, for the trappers' dogs
BELUGA WHALES IN AN ICE POT
into the whales' breathing hole Wednesday went forty lbs
of chopped fish and forty pounds of beef and lamb chops
BELUGA WHALES IN AN ICE POT

. . .

3.
BELUGA WHALES IN AN ICE POT
Skiers departing: John Turo, Harold Cook, Fred Kelly
Antoine Grandjambe, Rex Cockney, Turpin Cockney, Henry
Steen, George Grandjambe, Charles Tobac, Robert Kimiksana
Rose Ann Allen, and Anita Allen. Father Mouchet is going
as coach
BELUGA WHALES IN AN ICE POT
There's a first time for everything
BELUGA WHALES IN AN ICE POT
Father Franche almost rolled his bombardier near Fort
McPherson
BELUGA WHALES IN AN ICE POT
anti-freeze leaked out, but a jack, helping hand, and
the vehicle went back on its tracks
BELUGA WHALES IN AN ICE POT
at Tuk recently blowing snow so blinded him that he
missed his way and tracked back and forth through drift
wood and rough ice looking for the Tuk airport
flasher
BELUGA WHALES IN AN ICE POT

4.
the edge of the ice pot is crowded with forms of helplessness
whose only salvation is to help the doomed beyond help
BELUGA WHALES IN AN ICE POT
I think of teenage Eskimo girls being sent to jail for
repeated acts of intoxication in public places
BELUGA WHALES IN AN ICE POT
of unwed mothers in a context of neurotic social service
psychiatrists
BELUGA WHALES IN AN ICE POT
I try to forget the american bomber boiling in circles
over Hanoi
BELUGA WHALES IN AN ICE POT
compassion is unpredictable & as disreputable as thoughts
of mercy like helping
BELUGA WHALES IN AN ICE POT
I think of a role for the canadian theatre as Viet Cong yet
I have nightmares about
BELUGA WHALES IN AN ICE POT
the canadian artist in a centennial year poked at by the
forms of helplessness he is trying to save from a doom
beyond help

BELUGA WHALES IN AN ICE POT
the arctic is dotted with icepotsful of beluga whales
BELUGA WHALES IN AN ICE POT
thoughts in and of an ice pot
BELUGA WHALES IN AN ICE POT
I shall take my thoughts and shoot them and harpoon them
and use them for dogs' meat, for the trappers' dogs
BELUGA WHALES IN AN ICE POT

lines 1967

the caves dripping milk and honey
PORTRAIT OF THE STUDENT BODY AS MOUNT EISENHOWER
i stood under the mural
PORTRAIT OF THE STUDENT BODY AS MOUNT EISENHOWER
once upon a time the breasts of Tiresias were
lovely
PORTRAIT OF THE STUDENT BODY AS MOUNT EISENHOWER
but now the mammals of prophecy are as dry and
milkless as the tablets of the tablet chairs
PORTRAIT OF THE STUDENT BODY AS MOUNT EISENHOWER
damsels and damsons
if you smell a rat, it's the bad
air conditioning in the government-architected
buildings
PORTRAIT OF THE STUDENT BODY AS MOUNT EISENHOWER
and she cut me off a lock of her hair and she cut
me off one of her ears and she cut me off one of
her legs, it was so like her, so like her!
PORTRAIT OF THE STUDENT BODY AS MOUNT EISENHOWER
and in the afternoon she took off all her clothes
and as the sun was going down she ups and puts on
a pair of war-surplus army boots and jumped into
a laundry basket full of lamp bulbs and cried, **LET'S
PUT OUT THE LIGHT, LET'S PUT OUT THE LIGHT, LET'S
PUT OUT THE LIGHT**
PORTRAIT OF THE STUDENT BODY AS MOUNT EISENHOWER
and we all rushed into the street, crying, the
theatre of cruelty, it's so cruel, it sends you, but
it leaves you shredded, it's not for cabbages, it's
not for cabbages
PORTRAIT &c

lines september 1969

THE INVASION OF CANADA IS OVER
POEMS BEHIND THE SCENES ARE, WATER
the invasion of canada is over
THE RIVER WATER IS ROTTEN
the invasion of canada is over
STILL SOME WATER IS CLEAN ENOUGH TO DRINK
poems behind the scenes are, some waters are clean
enough to purify
THE INVASION OF CANADA IS OVER
THE INVASION OF CANADA IS OVER
POEMS BEHIND THE SCENES ARE, ACCESS TO OIL
THE INVASION OF CANADA IS OVER
but poems behind the scenes are, chiefly people
**WE CAN COMMAND THESE INTO AUDIENCES, THEY WILL
HAVE TO PASS EXAMINATIONS IN NOVELS, PLAYS, POEMS,
OUR BELLE-LETTRES, OUR BELLY-FARCICALS, OUR GOOFY-
GUT SUMMUM BONUMS**
the invasion of canada is over
**THE TOO MUCH POPULATED WORLD DEMANDS THE CLEAN
EXTERMINATION OF DEFEATED PEOPLES. WE ARE NOT
NAZIS NAGGED AT BY AN INSANE PROPAGANDA OF A
JUDEREIN FATHERLAND . WE ARE MEN OF GOOD
WILL BUT DRIVEN BY THE WHEEL OF NECESSITY. BUT
NEVERTHELESS**
THE INVASION OF CANADA IS OVER
FOR HISTORICO-PSYCHOLOGICAL REASONS
(their affinity with our negro populations)
**WE SHALL IN ALL LIKELIHOOD PHASE THEM OFF THE FACE
OF THE EARTH WITH OUR CULTURAL AND ECOLOGICAL
POGROMS
WE ARE FACING OFF THE NEGRO**
the invasion of canada is over
**TECHNIQUES WE HAVE DEVISED FOR OUR OWN
STRIPPING OFF OF SURPLUS POPULATION
FAT**
the invasion of canada is over
POEMS BEHIND THE SCENES ARE, THEY WILL BE FORCED
TO READ THOREAU, WHITMAN AND LINCOLN

. . .

2.
the invasion of canada is over
POEMS BEHIND THE SCENES ARE, CZECHOSLOVAKIA, THE MOON, THE DAY OF THE PIG IN CHICAGO, THE MURDER OF THE UNIVERSITY BY HAYAKAWA & CO, THE VIETNAMIZATION OF HANOI
the invasion of canada is over
POEMS BEHIND THE SCENES ARE, EXTERMINATION
the invasion of canada is over
BUT THE PREFERRED PROCESS THIS COMMITTEE RECOMMENDS IS CULTURAL ASSIMILATION, AN EDUCATIONAL GAS OVEN
the invasion of canada is over
THE CONCENTRATION CAMP IS CAMP, WE FEEL IT IS CONTRA-INDICATED, SINCE WE HAVE HAD SOME EXPERIENCE WITH CONCENTRATION CAMPUSES.
the invasion of canada is over
AND THANK GOD IT IS. IT HAS BEEN A PAINFUL CAMPAIGN
A COMPANY OF MEN HUNCHED DOWN IN THEIR DUNG AND DOWN-FILLED PARKAS, ALL THE WAY, FROM THE TRUMPETER-SWANS, TO THE GEESE, AND THE FLUSHING OUT OF THE ENGLISH SPARROWS
and now back to our women and our pigeon-holes

lines january 1971

the whalebone comb of love
**WAS IN THIS DEATH & HER BODY THE ESKIMO'S
HOUSE AFTER THE PRIMUS WAS WITHDRAWN**
the whalebone comb of love
**SMOOTHED THE STORM AND THE SMALL LIP OF THE WATER
SMOKING WITH SMASHED FISH SPOKE OF DRIFTWOOD
THE MOONCOMBED TIDE HAD GIVEN BACK THE
SEA**
the whalebone comb of love
**WHO COMBED CHRIST'S HAIR, ASKED THE ESKIMOS
OR DID SHE KNOW?**
the whalebone comb of love
**SHE THOUGHT WAS BEHIND GOD'S UNSMILING LIPS
THE WHALEBONE COMB OF LOVE
AFTER THE SEA HERON**
à Repulse Bay, par example, comme à Lake Harbour
où à Poste-de-baleine et dans les Iles Belcher
THE WHALEBONE COMB OF LOVE
dans presque toutes les autres régions
même Rankin Inlet
Tuktoyak, Aklavik, Coppermine, Holman, Bathurst
Inlet, Cambridge Bay, Pelly Bay, Whale Cove
THE WHALEBONE COMB OF LOVE
un objet de culte, poli par les vents et les vagues
THE WHALEBONE COMB OF LOVE
& the cast bones on the shore brushed by the
seabird's foot
**THE WHALEBONE COMB OF LOVE
THE WHALEBONE COMB OF LOVE
&
THE FINGERS AND TOES THEREOF WERE NINE OR
NINETEEN IN ACCORDANCE WITH THE MONTHS IN
THE WOMB OR THE NUMBER OF BICYCLES ON THE
MOON**

2.
elle était d'une simplicité étonnante
THE WHALEBONE COMB OF LOVE
she ran her hand through the child's hair
THE WHALEBONE COMB OF LOVE
two brute dogs plunging through the newfallen
snow
THE WHALEBONE COMB OF LOVE
un groupe de kayakeurs

. . .

étaient arrivés de bonne heure
THE WHALEBONE COMB OF LOVE
et il désire toujours bien faire sa survivance
THE WHALEBONE COMB OF LOVE
pour rendre ses sculptures plus heureuses
THE WHALEBONE COMB OF LOVE
Kaunak's bear, not his wife's, from Repulse Bay
THE WHALEBONE COMB OF LOVE
Mikkikak's cheval marin de Cap-Dorset
THE WHALEBONE COMB OF LOVE
Latcholassie's owl-man. Latcholassie, son of Tudlik.
Owl maker. Est maintenant aveugle
THE WHALEBONE COMB OF LOVE
les oiseaux d'Erkoolik de Rankin Inlet
THE WHALEBONE COMB OF LOVE
Angalakte, hiboux bois et fanon de baleine
from Repulse Bay
THE WHALEBONE COMB OF LOVE
Elisapee, from Arctic Bay, Fils conduisant son père
à la mort. Fanon de baleine. Note the age of the
father expressed in bends and curves, teeth of
the
WHALEBONE COMB OF LOVE
Christine Aaluk, mother and child in soapstone bitten
by
THE WHALEBONE COMB OF LOVE
& the mother and child of Kopapik, green serpentine
chez Cap-Dorset, toothed by
THE WHALEBONE COMB OF LOVE
le pécheur de baleines de Charlie Sheeguapik,
Kavik's hunter wearing a caribou across his
shoulders
et l'homme qui fait la culbute
THE WHALEBONE COMB OF LOVE
Tiktak's family group filed out of one piece of
one stone which is both sea and land, or the
woman with the bowl growing out of her belly
THE WHALEBONE COMB OF LOVE
Akulukjuk's family heavy with soap stone parkas
THE WHALEBONE COMB OF LOVE
&
Sheokjuk's two families sleeping beside their two
lamps in a snow house in a round stone

THE WHALEBONE COMB OF LOVE
&
Jonnie Inukpuk's mère allaitant son enfant
Akkanarshoonak's mother and child, Lukasi Usuitaijuk's
mother and child, with a fish lying
across her feet
THE WHALEBONE COMB OF LOVE

3.
o pâle Ophelia, belle comme la neige des neiges
THERE IS SNOW ON THE WATER THE SUN CANNOT MELT
the whalebone comb of love
 the soft squid swimming behind the eyes, she runs
her hand through the mud, pushes her fingers
through the soft whalebone mud
THE WHALEBONE COMB OF LOVE
une fange
de fanon de baleine
THE WHALEBONE COMB OF LOVE
she asked me for something
THE WHALEBONE COMB OF LOVE
WHAT WAS THE MATTER, I SAID, MY LIFE IS A TANGLE, SHE SAID. WHY, I SAID. OF SEA & SAND & SALT & THE FUTURE IS A DYING HERRING AT THE FOOT OF THE HERON'S NEST, SHE SAID. IN A FOOTPRINT CAKED WITH SALT, SHE SAID
the whalebone comb of love
FOOTPRINTS, SHE SAID, BY THE WATER LAP GONE LIKE DEW WITH THE NEXT TIDE
SHE SAID
the whalebone comb of love
BITES INTO THE SEA AND ITS TEETH ARE SALT, BONES ROTTING IN THE WIND, BONE ROT, AND THE LIVE WORM
A MILLION YEARS HAVE SHAPED THESE HANDS INTO COMBS, MASSACRES OF DAY AFTER DAY HAVE LEFT BONE DEBRIS OF WHALES WHERE THE TIDE WASHES AWAY THEIR BLOOD
the whalebone comb of love
O belle Ophelia, pâle comme les neiges & wiped
clean from
THE WHALEBONE COMB OF LOVE
WHEN THE MOONPULLED WATER WASHES AWAY THE BLOOD

. . .

4.
MY MOUTH IS FULL OF A (AND/OR THE) LOUD SAND
THE WHALEBONE COMB OF LOVE
MY HANDS ARE ROUGH, THEIR TOOTH FANGED OUT
BY THE SEA NAIL
the whalebone comb of love
Here were two girls, enfants de Sheokjuk, il me
semble, crying away the stone mouths of their
lives into a soft sand
THE WHALEBONE COMB OF LOVE
pushes them from egg to grave, and that's a short
throw, et la mer lui donne un coup de peigne de
fanon de baleine
THE WHALEBONE COMB OF LOVE
as quick as fingers or fungus, said the fox
THE WHALEBONE COMB OF LOVE
I don't know, I said. I don't know, said the giraffe
but no, it wasn't the giraffe, it was
Kaunak's bear stalking with the long giraffe neck
soapstone green shaped out by the pull of
THE WHALEBONE COMB OF LOVE
WHO HEARD THIS? I DID, MY MOUTH PRESSED TO THE
SAND
the whalebone comb of love
was speaking
AND I, SAGGIAK, CALL NULIAYUK THE WHALE-WOMAN
MY TALLULIYIK, MY MOUTH
the whalebone comb of love
AND I, KAMUK OF POVUNGNITUK, HAVE KEPT COMBING THE
LEGS OF NULIAYUK THE WHALE-WOMAN AND MY BOW DRILL
IN MY TEETH
the whalebone comb of love
AND I, ELIASEPIK, KEEP ON COMBING THE FAT THIGHS OF
NULIAYUK THE WHALE-WOMAN AND MY HACK
SAW
the whalebone comb of love
AND I, AISAH-ALAKOK OF POSTE-DE-BALEINE
KEEP ON COMBING THE BELLY AND BREASTS OF NULIAYUK
THE WHALE-WOMAN WITH MY ENTIRE BODY
the whalebone comb of love
AND I, LATCHOLASSIE, OWLMAKER OF CAP-DORSET KEEP
ON COMBING THE OWLS OF NULIAYUK
WITH
the whalebone comb of love

SAND
 & TIKTAK & TIKEAYKAK & ERKOOLIK & KAVIK
the whalebone comb of love
in their hands
went on combing the company of seagulls and
ptarmigan hair of Nuliayuk the whale-woman

lines 1968

SHE SHOOK HER HAIR AND SAID NO
it was an affirmation firm as the shadow of a star projected
into a fire bucket of quicksand
SHE SHOOK HER HAIR AND SAID NO
so he went into the garden and buried the moon.
SHE SHOOK HER HAIR AND SAID NO
he walked to the bus stop whistling:
                        stabat mater dolorosa
                        juxta crucem lacrimosa
                        dum pendebat, etc. etc.
SHE SHOOK HER HAIR AND SAID NO
what her mouth tastes like is nobody's business
SHE SHOOK HER HAIR AND SAID NO
whether the fragrance about her the odour of her body,
her peculiar fragrance, was the odour of sanctity, he
didn't know
SHE SHOOK HER HAIR AND SAID NO
HE LIFTED THE HAMMER, and drove the first nail through
God's hand
SHE SHOOK HER HAIR AND SAID NO
the president of the bethlehem steel complex which makes the
steel which composes the hammer head and nail said it couldn't
be done without the permission of God
she shook her hair and said no
he replied, it was God who crucified himself
SHE SHOOK HER HAIR AND SAID NO
but he heard her crying between her breasts, consummatum est
SHE SHOOK HER HAIR AND SAID NO
mea culpa, mea culpa, mea maxima culpa
SHE SHOOK HER HAIR AND SAID NO
was there, he asked, another Troy for her to burn?
SHE SHOOK HER HAIR AND SAID NO
but I, he said, I'm not Yeats and she is not Maud
Gonne
SHE SHOOK HER HAIR AND SAID NO
it was quite obvious she was looking for martyrdom,
others have done so, and he said so, but
she shook her hair and said no
**WHEN SHE POURED THE GASOLINE ON HER HEAD, GREASY TEARS
OF IT FELL DOWN ON HER CHEEKS AND RAN INTO HER BOSOM,
HE CRIED OUT, YOU DON'T KNOW WHAT YOU'RE DOING**
she shook her hair and said —
he didn't know what she said
SHE SHOOK HER HAIR AND SAID NO

lines 1967

the belly of the dragon was made of boiler plate
THEY KISSED THEIR ONLY LOVE GOOD BYE AND WHEN THEY STOOD ALONE THINKING, WELL, THAT'S A RELIEF, THERE SHE WAS AGAIN INSISTING THEY MUST PART FOREVER
THE BELLY OF THE DRAGON WAS MADE OF BOILER PLATE
they had climbed to the top of a long green hill and the mountain was a sheet of lead rising sheer above them
THE BELLY OF THE DRAGON WAS MADE OF BOILER PLATE
they cut off the large end of their boiled egg and there she sat smiling at him her two lips soaked in blood
THE BELLY OF THE DRAGON WAS MADE OF BOILER PLATE
HE STOOD COUNTING THE RIVETS IN THE BELLY OF THE MONSTER
le monstre chez moi
THE BELLY OF THE DRAGON WAS MADE OF BOILER PLATE
HE DREAMT THAT HE LOST HER OVER AND OVER AGAIN THOUGH HE LOOKED EVERYWHERE AND GROPED ABOUT IN CULVERT AND UNDERBRUSH. HE NEVER FOUND HER, AND YET THERE SHE WAS BESIDE HIM READY READY TO DISAPPEAR AS SOON AS HE REACHED OUT TOWARDS HER
the belly of the dragon was made of boiler plate
HE REALIZED HE COULD NEVER LOSE HER, YET THIS WAS THE PLOT
the belly of the dragon was made of boiler plate
THE BREASTS OF THE PIG
AS I STOOD RUMINATING ON THE IRON TITS ONE OF THE RIVETS GAVE WAY
the belly of the dragon was made of boiler plate
THEN A PLATE GAVE WAY AND SUPERHEATED STEAM AND SCALDING WATER COOKED MY FLESH TILL IT FLAKED AWAY FROM MY BONES
THE BELLY OF THE DRAGON WAS MADE OF BOILER PLATE
PATHOS HAS A FACE LIKE A WOUNDED BEAR IT WILL NOT GET OUT OF YOUR WAY WILL IT? IT WILL NOT GET OUT OF YOUR WAY   IT IS CLUMSY IT IS BRUTAL AND IT MOVES LIKE LIGHTNING
THE BELLY OF THE DRAGON IS MADE OF BOILER PLATE
THE SMELL OF HUMAN FLESH COOKING IS NAUSEATING I WANTED TO VOMIT I WANTED TO THROW UP BUT IT WAS MY OWN FLESH NO ONE LUSTED AFTER MY BROTH THE UNIVERSE HAD MADE A MISTAKE   IT SAID IT WAS SORRY IT WOULDN'T HAPPEN AGAIN

lines 1970

HE STOOD IN VENICE ON THE BRIDGE OF SIGHS
and somebody sighed, all the things of this
life are dead things
except the words
alas
HE STOOD IN VENICE ON THE BRIDGE OF SIGHS
and somebody sighed
                     Venice is no more.
the gondolas are gone. the gondoliers are
gone for ever
HE STOOD IN VENICE ON THE BRIDGE OF SIGHS
thinking. ah yes. but in Canada the trumpeter
swans are returning
with their loud trumpet-like, decidedly
gutteral ko-hoh uttered from one to a number
of times
the terrible honking that can be heard from
the interior of Canada to Hongkong Bay, Van-
couver Island, British Columbia
HE STOOD IN VENICE ON THE BRIDGE OF SIGHS
AND SOMEBODY SIGHED
                     THE WATER RISES
HE STOOD IN VENICE ON THE BRIDGE OF SIGHS
AND SOMEBODY WHEELING A PERAMBULATOR WITH A
SQUEAKING WHEEL SAID, SIGHING,
                           I AM SALVADOR
DALI
THE LIONS OF ST. MARK'S ARE SWIMMING
AND HE INTRODUCED ME TO THE WET NURSE
AND TOOK FROM THE PERAMBULATOR A DEAD
BABY
I STOOD IN VENICE ON THE BRIDGE OF SIGHS,
comment. I said, and he wheeled away. alas
whirling along the perambulator and the wet
nurse
I STOOD IN VENICE ON THE BRIDGE OF SIGHS
holding in my arms a dead baby.
it was very quiet.
                 but the canal water began
to cry.
and the sea began to cry.
the lions of St. Mark's were howling. all Venice
began to cry. all Europe
I STOOD IN VENICE ON THE BRIDGE OF SIGHS!
we were very quiet.
I and the dead baby

lines 1967

THE DRAGONS ARE CLIMBING OVER THE MANTEL PIECE
they have unplugged the clock
THE DRAGONS ARE CLIMBING ALL OVER THE MANTEL PIECE
they have knocked over the vases with their paper flowers
THE DRAGONS ARE CLIMBING ALL OVER THE MANTEL PIECE
they have scattered the roses
THE DRAGONS ARE SLOBBERING ALL OVER THE MANTEL PIECE
he went to the door to answer the knock, Come on in, he said
THE DRAGONS ARE CLIMBING ALL OVER THE MANTEL PIECE
it was an old woman wearing only a fur coat and on her
feet a pair of sneakers
THE DRAGONS ARE CLIMBING ALL OVER THE MANTEL PIECE
come on in, he said, and take off your coat
I cannot stay, she told him
THE DRAGONS ARE CLIMBING OVER THE MANTEL PIECE
I can't stay long enough to take off my coat, she said
THE DRAGONS ARE CLIMBING OVER THE MANTEL PIECE
when she took off her fur coat he saw that she indeed was
wearing only a fur coat
THE DRAGONS WERE CLIMBING ALL OVER THE MANTEL PIECE
she said in her nakedness you won't know who I am, I am
the goddess of love, Aphrodite
THE DRAGONS WERE CLIMBING ALL OVER THE MANTEL PIECE
nor will you know what to make of me, she added and kicked
off her sneakers
THE DRAGONS WERE CLIMBING ALL OVER THE MANTEL PIECE
she rubbed her foot on my foot
THE DRAGONS WERE CLIMBING ALL OVER THE MANTEL PIECE
I told her I remembered her face from way back and she
wept and said, look, feel this lump in my left breast, what
do you think it means, she said
THE DRAGONS WERE CLIMBING ALL OVER THE MANTEL PIECE
where Zeus the king of the gods kicked me, she said, feel it
THE DRAGONS WERE CLIMBING ALL OVER THE MANTEL PIECE
I put out my hand and felt her left breast
THE DRAGONS WERE CLIMBING ALL OVER THE MANTEL PIECE
make love to me she said don't think of telling me to see a doctor
THE DRAGONS WERE CLIMBING ALL OVER THE MANTEL PIECE
make love to me over and over again she said
THE DRAGONS WERE CLIMBING ALL OVER THE MANTEL PIECE
I have made love to the goddess of love I have done better than
Zeus Mars Haephestus and Anchises
I have kissed the immortal cancer in her left breast
THE DRAGONS WERE CLIMBING ALL OVER THE MANTEL PIECE

birthday lines 1965

THOU STILL UNRAVISHED BRIDE OF QUIETNESS
yesterday I met Paris crying, do you want to buy
some dirty pictures?
THOU STILL UNRAVISHED BRIDE OF QUIETNESS
and a year ago Hong Kong crying, would you like
white lady only a dollar
THOU STILL UNRAVISHED BRIDE OF QUIETNESS
and in the good old days, I heard America crying
would you like to sleep all night with this
young negress for only a hundred
dollars?
THOU STILL UNRAVISHED BRIDE OF QUIETNESS
and I met England crying, would you like to sleep
with Queen Victoria for only a thousand guineas
and cheap at that for the experience of
a lifetime
THOU STILL UNRAVISHED BRIDE OF QUIETNESS
I replied, though I admire the Quant and
have a sneaking admiration for Twiggy, no,
I wouldn't like to sleep with Queen Victoria
for only a thousand guineas and I would like
some dirty pictures and a white lady from
Hong Kong for only a dollar and all night with a
young negress for a hundred
dollars
THOU STILL UNRAVISHED BRIDE OF QUIETNESS
and I met Jerusalem crying, would you like to
have Pharaoh's wife for a concubine?
THOU STILL UNRAVISHED BRIDE OF QUIETNESS
I met Rome crying, I am Pontius Pilate, thou
shalt have no other gods but me!
THOU STILL UNRAVISHED BRIDE OF QUIETNESS
the breasts of Pilate's wife are small, hard
and warm I have bruised them, I have had sex
with Pilate's wife, we have laughed together,
we have rolled together
in the bed of Pilate!
THOU STILL UNRAVISHED BRIDE OF QUIETNESS

poem 1968

at eighteen the red youth from your mouth began
peeling
JE CHOISIS VOS SONNETS QUI SONT PLUS DOULEUREUX
you renewed the lipstick, I think to smear me with
the red mouth which is an extension of
Eve
JE CHOISIS VOS SONNETS QUI SONT PLUS DOULEUREUX
in the evening
the night before
JE CHOISIS VOS SONNETS QUI SONT PLUS DOULEUREUX
you turned the design of the cup towards me, and
your eyes turned to my feet were like the centres
of japanese flowers
JE CHOISIS VOS SONNETS QUI SONT PLUS DOULEUREUX
you gave me a french look
JE CHOISIS VOS SONNETS QUI SONT PLUS DOULEUREUX
you opened your mouth with this lever, the white
fury of a Chinese painted verb
JE CHOISIS VOS SONNETS QUI SONT PLUS DOULEUREUX
but I was won with a pathos
JE CHOISIS VOS SONNETS QUI SONT PLUS DOULEUREUX
I saw that life had victimized you before even
the first menstrual blood began to flower
JE CHOISIS VOS SONNETS QUI SONT PLUS DOULEUREUX

lines 1971

fils conduisant son père à la mort
I looked into the bathroom mirror
I was shaving furiously
fils conduisant son père à la mort
FILS CONDUISANT SON PERE A LA MORT
THERE WAS NO MORE ARROW MEAT
FILS CONDUISANT SON PERE A LA MORT
yes, she laughed obscenely because
she was crying inwardly
the tears in the heartlessness of things
FILS CONDUISANT SON PERE A LA MORT
tears not ours are always with us in
grief
FILS CONDUISANT SON PERE A LA MORT
m'sieu le fish doesn't always keep
truth with us
FILS CONDUISANT SON PERE A LA MORT
the ice pots are empty
FILS CONDUISANT SON PERE A LA MORT
she presses her fingers into the flesh
pots under his arms
FILS CONDUISANT SON PERE A LA MORT
every step of the way was anguish
dragging its feet
FILS CONDUISANT SON PERE A LA MORT
he placed his hands in the pot hole
of her back. her breasts are soft fire
o ma mère
FILS CONDUISANT SON PERE A LA MORT
tomorrow we look back on us as just
another day
FILS CONDUISANT SON PERE A LA MORT
fils conduisant son père à la mort
FILS CONDUISANT SON PERE A LA MORT
tomorrow is scalded with tears which
fell between us crushed between our
cheeks
FILS CONDUISANT SON PERE A LA MORT
I am not saying that Lord Aeneas is a
fake
FILS CONDUISANT SON PERE A LA MORT
but for those of us who are higher
than mob, and lower than the man of
talent, there is always the tribe
FILS CONDUISANT SON PERE A LA MORT
fils conduisant son père à la mort

lines january 1972

I am not ashamed, she said, but stood there
covered in such greek roots as logos and
mythos
OUR LOVE WAS CLEAN CONTRARY TO THE LOVE
EVERLASTING
Eve to Adam: open her legs like the good
book she is and there you may read strange
matters for the sense bleeds into the
hinge
in the beginning was the word
OUR LOVE WAS CLEAN CONTRARY TO THE LOVE
EVERLASTING
Eve to Everyman re appleskins: we stood
there clothed in the names of things, like
arm & eyebrow, cow & corn, sheep & grass,
bird & nest, fish & waterhole, wormwood &
weed, yin & yang
OUR LOVE WAS CLEAN CONTRARY TO THE LOVE
EVERLASTING
let's take them off, she said, and we did.
All we had on, in the white moon wash, was
one word
OUR LOVE WAS CLEAN CONTRARY TO THE LOVE
EVERLASTING
I don't know what word it was. She threw
it away. Ask her
OUR LOVE WAS CLEAN CONTRARY TO THE LOVE
EVERLASTING
we threw it away, she said. We don't know
what word it was
OUR LOVE WAS CLEAN CONTRARY TO THE LOVE
EVERLASTING
all coal and marble, cold and pelted, snow and
soot, noses watery, pockets full of chafe
OUR LOVE WAS CLEAN CONTRARY TO THE LOVE
EVERLASTING
mess muss moss moose mouse & muse

lines new year 1972

the sword dies slowly from age to age
BLOOD HARDENS INTO STONE HARDER THAN STONE
from age to age from age to age but
BLOOD HARDENS INTO STONE HARDER THAN STONE
it is not the teeth of the blade that
die first
BLOOD HARDENS INTO STONE HARDER THAN STONE
the mordant powers that strike forward and
BLOOD HARDENS INTO STONE HARDER THAN STONE
sink their stalk into the heart's opposite
BLOOD HARDENS INTO STONE HARDER THAN STONE
push backward on the handle and push backward
with subtle ferocity an ironic stroke
BLOOD HARDENS INTO STONE HARDER THAN STONE
the handle is the frail part of the
blade
until iron cannot tell enemy from enemy
this is the nature of the hardest steel
and so it is with the adulterer
BLOOD HARDENS INTO STONE HARDER THAN STONE
in the very moment of hard won success
BLOOD HARDENS INTO STONE HARDER THAN STONE
when he puts his flesh against her flesh
BLOOD HARDENS INTO STONE HARDER THAN STONE
and covers with his nakedness her nakedness
the grinning adulteress
this is the land of Richard and Bolingbroke
BLOOD HARDENS INTO STONE HARDER THAN STONE
the tragedy of Bolingbroke is only begun
Richard points his dead finger at the sun
BLOOD HARDENS INTO STONE HARDER THAN STONE
and his shadow is enormous everywhere
BLOOD HARDENS INTO STONE HARDER THAN STONE
into a wilderness is grown the dead garden
of the gardener of the gardener, hell's
husbandryman
BLOOD HARDENS INTO BLOOD HARDER THAN STONE
a wilderness of men's bones on men's bones
which have got themselves flung into a
garbage heap
white background for the long tailed magpie
BLOOD HARDENS INTO STONE HARDER THAN STONE
my crime is a pattern for our crime

our crime is a pattern for their crime
I hear the adulterer quoting the adulteress
BLOOD HARDENS INTO BLOOD HARDER THAN BLOOD
the sword dies slowly from age to age

white pelican poems (2)

Construction, May 1974

> *If such remarks were indeed scandalous, one could only reflect sadly on the peculiarities of Canadian writers. It is true, no doubt, that far deeper wounds than told in any fictions have been incurred in Canadian life, but what remains to be told, and I put this as a painful question, is whether the sociology of either critics or historians in this country has been or indeed could be adequate to those wounds, that suffering.*
> Eli Mandel

someone or other was out to hang a student, still
    it was a committee that no one wanted to serve on
The choke cherry was coming into blossom. The grosbeaks had disappeared. The first robin had multiplied into an invasion. The time was unripe
    it was a committee that no one wanted to serve on
Night holds Hippolytus the pure of stain, etc. etc., we had muttered. plagiarizing in our hearts the English translator's plagiaries
    it was a committee that no one wanted to serve on
I repeat it,
    it was a committee that no one wanted to serve on
We were departing for various places and in no mood to be justice's wage-earners. The small sums in our pockets were more than enough for the entertainment we had in our mind's eye
    it was a committee that no one wanted to serve on
We had voted it into being earlier, in a narrow morning, when justice had surprised us, but that was something else
    it was a committee that no one wanted to serve on
'The Saratoga trunk was packed, the Gladstone bag bulged poignantly, like a repeated pregnancy, and in our hands the silver-mounted Banbury Park umbrella, in case of rain': we were Miriam
    it was a committee that no one wanted to serve on
Let the student who had to be hanged go hang himself — let all students go hang themselves. The chairman of the committee was named Ms. Sackcloth
    it was a committee that no one wanted to serve on
The other committee members were Dr Pickaxe, Dr Spade, Mrs Shroud, and Professor Hearse.
    it was a committee that no one wanted to serve on
Figliuol mio, Virgil said, qui può esser tormento, ma non morte. Ricordati, ricordati — here my son may be torment but not death. Keep that in your heart . . .
    it was a committee that no one wanted to serve on
But then there was the difficulty of finding a committee room —

          . . .

purgatory had closed for the summer. The only available place was the hell that opens up its offices of terror in the hearts of the mercenaries of justice.
 it was a committee that no one wanted to serve on
Don't think this is just another exercise in minimal art, to crucify meaning and non-meaning on the same cross
 it was a committee that no one wanted to serve on

construction, untitled

17 ways of not looking at the face of margaret atwood on the dust jacket of survival.
the first is, not through the eyes of the west coast halibut.
the west coast halibut will not survive.
17 ways of not looking at the face of margaret atwood on the dust jacket of survival.
& the second is, not through the eyes of jack shadbolt.
jack shadbolt will not survive.
17 ways of not looking at the face of margaret atwood on the dust jacket of survival.
& the third is, not through the eyes of the chemainus black bear.
the chemainus black bear will not survive.
17 ways of not looking at the face of margaret atwood on the dust jacket of survival.
& the fourth is not through the eyes of roy kiyooka.
roy kiyooka will not survive.
17 ways of not looking at the face of margaret atwood on the dust jacket of survival.
& the fifth is, not through the eyes of the peregrin falcon or duck hawk.
the duck hawk will not survive.
17 ways of not looking at the face of margaret atwood on the dust jacket of survival.
& the sixth is, not through the eyes of guido molinari, not through the eyes of claude tousignant.
guido molinari will not survive.
claude tousignant will not survive.
17 ways of not looking at the face of margaret atwood on the dust jacket of survival.
& the seventh is, not through the eyes of the cap dorset polar bear.
the cap dorset polar bear will not survive.
17 way of not looking at the face of margaret atwood on the dust jacket of survival.
& the eighth is, not through the eyes of jeremy sadness, not through the eyes of robert kroetsch.
jeremy sadness will not survive.
robert kroetsch will not survive.
17 ways of not looking at the face of margaret atwood on the dust jacket of survival.
& the ninth is not through the eyes of the evening grosbeak, not through les yeux du gros-bec errant.
le gros-bec errant will not survive.
17 ways of not looking at the face of margaret atwood on the dust

. . .

jacket of survival.
& the tenth is, not through the eyes of marshall mcluhan, not through the eyes of norman yates.
marshall mcluhan will not survive.
norman yates will not survive.
17 ways of not looking at the face of margaret atwood on the dust jacket of survival
& the eleventh is, not through the eyes of the siberian tiger (posing on a plywood slab out at al oeming's animal farm)
the siberian tiger will not survive.
17 ways of not looking at the face of margaret atwood on the dust jacket of survival.
& the twelfth is, not through the eyes of tac tanabe.
tac tanabe will not survive.
17 ways of not looking at the face of margaret atwood on the dust jacket of survival.
& the thirteenth is, but i am not saying what the thirteenth is.
17 ways of not looking at the face of margaret atwood on the dust jacket of survival.
& the fourteenth is, not through the eyes of the coyote.
the coyote will not survive.
17 ways of not looking at the face of margaret atwood on the dust jacket of survival.
& the fifteenth is, not through the eyes of charles gagnon (for all their eschatological whites).
chas. gagnon will not survive.
17 ways of not looking at the face of margaret atwood on the dust jacket of survival.
& the sixteenth is, not through the eyes of the nanaimo she-cougar.
the nanaimo she-cougar will not survive.
17 ways of not looking at the face of margaret atwood on the dust jacket of survival
& the seventeenth way is, not through the eyes of alice munro, not through the thirteen year old girl's eyes of alice munro blinded with the horror and the wonder of it all.
i have not forgotten the thirteenth way. the thirteenth way of not looking at the face of margaret atwood on the dust jacket of survival was unsuccessful. I am not saying what i saw.

construction with horizontal columns / construction avec colombes mortes

1.
the coming of robert creeley to vancouver in february 1962
to read poetry at the festival of contemporary arts, sponsored by the university of british columbia, wasn't exactly an unprecedented national disaster

les colombes britanniques, où sont-elles, cantatriced la
cantatrice chauve alias the bald soprano

the coming of robert creeley to vancouver in february 1962
wasn't exactly an unprecedented national disaster

but why did I come here at all, asked la cantatrice chauve
dropping her eyes into the fresh canadian snow. Because,
she said, you are the only people on earth whose national
identity has grown out of the recognition that you are not
americans, and whose glorious tradition is from the beginning to have elected not to be governed by the american
people or by any government of the american people for the
american people, whatever the american people in their wisdom might want

the coming of robert creeley to vancouver in february 1962
wasn't exactly an unprecedented national disaster

we excused ourselves profusely

the coming of robert creeley to vancouver in february 1962
wasn't exactly an unprecedented national disaster

I have been giving this speech all over canada, said the
bald soprano alias la cantatrice chauve

the coming of robert creeley to vancouver in february 1962
wasn't exactly an unprecedented national disaster

not like the americanization of the vancouver island forest, we cantatriced

. . .

2.
the coming of robert creeley to vancouver in february 1962
wasn't exactly an unprecedented national disaster

he appeared before us like the ghost of edgar allen poe

the coming of robert creeley to vancouver in february 1962
wasn't exactly an unprecedented national disaster

these readings weren't run of the mill board footage

the coming of robert creeley to vancouver in february 1962
wasn't exactly an unprecedented national disaster

not like the poetry that the victoria lumber and manufact-
uring company's sawmill read to the chemainus forests

the coming of robert creeley to vancouver in february 1962
wasn't exactly an unprecedented national disaster

apropos the devastation of the chemainus forests, began
la cantatrice chauve

the coming of robert creeley to vancouver in february 1962
wasn't exactly an unprecedented national disaster

the poetry that the victoria lumber and manufacturing com-
pany's sawmill read to the chemainus forests wore clothes
appropriate to emerson and thoreau

the coming of robert creeley to vancouver in february 1962
wasn't exactly an unprecedented national disaster

apropos the chemainus forests, soprano'd the cantatrice,
was it a case of manifest american destiny or of manif-
est canadian stupidity?

the coming of robert creeley to vancouver in february 1962
wasn't exactly an unprecedented national disaster

it's difficult to say yes or no to that one, I replied. But
the keyboard metrics of the number two trimsaw (which I
mastered at the age of seventeen) sliced things up much
more effectively than chas. olson

the coming of robert creeley to vancouver in february 1962
wasn't exactly an unprecedented national disaster

how soft a pad is american friendship and mutual self interest — as long as you don't mind being fucked, montaigned la cantatrice chauve, mais . . .

les héros canadiens, elle s'écria, où sont-elles?

the coming of robert creeley to vancouver in february 1962
wasn't exactly an unprecedented national disaster

I have never learned how to parse that word, said the cantatrice chauve. Did I say the wrong thing?

the coming of robert creeley to vancouver in february 1962
wasn't exactly an unprecedented national disaster

I should hope not, said la cantatrice. — There were some uprisings, we equivocated. — I should hope so, said la cantatrice

the coming of robert creeley to vancouver in february 1962
wasn't exactly an unprecedented national disaster

there were uprisings of dislocated herons, which we fed to the herrings, we counter-cantatriced

3.
the coming of robert creeley to vancouver in february 1962
wasn't exactly an unprecedented national disaster

they claimed he was the mid-twentieth century american jo: donne

the coming of robert creeley to vancouver in february 1962
wasn't exactly an unprecedented national disaster

the ravens which flew out of his mouth were bred in the desolate tarns and abandoned ruins of the american nineteenth century

the coming of robert creeley to vancouver in february 1962
wasn't exactly an unprecedented national disaster

. . .

the bobby watsons would never believe it, the bobby watsons would never believe it, the bobby watsons would never believe it, re-cantatriced la cantatrice chauve . . .

thereat the english clock struck seventeen strokes of english silence

the point atkinson foghorn blew seventeen worried blasts of port atkinson english silence. — The english bay clocks struck seventeen strokes of densely populated english bay silence. — At new westminster the new westminster penitentiary chimed out the new westminster chimes. — The provincial government carillon at edmonton bible-belted out seventeen bars of god our help in ages past. — The CN telecommunications clock at toronto telexed out seventeen strokes of ontario english silence. — The control clock at the dorval international airport struck seventeen strokes of aviation english silence. — From godwin in ontario to jubilee in victoria, the post office clocks at all the major postal centres in canada, struck seventeen strokes of official small town post office english silence

the coming of robert creeley to vancouver in february 1962 wasn't — in itself — an unprecedented national disaster

il y a personne dans cette maison, cantatriced the bald soprano

thereat the parliament hill clock at ottawa (never giving in to pressure, but always responsive to the wishes of the people) struck seventeen strokes of national silence — un, dong, deux, dong, trois, dong, quatre, dong, cinq, dong, six, dong, sept, dong, huit, dong, neuf, dong, pont neuf, dong, richard dix, dong, louis onze, dong, irma la douce, dong, la trahison des clercs, dong, louis quatorze, dong, les quinze joies de mariage, dong, cessez le feu, dong, dong, d-dong, etc

the coming of robert creeley to vancouver in february 1962 wasn't exactly an unprecedented national disaster

it is these frightful english silences that appall me, cantatriced la cantatrice chauve

4.
les silences anglaises, ajouta-t-elle

the coming of robert creeley to vancouver in february 1962
wasn't exactly an unprecedented national disaster

we were afraid she might get the frostbite — oui, she con-
fessed, we had romped together in the fresh canadian snow
— she was pregnant

the coming of robert creeley to vancouver in february 1962
wasn't exactly an unprecedented national disaster

of course I was on the pill, she said. If I hadn't been it
wouldn't have happened, would it?

perhaps not, we recantatriced

the coming of robert creeley to vancouver in february 1962
wasn't exactly an unprecedented national disaster

it wasn't that we had fallen out of love with nineteenth
century poetry — the CPR was our homer, our tribal hoe-
mother

the coming of robert creeley to vancouver in february 1962
wasn't exactly an unprecedented national disaster

it wasn't that we had fallen out of love with the act of
love

the coming of robert creeley to vancouver in february 1962
was not an unprecedented national disaster

it wasn't that we had fallen out of love with love

the coming of robert creeley to vancouver in february 1962
wasn't exactly an unprecedented national disaster

we had fallen in love with the bald soprano

the coming of robert creeley to vancouver in february 1962
wasn't exactly an unprecedented national disaster

. . .

après moi, le mois de mai, mais, mau-mau'd the bald soprano, mais —

5.
le peuplement de la terre est toujours comme ça, madeleine-ferron'd la cantatrice — après moi, encore moi, recantatriced la cantatrice chauve

et après toi, encore toi, ajouta-t-elle

the coming of robert creeley to vancouver in february 1962 wasn't exactly an unprecedented national disaster

and after the pill, marian engel'd la cantatrice, the population explosion —

if I take one pill or a hundred or a thousand pills a day, will that prevent the population explosion?

elle hocha les mamelles

they'll keep on having babies, they can't help it, said la cantatrice, alice-munro-ing from point no point to foul bay

the fertility myth in their minds keeps on exploding, and it's the pill that puts it there

the coming of robert creeley to vancouver in february 1962 wasn't exactly an unprecedented national disaster

will someone tell me, recantatriced la recantatrice chauve, where I can get an abortion for the thought in my heart that abortion is an elephant refusing to support the world on a tortoise refusing to support the elephant

6.
the marriage took place on aristophanes street at zero nine three zero hours

that was in 1957, anno domino'd the bald soprano

the coming of robert creeley to vancouver in february 1962 wasn't exactly an unprecedented national disaster

the bridesmaids were mary and terry and stephanie and eli-
zabeth and billy the coyote held up the bridal train

the coming of robert creeley to vancouver in february 1962
wasn't exactly an unprecedented national disaster

the father of the bride wore a fleur-de-lys in his lapel
and morning clothes of asbestos board

the coming of robert creeley to vancouver in february 1962
wasn't exactly an unprecedented national disaster

the bridal veil was composed of twenty odd metres of doub-
ble width pink broad wale edible corduroy

the coming of robert creeley to vancouver in february 1962
wasn't exactly an unprecedented national disaster

le prétendu porta bien son vin dans un bikini de bronze à
canon poli

the coming of robert creeley to vancouver in february 1962
wasn't exactly an unprecedented national disaster

in my mind I fear a marriage of sea-damaged sheep, la can-
tatrice chauve told the marriage priest, but when I have
his cock-boat safe in my marina, I know what the rent of a
woman comes to, I am as brave as two lionesses, except for
certain reservations, mon père

7.
father joseph payola était le desservant de la bénédiction
nuptiale

the coming of robert creeley to vancouver in february 1962
wasn't exactly an unprecedented national disaster

but why do I have to be married by an american, robin mat-
thews'd the bald soprano

the coming of robert creeley to vancouver in february 1962
wasn't exactly an unprecedented national disaster

. . .

my friends, said father payola, by way of marriage homily —
the wages of sin are death, but, he ezra pounded, the wages
of marriage are the united states of america

this is true wherever you happen to live in the free world,
he explained, unless you happen to be a draft dodger

I do not speak without irony, said father payola

of course the church comes between the bride and the bride-
groom, contra naturam, propounded father payola

the coming of robert creeley to vancouver in february 1962
wasn't exactly an unprecedented national disaster

father payola added, I pronounce you man and wife. Woman
submit to your husband. Husband, cherish your wife. I am
glad to see you are not on the pill

but I was, decantatriced la cantatrice

toute la plâterie est lézardée, ionesco'd father payola
c'est drôle — all the plaster is cracked

to a man it is drôle, elle dit

the coming of robert creeley to vancouver in february 1962
wasn't exactly an unprecedented national disaster

8.
nox erat. The city square slept. The horse stood stiff in
its wood with its belly full of pricks

their names were: mannix, cannon, inspector erskine, kojak
steve mcgarrett, banacek, sergeant mccloud, commissioner
mcmillan, lieutenant colombo and chief dan george

the coming of robert creeley to vancouver in february 1962
wasn't exactly an unprecedented national disaster

the wedding ceremony itself, the wedding reception, to say
nothing of the rehearsals for the wedding photographs has
made me so horny, I could eat you, the bridegroom told the
bald soprano

the coming of robert creeley to vancouver in february 1962
wasn't exactly an unprecedented national disaster

what a frightful wedding, michel tremblay'd la cantatrice
chauve

the coming of robert creeley to vancouver in february 1962
wasn't exactly an unprecedented national disaster

mon pauvre mari, decantatriced la cantatrice chauve, turn-
ing blue eyes large as snowballs towards the marie claire
blais-ing eyes of the bowler-hatted groom

the coming of robert creeley to vancouver in february 1962
wasn't exactly an unprecedented national disaster

o my more than sister, o my more than myself, o my darling
wife, said le prétendu, the snow of the whites of your eyes
stretches out for thousands of miles into the canadian win-
ter landscape, and we are so utterly alone

ah, circumcantatriced la cantatrice chauve, tonight of all
tonights when an audience of more than one unpopulated key-
hole, would be a mischance all too cruel!

9.
the coming of robert creeley to vancouver in february 1962
wasn't exactly an unprecedented national disaster

at the words 'malchance si cruelle' the bald soprano threw
aside her edible wedding veil, her edible wedding dress,
her wedding wig, bikini, stockings and shoes, which were
also edible —

she gave him a japanese look, but her large cunt, even with
the knees held shut, established, for her, the necessary
sexual identity. The large belly could have meant japan-
ese wrestler. But even when she had wrestled with her bik-
ini, she was female post-procreant, not male bellied wrest-
ler

the coming of robert creeley to vancouver in february 1962
wasn't exactly an unprecedented national disaster

. . .

circumstance si cruelle et si absurde, she marian angleter-
red, but no, she laughed, I didn't get this looping the
loop in an imported de haviland moth

the coming of robert creeley to vancouver in february 1962
wasn't exactly an unprecedented national disaster

homo homini lupus lupi, incantatriced le prétendu, and wolfed
down her edible wedding veil, wig, wedding dress, gloves,
stockings and shoes

stop, contralto'd the bald soprano, and snatched back her bi-
kini

the coming of robert creeley to vancouver in february 1962
wasn't exactly an unprecedented national disaster

le théâtre de cruauté c'est moi, counter-contralto'd la can-
tatrice. She gave him back the bikini. This reversal whet-
ted his hunger afresh. He devoured it greedily

your wild body, she told the groom, will be my theatre of the
absurd, and my magical body will be your theatre of the absurd

the coming of robert creeley to vancouver in february 1962
wasn't exactly an unprecedented national disaster

la cantatrice chauve alias the bald soprano shuddered. Every
thing is so metaphysical, she heard herself saying in a can-
tatricious voice. Le prétendu paid no attention. Le préten-
du was asleep, spaced out, one arm in one corner of the bri-
dal bed, one arm in the other, his feet in each of the other
corners. In her belly was his foetus. Your father-in-law,
she told her bridegroom, is the multi-national corporation
and your mother-in-law is the mechanical bride

construction with herring bones / c. des harengs saurs

portrait of myself aged seventeen

in my birth certificate my father
is denoted leading seaman

portrait of myself aged seventeen

everynight we'd go swimming, my
father and I

portrait of myself aged seventeen

regardless of what the moon her
shrink said to the sea, our mother

portrait of myself aged seventeen

at chemainus bay the sand is ground
clam-shell

portrait of myself aged seventeen

the sun dropped down into the smoke
behind the beach-house

portrait of myself aged seventeen

we'd undress on the beach while the one
officer of the old law was having
supper

portrait of myself aged seventeen

the inside water was still clean,
except for the crab, gull and human
shit of a sawmill culture

portrait of myself aged seventeen

families of sawmill herons provided
us with replacement cousins

portrait of myself aged seventeen

. . .

**the body of my father was hard as
iron**

portrait of myself aged seventeen

**our words rarely strayed from the
rocks covered with barnacles sharp
as razors**

portrait of myself aged seventeen

**but we shouted at the sliding woman-
hood of the sea, an accomplished
murderess**

portrait of myself aged seventeen

**a whore with as many holes as there
are punks and sailors**

portrait of myself aged seventeen

**yet she washed away the agony between
us**

portrait of myself aged seventeen

**time past and time future fell from
us like sand from our feet**

portrait of myself aged seventeen

**flowed away into the chafe and abrasions
of the sand**

portrait of myself aged seventeen

**we sat with wet shoulders and shriveled
cocks counting the salmon jump**

portrait of myself aged seventeen

I dug my fingers into the sharp sand
which levered us into the waiting
water

portrait of myself aged seventeen

saying nothing — the silence between us
was a tidewater cedar crying out for
the totem pole maker

portrait of myself aged seventeen

made in the image of god the son
sitting on the beach at the right
hand of my father made in the image
of god the father

portrait of myself aged seventeen

drying myself off in the shadow of
the chemainus beach-house

portrait of myself aged seventeen

the eyes of my father were seagull
eggshell blue

portrait of myself aged seventeen

the beach-house at chemainus comprised
a shed with two rooms back to back to
hold the two main nations of mankind
and womankind, comprised a waspnest,
various graphiti plus a drawing in
lumber chalk of aphrodite with her legs
opened out, thrusting upward and out-
ward, presenting in reverse perspective

portrait of myself aged seventeen

a knot-hole elaborated with chalk and
flame into cro-magnon cunt, recently
renovated

. . .

portrait of myself aged seventeen

my father's towel flailing out at the
wasps fat with fish-blood

portrait of myself aged seventeen

the longer tides splashing right over
the hemlock boom pole honeycombed with
teredos into the beach-house

portrait of myself aged seventeen

the whites of my father's eyes were
frozen milk

portrait of myself aged seventeen

even if you have lost a good deal of
blood, the sawmill doctor told my
mother, you should consider yourself
a lucky woman

portrait of myself aged seventeen

why, asked my father, what's wrong
with her carrying a baby at her age?

portrait of myself aged seventeen

for answer, skipping a rock out across
the flat belly of the water

portrait of myself aged seventeen

white cormorants drying our wet feather

portrait of myself aged seventeen

construction with driftwoods

she gave me an indigenous look

from the head to the waist she had the shape of woman

she gave me an indigenous look

but beneath she was a vegetable

she gave me an indigenous look

horror (like beauty) lies in the eye of the beholder

she gave me an indigenous look

when I looked into her eyes I saw that she was looking into mine

she gave me an indigenous look

horror met horror in the meeting of our eyes

she gave me an indigenous look

from the waist down she was radish, turnip, carrot

she gave me an indigenous look

I swear to socrates, I understand my animal soul less than my rational soul my vegetable soul less than my animal one

she gave me an indigenous look

I was no shaman to read in that green water the incredible deaths of the earth

she gave me an indigenous look

WILFRED WATSON

ngv

from I begin with counting

after the snow fell

november	1	twenty-sixth					
nineteen	2	seventy-seven					
at	3	0937					
				hours	4	after	
the	5	night's					
				snow	6	absalom	
trapped	7	in					
				the	8	choke	

9 cherry

hanging	1	head				
down	2	caught				
by	3	the				
			feet	4	in	
the	5	branch				
			his	6	beautiful	
hair	7	gilding				
			the	8	tree's	

9 crotch

essay on castle mountain

	one	**1**	reason			
	for	**2**	calling			
	the	**3**	well-known			
				mountain	**4**	castle
mountain	**5**	its				
				old	**6**	name
	is	**7**	that			
				the	**8**	word

9 castle

	is	**1**	fairly			
	easy	**2**	to			
	spell	**3**	— it			
				is	**4**	also
an	**5**	emblem				
				symbol	**6**	archetype
	or	**7**	ancestral			
				image	**8**	of

9 shelter

	a	**1**	castle			
	is	**2**	the			
primordial	**3**	private				
				place	**4**	hence
	the	**5**	old			
				byword	**6**	an
englishman's	**7**	home				
				is	**8**	his

9 castle

	which	**1**	means			
	that	**2**	the			
	RCMP	**3**	cannot			
				reach	**4**	there
	hence	**5**	the			
				never	**6**	ending
	hostility	**7**	between			
				the	**8**	RCMP

9 and

	the	**1**	castle			
	system.	**2**	It			
	was	**3**	early			
				one	**4**	beautiful
morning	**5**	and				
				the	**6**	moon
	still	**7**	up			
				when	**8**	the

9 RCMP

	knocked	**1**	on			
	my	**2**	castle			
	door.	**3**	Who's			
				there,	**4**	I
	asked.	**5**	We			
				are,	**6**	said
	the	**7**	RCMP,			
				open	**8**	up,
9	they					
	shouted.	**1**	Have			
	you	**2**	a			
	search	**3**	warrant,			
				I	**4**	asked.
	No,	**5**	they			
				said	**6**	we
	just	**7**	haven't			
				bothered	**8**	to
9	get					
	a	**1**	warrant			
	because	**2**	we're			
	the	**3**	RCMP			
				the	**4**	RCMP
	don't	**5**	need			
				a	**6**	warrant
	all	**7**	we			
				need	**8**	is
9	reasonable					
	suspicion	**1**	what's			
	reasonable	**2**	suspicion,			
	I	**3**	asked			
				we	**4**	suspect
	this	**5**	castle's			
				full	**6**	of
	drug-pushers	**7**	and			
				worse,	**8**	they
9	said.					
	This	**1**	is			
	my	**2**	castle,			
	I	**3**	said.			
				But	**4**	you
	are	**5**	not			
				an	**6**	englishman,
	said	**7**	a			
				corporal,	**8**	a
9	rectangular					

. . .

```
              faced   1   man
                 of   2   marked
       intelligence   3   but
                            whose   4   mind
                was   5   scarred
                               by   6   the
            ethical   7   sensibility
                            often   8   found
9    in
            typical   1   visitors
                 to   2   museums
                 of   3   instruments
                               of   4   torture.
                 He   5   resented
                               my   6   castle
                and   7   my
                           castle   8   resented
9    him.
            b-bingo   1   b-bango
            b-bongo   2   b-bungo
              crash   3   b-bingo
                          b-bango   4   b-bongo
            b-bungo   5   crash
                           crunch:  6   they
             rammed   7   down
                               my   8   castle
9    door
              which   1   wasn't
                 so   2   much
                  a   3   burglar
                          stopper   4   as
                  a   5   feudal
                         monument   6   to
            ancient   7   privacy.
                             They   8   lined
9    up
                 my   1   family
                 in   2   the
             castle   3   courtyard
                              and   4   subjected
                the   5   males
                               to   6   rectal
                and   7   the
                          females   8   to
9    rectal
```

	and	1	vaginal			
	search,	2	as			
	a	3	result			
				of	4	which
	my	5	youngest			
				daughter	6	whose
	passion	7	was			
				to	8	become
9	a					
	nun	1	was			
	charged	2	with			
	obstructing	3	an			
				officer	4	in
	the	5	performance			
				of	6	his
	duty,	7	with			
				assaulting	8	an
9	officer					
	of	1	the			
	law	2	and			
	with	3	resisting			
				arrest,	4	charges
	which	5	were			
				later	6	dismissed
	as	7	preposterous:			
				No	8	evidence
9	was					
	found.	1	My			
	wife	2	was			
	clean	3	my			
				boys	4	were
	clean	5	my			
				girls	6	were
	clean	7	my			
				old	8	father
9	anchises					
	was	1	clean			
	my	2	castle			
	was	3	clean,			
				and	4	dirtiest
	thrust	5	of			
				all,	6	I
	was	7	said			
				to	8	be
9	clean.					

```
                  The    1   incident
              however    2   left
               mental    3   scars
                                         on    4   all
            concerned    5   though
                                        the    6   RCMP
               blamed    7   most
                                         of    8   the
9   distress
                   on    1   the
               castle    2   mentality
                   of    3   the
                                   suspects.    4   (Now
                   my    5   second
                                   youngest    6   deviant
                  boy    7
                                      wants    8   to
9   play
                   at    1   RCMP
                 with    2   his
             sisters.)   3   My
                                 complaints    4   led
                   to    5   an
                                    official    6   investigation
                  and    7   the
                                       RCMP    8   justified
9   their
           procedures    1   vis-à-vis
                  the    2   viciousness
                   of    3   traffickers
                                         in    4   hard-drugs
                  and    5   the
                               ever-growing    6   number
                   of    7   drug
                                    addicts.   8   Fascist
9   pigs,
             muttered    1   my
                  old    2   father
            anchises.    3   My
                                     castle    4   was
            violated.    5   My
                                       sons    6   and
            daughters    7   dishonoured
                                         as    8   they
9   were
```

		by	1	the			
		RCMP	2	side			
		with	3	their			
					mother	4	against
		me.	5	I			
					am	6	mocked
		at	7	on			
					all	8	sides
9	by						
		my	1	flesh			
		and	2	blood.			
			3		In	4	the
		ruins	5	of			
					my	6	ancestral
		castle	7	my			
					kinswoman	8	cassandra
9	sings						
		her	1	mad			
		song	2	O			
		apollo	3	apollo			
					my	4	swallow
		my	5	swallow			
					apollo	6	mon
		apollon	7	apollon			
					mon	8	apollon
9	apollon						

portrait of my mother the fox

	portrait	**1**	of					
	my	**2**	mother					
	aged	**3**	ninety-two					
				years	**4**	become		
	a	**5**	vegetable					
				and	**6**	how		
	is	**7**	your					
				mother	**8**	asked		
9	my							
	mother-in-law,	**1**	is					
	she	**2**	still					
	alive?	**3**	I					
				complained	**4**	to		
	eternity	**5**	that					
				upon	**6**	the		
	death	**7**	of					
				my	**8**	father		
9	my							
	mother	**1**	a					
	wise	**2**	enough					
	woman	**3**	at					
				times	**4**	but		
	at	**5**	times					
				foolish	**6**	and		
	occasionally	**7**	very					
				foolish	**8**	had		
9	given							
	up	**1**	hope					
	and	**2**	become					
	a	**3**	vegetable.					
				The	**4**	grass		
	is	**5**	holy,					
				said	**6**	eternity.		
	Do	**7**	you					
				mean	**8**	to		
9	tell							
	me,	**1**	I					
	replied,	**2**	that					
	turnips	**3**	are					
				saints.	**4**	The		
	grass	**5**	is					
				holy,	**6**	repeated		
	eternity.	**7**	I					
				know	**8**	that		
9	at							

	the	1	funeral			
	of	2	my			
	father,	3	I			
				retorted,	4	a
	hireling	5	preacher			
				recited,	6	all
	flesh	7	is			
				grass,	8	and
9	the					
	days	1	of			
	man	2	as			
	the	3	flower			
				thereof.	4	Grass
	is	5	holy,			
				bellowed	6	eternity
	and	7	slammed			
				the	8	kitchen
9	door					
	as	1	he			
	left	2	and			
	disappeared	3	into			
				the	4	choke
	cherry.	5	Portrait			
				of	6	my
	mother	7	the			
				fox	8	become
9	a					
	vegetable.	1	And			
	how	2	is			
	your	3	mother,			
				asked	4	my
	mother-in-law.	5	The			
				grass	6	is
	holy,	7	she			
				said	8	looking
9	away					

re spences bridge

		if	**1**	god		
		asked	**2**	me		
		to	**3**	set		
					a	**4** place
		to	**5**	meet		
					him	**6** I
		wd	**7**	suggest		
				spences	**8**	bridge
9	there					
		is	**1**	hwy		
		no.	**2**	one		
		and	**3**	there		
					is	**4** hwy
		no.	**5**	eight		
					and	**6** spences
		bridge	**7**	itself		
					there	**8** is
9	the					
		canadian	**1**	national		
		railroad	**2**	and		
		there	**3**	is		
					the	**4** canadian
		pacific	**5**	railroad		
					there	**6** is
		the	**7**	thompson		
					river	**8** and
9	there					
		is	**1**	the		
		nicola	**2**	river		
		and	**3**	valleys ...		
					the	**4** possibilities
		of	**5**	arrival		
					are	**6** considerable
		by	**7**	water		
					road	**8** and
9	air					

at spences bridge

	they	**1**	have				
	turned	**2**	the				
	confluence	**3**	of				
				the	**4**	thompson	
	and	**5**	the				
				nicola	**6**	rivers	
	at	**7**	spences				
				bridge	**8**	into	
9	an						
	enormous	**1**	garbage				
	dump,	**2**	an				
	ashcan	**3**	of				
				which	**4**	the	
	sides	**5**	are				
				mountains.	**6**	I	
	do	**7**	not				
				blame	**8**	them,	
9	no						
	one	**1**	told				
	them	**2**	that				
	the	**3**	meeting				
				of	**4**	two	
	rivers	**5**	was				
				the	**6**	meeting	
	of	**7**	two				
				harmonic	**8**	forms.	
9	By						
	them	**1**	I				
	do	**2**	not				
	mean	**3**	merely				
				the	**4**	road	
	gangs	**5**	they				
				are	**6**	sleeping	
	in	**7**	their				
				campers	**8**	and	
9	trailers						
	beside	**1**	my				
	cabin	**2**	among				
	the	**3**	moon-struck				
				acacias	**4**	I	
	looked	**5**	up				
				and	**6**	overhead	
	the	**7**	sky				
				was	**8**	the	
9	sky						

. . .

		in	**1**	el		
		greco's	**2**	toledo		
		it	**3**	was		
					as	**4**	if
		the	**5**	full		
					moon	**6**	with
		its	**7**	troubled		
					face	**8**	was
9	the					
		face	**1**	of		
		god	**2**	looking		
		into	**3**	the		
					garbage-can	**4**	at
		the	**5**	garbage		
					can	**6**	and
		the	**7**	garbage		
					can	**8**	maker
9	at					
		fresh	**1**	horse-droppings		
		splashes	**2**	of		
		dried	**3**	bird		
					shit	**4**	condoms
		sanitary	**5**	napkins		
					engine-oil	**6**	tins
		wagon	**7**	wheels		
					yellow	**8**	blossoming
9	tumble-weeds					

la tête nouvelle de mimi mandel

```
                the    1   new
            starved    2   face
                 of    3   mimi
                             mandel   4   la
               tête    5   la
                               tête   6   nouvelle
                 de    7   femme
                              poète   8   on
9   a
            starved    1   jewish
               neck    2   the
               eyes    3   the
                               eyes   4   of
          byzantine    5   cow
                               eyed   6   madonna
                the    7   mouth
                                the   8   crucified
9   mouth
                 of    1   mary
              jesus    2   christ's
             mother    3   the
                               hair   4   and
              skull    5   the
                               hair   6   and
              skull    7   of
                             caesar   8   whose
9   ghost
           accosted    1   made
          beatrice's   2   majestic
            officer    3   dead
                             virgil   4   at
            dante's    5   knee
                                 as   6   if
              alive    7   catch
                             breath   8   and
9   shudder
```

things I've noticed about gail

```
                the    1   laughing
              .voice   2   of.
                  I    3   suppose
                              there's   4   a
               pond    5   of
                              frogs     6   in
                her    7   belly
                              not       8   that
9   gail
            osachoff   1   laughs
                much   2   I
               can't   3   remember
                              her       4   laughing
                but    5   she
                              has       6   a
            laughing   7   voice
                              which     8   is
9   strange
               since   1   laughter
                  is   2   the
                body   3   thinking
                              and       4   she
                  is   5   a
                              bird      6   and
                 has   7   the
                              strong    8   bird's
9   skeleton
                 the   1   bird's
             economy   2   of
               flesh   3   yet
                              her       4   voice
                  is   5   a
                              laughing  6   voice
             despite   7   the
                              sad       8   bones
9   of
```

re paula anderson and the colonization of women

	her	**1**	intelligence				
	english	**2**	the				
	intelligence	**3**	of				
				thomas	**4**	hobbes
	of	**5**	john				
				locke	**6**	of
	berkeley	**7**	burke				
				butler	**8**	george
9	bernard						
	shaw	**1**	phrasing				
	itself	**2**	in				
	a	**3**	body				
				of	**4**	musk
	so	**5**	rhetorical				
				that	**6**	the
	sense	**7**	ached				
				at	**8**	the
9	appalling						
	contradiction	**1**	of				
	thought	**2**	and				
	bodily	**3**	gesture				
				her	**4**	imagination
	the	**5**	imagination				
				of	**6**	frantz
	fanon	**7**	limbing				
				black	**8**	figures
9	with						
	white	**1**	shadows				
	her	**2**	head				
	crowned	**3**	with				
				african	**4**	verticals
	of	**5**	white				
				mahogany	**6**	hair
	her	**7**	medieval				
				eyes	**8**	the
9	eyes						
	of	**1**	logical				
	abelard	**2**	her				
	teeth	**3**	the				
				bright	**4**	white
	teeth	**5**	of				
				heloise	**6**	to
	bite	**7**	off				
				the	**8**	rattlesnake
9	head						

. . .

247

	of	1	atonement			
	her	2	countervailing			
	laughter	3	not			
			heloise's	4	consummatum
	est	5	nor			
			hobbes's	6	basic
	political	7	act			
			but	8	as
9	if					
	true	1	she			
	saw	2	the			
	sexual	3	act			
			as	4	an
	episode	5	in			
			the	6	colonization
	of	7	women			
			the	8	male
9	appearing					
	like	1	a			
	british	2	trader			
	with	3	petty			
			gifts	4	of
	beads	5	and			
			knives	6	to
	expropriate	7	vast			
			territories	8	not
9	his					

the colonization of florence steed

```
                    I   1  complained
                   to   2  eternity
                about   3  florence
                             steed  4  that
                  she   5  was
                               a    6  really
                 weird  7  example
                               of   8  the
9  colonization
                   of   1  women
                   in   2  paula
            anderson's  3  sense
                            — it's  4  weird,
                weird,  5  everything's
                             weird, 6  eternity's
                weird — 7  it
                             seems  8  that
9  eternity
                  has   1  an
                  eye   2  for
                  mrs   3  steed
                               my   4  god
                    I   5  know
                              that  6  eternity
                isn't   7  a
                             roman  8  catholic
9  priest
              haunting  1  after
               women,   2  hasn't
                  the   3  charging
                               eye  4  of
                    a   5  lasciviously
                          celibate  6  elk —
                  mrs   7  steed,
                                I   8  began —
9  mrs
               steed,   1  said
             eternity,  2  is
                    a   3  devoted
                            mother  4  and
                    a   5  model
                             wife — 6  ontario
               style,   7  I
                             asked  8  — admittedly
9  ontario
```

. . .

249

		style,	**1**	said				
		eternity —	**2**	the				
		colonized	**3**	mrs				
					steed,	**4**	I	
		said	**5**	à la				
					frantz	**6**	fanon	
		has	**7**	become				
					the	**8**	colonizer	
9	until							
		her	**1**	colonized				
		colonizing	**2**	mind				
		stands	**3**	up				
					like	**4**	mount	
		ishbel —	**5**	or				
					like	**6**	mount	
		edith	**7**	cavell,				
				interposed	**8**	eternity,		
9	adding							
		and	**1**	what				
		have	**2**	you				
		got	**3**	to				
					say	**4**	about	
		the	**5**	colonization				
					of	**6**	women	
		apropos	**7**	the				
					blessed	**8**	virgin	
9	mary?							

self portrait

```
            portrait   1   of
             myself    2   aged
           seventeen   3   going
                                    swimming   4   nights
                with   5   my
                                      father   6   the
              sailor   7   on
                                        land   8   we
9   maintained
                 the   1   silence
                  of   2   an
          antagonism   3   so
                                    absolute   4   that
                  it   5   must
                                        have   6   had
                 its   7   roots
                                          in   8   hell
9   mitigated
                only   1   by
            requests   2   for
               pitch   3   for
                                    kindling   4   — granted —
                  or   5   for
                                   mill-ends   6   for
                 the   7   kitchen
                                       stove.  8   But
9   in
                 the   1   sea
                 the   2   sea
               spoke   3   for
                                          us   4   the
          salt-water   5   was
                                          my   6   father's
       mother-tongue   7   he
                                        knew   8   all
9   the
               sea's   1   languages
           including   2   even
                 the   3   kwakiutl
                                     dialect   4   of
                 the   5   saltchuk
                                          at   6   chemainus
                bay.   7   Now
                                        even   8   as
9   then
                                                        . . .
```

```
                    the      1    sea
                 speaks      2    for
                    him      3    wherever
                                            its      4    long
                 tongue      5    reaches
                                          rough      6    or
                 smooth      7    even
                                             in      8    my
9    tears
                    for      1    the
                 living      2    and
                    the      3    dead,
                                           even      4    in
                     my      5    tears
                                            for      6    alfred
                  hailey      7    master
                                         mariner      8    and
9    harbour
                master,      1    lashed
                     to      2    his
                  craft      3    capsized
                                            off      4    lasqueti
                  whom       5    the
                                            sea      6    spoke
                    for      7    alright
                                            but      8    couldn't
9    drown
```

re myrna kostash

		I	**1**	recall				
		myrna	**2**	kostash				
		aged	**3**	seventeen				
					rising	**4**	up	
		from	**5**	the				
					tablet	**6**	chairs	
		in	**7**	front				
					of	**8**	me	
9	like							
		communist	**1**	russia				
		to	**2**	a				
		tactical	**3**	question				
					on	**4**	milton	
		re	**5**	god				
					the	**6**	father	
		and	**7**	his				
					accuser.	**8**	I	
9	recall							
		her	**1**	not				
		harrowingly	**2**	beautiful				
		as	**3**	now				
					but	**4**	most	
		harrowingly	**5**	young				
					harrowingly	**6**	sexual	
		harrowingly	**7**	someone				
					important's	**8**	daughter —	
9	god's							
		justice,	**1**	I				
		began —	**2**	what				
		is	**3**	justice,				
					came	**4**	her	
		counter	**5**	question?				
					The	**6**	words	
		fell	**7**	like				
					a	**8**	lash	
9	energized							
		by	**1**	sexual				
		pleasure	**2**	of				
		female	**3**	against				
					male	**4**	and	
		accelerated	**5**	by				
					the	**6**	pain	
		of	**7**	truth.				
					And	**8**	I	
9	recall							

. . .

```
            her     1   smile
            more    2   like
            a       3   show
                            of    4   teeth
            than    5   a
                            smile 6   I
            recall  7   her
                            teeth 8   tiny
9   and
            white   1   and
            cruel   2   pearl
            by      3   pearl
                            I     4   read
            what    5   their
                            white 6   lettering
            said    7   pearl
                            by    8   pearl
9   I
            read    1   this:
            you     2   mean
            don't   3   you
                            the   4   unjust
            man     5   justices?
                            what  6   justice
            has     7   the
                            female 8  got
9   but
            sexual  1   justice?
            what    2   exactly
            is      3   man's
                            justice 4 vis-à-vis
            the     5   female
                            but    6  the
            pimp    7   of
                            all    8  that's
9   cruel?
```

answering john stuart mill

	and	**1**	sure		
	as	**2**	oft		
	as	**3**	women		
				weep	**4**	it
	is	**5**	to		
				be	**6**	supposed
	they	**7**	grieve,		
				said	**8**	the
9 honourable					
	member	**1**	of		
	parliament	**2**	for		
	hull	**3**	concerning		
				the	**4**	subjection
	of	**5**	women		
				and	**6**	their
	behaviour	**7**	as		
				great	**8**	nature's
9 slaves					
	the	**1**	remedy		
	a	**2**	new		
	mankind	**3**	and		
				a	**4**	new
	nature	**5**	towards		
				which	**6**	by
	the	**7**	sweat		
				of	**8**	our
9 brows					
	we	**1**	have		
	so	**2**	far		
	achieved	**3**	broken		
				men	**4**	broken
	women	**5**	a		
				state	**6**	of
	schizophrenia	**7**	and		
				a	**8**	fragmented
9 nature					

re pauline boote, activist, ex-potter

```
                    I   1  think
                   of   2  pauline
                boote   3  as
                              a   4  squad
                   of   5  activist-angels
                              committed   6  to
                   an   7  errand
                              of   8  mercy
9  or
           compassion   1  or
           consolation  2  which
                  has   3  lost
                              its   4  way
                  and   5  is
                              bloody   6  angry
                about   7  it
                              the   8  angelic
9  hair
                 nail   1  fur
                teeth   2  tongue
                elbow   3  spit
                              fist   4  foot
            imploding   5  from
                              all   6  directions
              towards   7  a
                              point   8  with
9  neither
             purchase   1  nor
             position   2  but
                 with   3  a
                              magnitude   4  of
               motion   5  generating
                              a   6  locus
           resembling   7  a
                              labyrinth   8  — do
9  you
                speak   1  english
                    I   2  ask
                   it   3  and
                              it   4  answers
                   me   5  in
                              the   6  voice
                   of   7  glenda
                              jackson   8  as
9  if
```

		it	**1**	were				
		an	**2**	(unknown)				
		early	**3**	play				
					of	**4**	shakespeare's	
		written	**5**	between				
					richard	**6**	the	
		second	**7**	and				
					romeo	**8**	and	
9	juliet							
		very	**1**	english				
		the	**2**	wit				
		love's	**3**	labour's				
					lost	**4**	with	
		a	**5**	passionate				
					sense	**6**	of	
		the	**7**	injustice				
					of	**8**	the	
9	world's							
		melancholy	**1**	role				
		its	**2**	cupiditas				
		its	**3**	rationales				
					of	**4**	deceit	
		and	**5**	greed				
					its	**6**	putting	
		one	**7**	agony				
					around	**8**	another	
9	agony							
		she	**1**	is				
		also	**2**	a				
		bowl	**3**	the				
					perfect	**4**	and	
		everyday	**5**	aesthetic				
					to	**6**	the	
		soup	**7**	I				
					eat	**8**	everyday	
9	for							
		lunch	**1**	a				
		potage	**2**	québécois				
		of	**3**	vegetables				
					in	**4**	season	
		taken	**5**	with				
					a	**6**	slice	
		of	**7**	bee-bell's				
					seven	**8**	grain	
9	bread							

re nino gramsci

all	**1**	pleasure			
whether	**2**	of			
sex	**3**	or			
			food	**4**	territory
or	**5**	roof			
			of	**6**	road
or	**7**	sea			
			or	**8**	field

9 or

beach	**1**	or			
crowd	**2**	or			
mountain	**3**	top			
			or	**4**	sun
or	**5**	moon			
			is	**6**	the
interiorization	**7**	of			
			some	**8**	rising

9 or

falling	**1**	power.			
Nino	**2**	gramsci			
experienced	**3**	all			
			these	**4**	under
a	**5**	constraint			
			to	**6**	death
of	**7**	utter			
			powerlessness	**8**	and

9 enjoyed

julcha	**1**	and			
tatiana	**2**	word			
and	**3**	crumb			
			behind	**4**	a
wall	**5**	which			
			as	**6**	it
excluded	**7**	cure			
			scrupulously	**8**	prolonged

9 life.

What	**1**	a			
marvelous	**2**	pleasure			
the	**3**	power			
			of	**4**	irony
like	**5**	a			
			drug	**6**	injects —
the	**7**	attempt			
			to	**8**	stop

9 his

	brain	1	from		
	functioning	2	for		
	twenty	3	years		
			despite	4	the
	prognostic	5	of		
			prostitute	6	medical
	care	7	accelerated		
			it	8	for
9	seven				
	eight	1	nine		
	ten,	2	into		
	the	3	hundreds		
			and	4	thousands
	of	5	years		
			the	6	martyrs
	claim	7	from		
			us	8	and
9	ours				

re the names of harbours and mountains

	forward	**1**	inlet				
	quatsino	**2**	sound				
	forward	**3**	harbour				
				wellbore	**4**	channel	
	forward	**5**	bay				
				johnstone	**6**	strait	
	which	**7**	I				
				sailed	**8**	down	
9	aboard						
	the	**1**	minesweeper				
	courtenay	**2**	may				
	1946	**3**	after				
				the	**4**	gunboats	
	forward	**5**	and				
				grappler	**6**	under	
	convoy	**7**	of				
				hms	**8**	termagant	
9	twenty-five						
	guns	**1**	lieutenant				
	lascelles	**2**	commanded				
	the	**3**	forward				
				largely	**4**	instrumental	
	in	**5**	bringing				
				several	**6**	kwakiutl	
	murderers	**7**	to				
				justice	**8**	which	
9	justice						
	mr	**1**	allen				
	of	**2**	the				
	victoria	**3**	evening				
				express	**4**	cast	
	doubts	**5**	upon,				
				was	**6**	kidnapped	
	half	**7**	drowned				
				but	**8**	couldn't	
9	bring						
	lascelles	**1**	mountain				
	forward	**2**	harbour				
	to	**3**	heel				
				as	**4**	for	
	the	**5**	aboriginals				
				lascelles	**6**	justly	
	or	**7**	unjustly				
				hanged	**8**	they	
9	hanged						

the offshore canadians

```
                my      1   father
                he      2   took
                                me      3   swimming
                on      4   his
                                back    5   I
                met     6   the
                                sea     7   at
                                portsmouth  8   clinging
9   to
                the     1   neck
                of      2   my
                                father  3   I
                shut    4   my
                                mouth   5   tight
                I       6   didn't
                                want    7   to
                                drink   8   the
9   salt
                channel 1   I
                couldn't 2  cry
                                out     3   in
                fear    4   the
                                body    5   of
                my      6   father
                                was     7   lean
                                it      8   smelled
9   of
                would   6   drown
                thought 5   I
                                tea     4   I
                strong  3   milky
                                biscuits 2  and
1   sweet
```

re the names of mountains

		hms	1	warspite			
		hms	2	indefatigable			
		hms	3	inflexible			
					hms	4	invincible
		and	5	too			
					hms	6	valiant
		on	7	board			
					which	8	I
9	first						
		tasted	1	reconstituted			
		milk	2	have			
		disappeared	3	with			
					the	4	buffalo
		and	5	the			
					british	6	empire
		and	7	blackfoot			
					power	8	but
9	alberta						
		a	1	conservative			
		province	2	retains			
		in	3	symbols			
					of	4	erosion
		the	5	memory			
					of	6	these
		forces	7	however			
					indefensible	8	namely
9	mount						
		jutland	1	mount			
		jellico	2	mount			
		beatty	3	mount			
					evan-thomas	4	mount
		packenham	5	mount			
					warspite	6	mount
		inflexible	7	mount			
					indefatigable	8	mount
9	invincible						

a vision of whooping cranes

	kayakyak,	1	kayakyak,			
	cry	2	the			
	magpies	3	and			
				the	4	bluejays
	answer	5	trombone			
				brass	6	with
	doublereed	7	octave			
				kiyekyek	8	kiyekyek
9	kiyekyek					
	kiyekyek	1	but			
	there	2	flies			
	up	3	before			
				me	4	an
	endless	5	succession			
				of	6	whooping
	cranes	7	flying			
				each	8	the
9	same					
	flying	1	machine			
	male	2	or			
	female	3	yet			
				every	4	bird
	of	5	this			
				timelessly-long	6	white
	bird-rope	7	an			
				absolutely	8	new
9	individual					
	perhaps	1	and			
	perhaps	2	only			
	in	3	the			
				haunted	4	mind
	uttering	5	over			
				and	6	over
	again	7	the			
				same	8	horn
9	cry					

re ponziopilatismo

		march	**1**	twelfth				
		1977	**2**	I				
		bought	**3**	five				
					tightly	**4**	closed	
		daffodils	**5**	at				
					the	**6**	corner	
		safeway	**7**	store				
					for	**8**	fifty-nine	
9	cents							
		to	**1**	bring				
		home	**2**	to				
		subtle	**3**	gramsci's				
					scholar	**4**	to	
		meditate	**5**	upon				
					their	**6**	opening	
		and	**7**	open				
					out	**8**	the	
9	metaphysics							
		of	**1**	their				
		cut-being	**2**	she				
		put	**3**	them				
					sub	**4**	judice	
		one	**5**	by				
					one	**6**	into	
		a	**7**	pot				
					of	**8**	frank	
9	kiyooka's							

memo to sylvia vance

how	**1**	people				
become	**2**	accomplices				
in	**3**	their				
			own	**4**	subjugation,	
how	**5**	domination				
			is	**6**	anchored	
in	**7**	the				
			hearts	**8**	of	

9 the

dominated	**1**	(I				
quote	**2**	jessica				
benjamin)	**3**	is				
			adorno's	**4**	question	
of	**5**	marx				
			and	**6**	freud.	
And	**7**	evening				
			grosbeaks	**8**	too,	

9 I

suppose,	**1**	male				
and	**2**	female				
complicate	**3**	this				
			problem	**4**	with	
their	**5**	too-apposite				
			images	**6**	of	
			domination,			
			female	**8**	submissiveness.	

9 Non-predatory,

seed-eaters,	**1**	does				
the	**2**	male				
grosbeak	**3**	interiorize				
			the	**4**	brute	
authority	**5**	of				
			nature	**6**	over	
beast	**7**	and				
			man	**8**	and	

9 then

exteriorize	**1**	it				
in	**2**	flag				
and	**3**	sword-beak?				
			and	**4**	she —	
what	**5**	about				
			her	**6**	image?	
does	**7**	it				
			extravert	**8**	great	

9 nature's

		power	1	and				
		authority	2	refracted				
		(and	3	gutted)				
					in	4	him?	
		Let	5	jessica				
					benjamin	6	and	
		adorno	7	marx				
					and	8	freud	
9	answer							
		to	1	this.				
		Non-fierce,	2	the				
		grosbeak	3	is				
					more	4	brutal,	
		more	5	stupid;				
					the	6	worm-abusing	
		robin	7	more				
					delicate,	8	more	
9	fierce							

re the faces of doom every evening

		past	1	the			
		anguish	2	however			
		great	3	of			
					the	4	cross
		of	5	wood			
					tv	6	makes
		images	7	into			
					a	8	cross
9	harder						
		then	1	the			
		knuckles	2	and			
		elbows	3	of			
					a	4	tree
		and	5	last			
					night	6	looking
		at	7	the			
					news	8	I
9	recalled						
		as	1	if			
		it	2	were			
		a	3	crucifixion			
					the	4	wooden
		faces	5	of			
					roman	6	soldiers
		drafted	7	into			
					the	8	agony
9	squad						
		for	1	their			
		bread	2	and			
		butter's	3	sake			
					frank	4	dolphin
		joe	5	schlessinger			
					ken	6	colby
		paddy	7	gregg			
					don	8	mcneill
9	jason						
		moscovitch	1	brian			
		stewart	2	colin			
		howth	3	mark			
					phillips	4	bill
		laing	5	david			
					halton	6	in
		hard	7	focus			
					versus	8	us
9	all						

re elizabeth the second of england as leader of the peoples of the commonwealth

		I	1	complained				
		to	2	eternity				
		that	3	however				
					much	4	I	
		was	5	haunted				
					by	6	the	
		sad	7	face				
					of	8	this	
9	woman							
		who	1	is				
		my	2	sovereign				
		mistress	3	and				
					my	4	king	
		I	5	could				
					not	6	feel	
		any	7	the				
					least	8	spot	
9	of							
		loyalty	1	towards				
		the	2	flunkies				
		of	3	power				
					she	4	has	
		sacrificed	5	flesh				
					and	6	blood	
		to,	7	mind				
					and	8	heart	
9	and							
		soul.	1	The				
		compassions	2	of				
		eternity	3	are				
					strange	4	and	
		harsh	5	and				
					full	6	of	
		resentment	7	for				
					the	8	opaque	
9	of							
		conscience.	1	Do				
		not	2	gainsay				
		her,	3	said				
					eternity,	4	the	
		beauty	5	of				
					a	6	sacrifice	
		so	7	motivated				
					in	8	desolation	
9	of							

	self.	**1**	I				
	reflect	**2**	upon				
	her	**3**	smile				
				which	**4**	does	
	not	**5**	smile,				
				her	**6**	hands	
	which	**7**	do				
				not	**8**	wave	
9 as

	ablated	**1**	functions				
	of	**2**	an				
	england	**3**	which				
				in	**4**	its	
	salad	**5**	days				
				boy-aping	**6**	high-flown	
bird-cleopatras	**7**	would				
				have	**8**	wept	
9 majestic

	tears	**1**	for				
	her	**2**	voice				
	which	**3**	cannot				
				break	**4**	for	
	her	**5**	class-mouth				
				compressed	**6**	by	
	its	**7**	own				
				poverty	**8**	and	
9 theirs

re the haiku as analog methodology

		july	**1**	fourteenth				
		1978	**2**	at				
		0827	**3**	hours				
					portrait	**4**	of	
		mary	**5**	hamilton				
					as	**6**	japanese	
		haiku	**7**	the				
					first	**8**	syllable	
9	is							
		the	**1**	straight				
		black	**2**	hair				
		the	**3**	second				
					syllable	**4**	is	
		the	**5**	eyes				
					the	**6**	third	
		syllable	**7**					
					is	**8**	the	
9	mouth							
		the	**1**	fourth				
		syllable	**2**	is				
		the	**3**	teeth				
					the	**4**	fifth	
		syllable	**5**	is				
					the	**6**	skin	
		the	**7**	sixth				
					syllable	**8**	is	
9	the							
		kabuchi	**1**	soul				
		of	**2**	and				
		the	**3**	seventh				
					syllable	**4**	is	
		the	**5**	will				
					like	**6**	a	
		sheathed	**7**	sword				
					the	**8**	eighth	
9	syllable							
		is	**1**	the				
		neck	**2**	like				
		a	**3**	crane's				
					the	**4**	ninth	
		syllable	**5**	is				
					the	**6**	backbone	
		stiff	**7**	with				
					spirit	**8**	the	
9	tenth							

	syllable	1	is			
	the	2	hands			
	and	3	wrists			
				supple	4	as
	a	5	willow-bough			
				the	6	eleventh
	syllable	7	is			
				the	8	wit
9 a						
	pine-tree	1	reflected			
	in	2	unbroken			
	water	3	the			
				twelfth	4	syllable
	is	5	the			
				feet	6	like
	rain	7	falling			
				in	8	grass
9 the						
	thirteenth	1	syllable			
	the	2	voice			
	dropping	3	like			
				a	4	moon
	through	5	clouds			
				the	6	fourteenth
	syllable	7	is			
				the	8	laughter
9 like						
	a	1	whole-tone			
	scale	2	portrait			
	of	3	mary			
				hamilton	4	as
	japanese	5	haiku			
				the	6	fifteenth
	syllable	7	is			
				the	8	turning
9 of						
	the	1	head			
	towards	2	the			
	sixteenth	3	the			
				turning	4	of
	the	5	head			
				away	6	from
	portrait	7	of			
				mary	8	hamilton
9 as						

. . .

	japanese	**1**	haiku					
	the	**2**	seventeenth					
	syllable	**3**	is					
				all	**4**	the		
	other	**5**	syllables					
				conjoined	**6**	in		
	stasis	**7**	the					
						bright	**8**	sadness
9	of							

meditation on the godfathers

```
            seigneur   1
                       1
                       1   les
                       2
            les        2   lauriers
            lauriers   2   sont
                       3
            sont       3   coupables
            coupables  3   new
                              seigneur,   4   you
                                          4
                              technology  4   turns
            were       5   beset
                       5   organized
            old        5   environments
                              with        6   only
                              crime       6   is
                              into        6   art-form
            two        7   thieves
            computerized 7 into
                       7

                                          8   help
                              art-form    8
                              the         8   banks
9   help
9   the
9   have
            help       1   stop
            finance    1   ministers
            become     1   the
            thief      2   help
            have       2   absconded
            bank       2   robbers
            help       3   stop
                       3
            the        3   neutralization
                              thief       4
                                          4
                              of          4   dread
            help       5
                       5
            induces    5   in
                                          6
                                          6
                              the         6   private
```

	seigneur	7	ayez			
	a	7	rapacity			
	sector	7	les			
				pitié	8	seigneur
				totally	8	without
				lauriers	8	sont

9 seigneur
9 shame
9 coupables

concerning beautiful people

		1				
	demeter's	**1**	tragic			
		2	demeter's			
	chicken	**2**				
	tragic	**3**	chicken			
		3				
				and	**4**	demeter
					4	making
		5	the			
	love	**5**	together			
				beautiful	**6**	people
				on	**6**	that
	making	**7**	love			
	ugly	**7**	morning			
				together	**8**	o
					8	in
9	jonas					
9	the					
	o	**1**	barbara			
	beautiful	**1**	imaginations			
	o	**2**	amiel			
	of	**2**	george			
	then	**3**	lying			
	jonas	**3**	and			
				plucked	**4**	and
				barbara	**4**	amiel
	eviscerated	**5**	demeter's			
	o	**5**	demeter			
				tragic	**6**	chicken
				o	**6**	barbara
	in	**7**	that			
	o	**7**	jonas			
				same	**8**	conjugal
					8	o
9	imagination					
9	amiel					

les colonels sont toujours très polis

mankind has three wishes the first is for wealth the second for justice the third wish is for the colonels wish for wealth impoverishes the wish for justice leads to the rule of law with all the majesty and slow delay of counsel courts juries

		judges	**7**	as				
			7					
					for	**8**	the	
						8		
9	third							
9								
		wish	**1**	only				
		left	**1**	left				
		it	**2**	is				
		left	**2**	right				
		realised	**3**	the				
		left	**3**	left				
					colonels	**4**	are	
					left	**4**	left	
		polite	**5**	and				
		right	**5**	left				
					never	**6**	disappoint	
					left	**6**	left	
		us	**7**					
		left	**7**	right				
						8		
					left	**8**	left	
9								
9	left							

re the blue jays of april fifteenth

		kyrie	**1**	kyrie			
		blue	**1**	jay			
		kyrie	**2**	crying			
		blue	**2**	jay			
		crying	**3**	crying			
		blue	**3**	jay			
					crying	**4**	crying
					kyrie	**4**	kyrie
		crying	**5**	crying			
		kyrie	**5**	kyrie			
					crying	**6**	crying
					kyrie	**6**	blue
		kyrie	**7**	kyrie			
		jay	**7**	blue			
					kyrie	**8**	crying
					jay	**8**	eleison
9	crying						
9	eleison						
		waking	**1**	up			
			1				
		years	**2**	ago			
			2				
		in	**3**	a			
			3				
					now	**4**	deserted
						4	
		shipyard	**5**				
		and	**5**	the			
						6	
					tomorrowing	**6**	sun
			7				
		crashing	**7**	through			
					and	**8**	the
					transparent	**8**	gantries
9	welders						
9	wet						
		cemeteried	**1**	beside			
		with	**1**	april			
		drowned	**2**	ships			
		morning	**2**				
		their	**3**	flaming			
			3				
					flaring	**4**	torches
					and	**4**	the
		quenched	**5**				
		honking	**5**	cry			

```
                                          6
                             of           6      the
             7
      blue   7    jay
                             calling      8      blue
                                          8      from
9  jay
9  tree
                  1
           to    1    tree
                  2
           and   2    over
           my    3    roof
                  3    and
                                          4
                              the         4

                                          6      blue
                            honking       6      blue
      blue    5    jay
             5
      jay    7    blue
      jay    7    in
                                          8      blue
                              jay         8      deserted
                               a
9  jay
9  shipyard
```

norman yates

```
         hosannah   1
                    1    the
              the   1    ballad
                    2
           ballad   2    of
               of   2    born
        benedictus  3    benedictus
             born   3    again
            again   3    space
                                         4
                                space    4
                                  the    4    inhabitants
            glory   5
                    5    singing
          thereof   5    singing
                                benedictus   6
                                   sanctus   6
                                   singing   6    sanctus
                    7    hosannah
               in   7    pipe
                    7    norman
                                         8    glory
                                lines    8    of
                                yates    8    looking
9
9    born
9    at
                    1
            again   1    space
              his   1    watch
                    2
           norman   2    yates
                    2
                    3
         hurrying   3    away
             like   3    a
                                         4
                                 like    4    a
                         construction    4    worker
       benedictus   5
     construction   5    worker
               in   5    a
                                hosannah    6    glory
                                     who    6    is
                                    hard    6    hat
```

glory	**7**	glory
late	**7**	the
	7	
	8	
ballad	**8**	of
born	**8**	again

9 benedictus
9
9 space

putting one environment around another

	1	the		
	1	the		
the	**1**	military		
the	**1**	victim		
interrogation	**2**	of,		
victim	**2**	whether		
standing	**2**	around		
as	**2**	pop		
the	**3**	torture		
jew,	**3**	or		
as	**3**	midwives		
art . . .	**3**			
		of,	**4**	the
		japanese,	**4**	or
		the	**4**	military
			4	putting
murder	**5**	of,		
vietnamese,	**5**	man		
	5			
one	**5**	environment		
		the	**6**	gawking
		woman	**6**	or,
		becoming	**6**	human . . .
		around	**6**	another . . .
at,	**7**	the		
woman	**7**	with		
the	**7**	military		
the	**7**	victim		
		military	**8**	helping
		child	**8**	
		standing	**8**	around
		as	**8**	pop

9 to . . .
9
9 the-birth-of.
9 art

bessai topology

```
                        1   portrait
                        1   diane
             of         2   bessai
         bessai         2
            qua         3   gondola
          drunk         3   the
                                            4   her
                            venetian        4   beauty
           prow         5   tottering,
            of,         5   the
                                her         6   keel and plank
                              sea's         6   ring
            the         7   rump
             on         7   her
                                 of         8   the
                             finger         8   alleluia
9   lion
9   alleluia
             of         1   saint
        alleluia        1   remarrying
         mark's         2   the
            the         2   sea
         city's         3   gorgeous
        alleluia        3   alleluia
                           daughter         4   her
                                her         4   legs
           feet         5   like
        alleluia        5   with
                                  a         6   bride's
                            anguish         6   of
        pitching        7   careening
            the         7   wine
                              under         8   her
                            portrait        8   of
9   alleluia
9   bessai
```

returning to square one

```
                        1
                        1   at
                        2
            the         2   fourteenth
                        3
            station     3   we
                                            4
                                    begin   4   by
                        5
            turning     5   back
                                            6
                                    to      6   the
                        7
            thirteenth  7   station
                                    the     8   taking
                                            8
9   down
9
            of          1   the
                        1
            dead        2   body
                        2
            of          3
                        3   at
                                            4
                                    the     4   thirteenth
                        5
            station     5   we
                                            6
                                    turn    6   back
                                            8   the
                                    twelfth 8   station
9   putting
9
            up          1   with
                        1
            the         2   death
                        2
            of          3
                        3   at
                                            4
                                station     4   twelve
```

```
                    5
            we      5    turn
                                            6
                                   back     6    to
                    7
            station 7    eleven
                                   the      8    getting
                                            8
9   used
9
            to      1    the
                    1
            nailing 2    up
                    2
            of      3
                    3    at
                                            4
                                   station  4    eleven
                    5
                    5    we
                                            6
                                   turn     6    back
                    7
            to      7    station
                                   the      8    stripping
                                   ten      8
9   off
9
            of      1    the
                    1
            clothes 2    of
                    2
                    3
            at      3    station
                                            4
                                   ten      4    we
                    5
            turn    5    back
            the     7
            nine    7
                                            6
                                   to       6    station
                                   third    8    falling
                                            8
9   down
9
                                                     . . .
```

```
                    of    1
                          1    at
                          2
            station       2    nine
                          3
                 we       3    turn
                                              4
                                      back    4    to
                          5    the
            station       5    eight
                                              6
                                   telling    6    off
                                              6
                    of    7    the
                          7
                                       city   8    women
                                              8
     9    of
     9
                          1
                    at    1    station
                          2
             eight        2    we
                          3
                   are    3    not
                                              4
                                 discouraged  4    by
                          5
                the       5    thought
                                              6
                                         of   6    turning
                          7
                back      7    to
                                              8    the
                                    station   8    seven
     9    second
     9
             falling      1    down
                          1
                    of    2
                          2    at
                          3
            station       3    seven
                                              4
                                         we   4    turn
```

```
                    5
        back        5    to
                                         6    the
                              station    6    six
        wiping      7    the
                    7
                                   face  8    of
                                         8
9
9   at
                    1
        station     1    six
                    2
        we          2
                    3
        turn        3    back
                                         4
                              to         4    station
        the         5    beautiful
        five        5
                              simon's    6    taking
                                         6
        up          7    the
                    7
                              weight     8    of
                                         8
9
9   at
                    1
        station     1    five
                    2
        we          2    turn
                    3
        back        3    desolate
                                         4
                              to         4    station
        the         5    meeting
        four        5
                              up         6    with
                                         6
        the         7    miserable
                    7
                              mother     8    of
                                         8
9
9   at                                              . . .
```

287

		1	
station	1	four	
	2		
we	2	are	
	3		
almost	3	there	

		4	
and	4	turn

		5	
back	5	to

		6	the
station	6	three

| first | 7 | falling |
| | 7 | |

		8	of
down	8

9	
9	at

		1	
station	1	three
	2	
we	2	turn
	3	
back	3	to

		4	the
station	4	two

| acceptation | 5 | of |
| | 5 | |

		6	full
the	6

| expense | 7 | of |
| | 7 | here |

		8	the
comes	8

9	
9	crisis

		1	
of	1	expected
	2		
defeat	2	at
	3	
station	3	two

```
                                   4
                          we       4     turn
                  5
           back   5
                                   6
                          to       6     the
                  7       the
           first  7       station
                                   8
                                   8
9   washing
9
           of     1       the
                  1
           hands  2       of
                  2
                  3
           and    3       the
                                   4
                          condemnation   4     of
                  5
           by     5       pontius
                                   6
                          pilate   6     it
                  7
           is     7       here
                                   8
                          we       8     must
9
9   begin
```

from mass on cowback

re counting

```
                one     1   two
                        1
              three     2   four
                        2
               five     3   six
                        3
                                    seven   4   eight
                                            4   one
               nine     5
                two     5
                                                6
                                    three   6   four
                        7
                        7   five
                                                8
                                      six   8
 9
 9   seven
                        1   one
              eight     1
                two     2   three
               nine     2
               four     3   four
                        3
                                     five   4   six
                                            4
             seven     5   eight
                       5
                                     nine   6   seven
                                            6
             eight     7   nine
                 I     7   begin
                                    seven   8   eight
                                            8   with
 9   nine
 9   counting
                       1   I
                 I     1   begin
             begin     2   with
              with     2   counting
          counting     3
                 I     3   count
                                            4   Count
                                      my    4   fingers
              your     5   blessings
              toes     5   eyes
                                                    . . .
```

293

					said	6	my
					ears	6	my
		mother	7	and			
		vanished	7	teeth			
				I	8	count
					the	8	hairs
9	them						
9	of						
		one	1	by			
		my	1	head			
		one	2				
		my	2	kinspeople			
			3	all			
		friends	3				
					the	4	years
					all	4	the
		I	5	begin			
		years	5	of			
					with	6	counting
					my	6	age
		and	7	the			
			7	I			
					years	8	to
					begin	8	with
9	come						
9	counting						
		onetwo	1				
			1	threefour			
		fivesix	2				
			2	seveneight			
		nine	3				
			3	nine			
						4	seveneightnine
					nine	4	
	seveneightnine		5				
			5	nine			
				seveneightnine		6	
						6	nine
			7				
		nine	7	nine			
						8	seveneightnine
					nine	8	nine
9	nine						
9	nine						

letter to marian engel

```
                they      1  invented
                          1
                  a       2  new
                          2
            woman.        3
               One        3  for
                                                    4
                                         whom       4  the
                          5
             slogan       5  abortion
                                                    6
                                            on      6  demand
                          7
                 wd       7  be
                                                    8  They
                                    meaningless     8  battlecry.
9  invented
9  They
                  a       1  new
           invented       1  a
            woman.        2
               new        2  woman.
                          3  One
                          3
                                           for      4  whom
                                                    4
                the       5  wild
                          5
                                          body      6  and
                                                    6
            magical       7  mind
                          7  they
                                            of      8  irving
                                      invented      8  a
9  layton
9  new
                 wd       1  be
              woman       1
             totally      2  inadequate.
                          2
                they      3  invented
                          3  They
                                             a      4  new
                                      abolished     4  love
                                                          . . .
```

295

```
                       woman.   5   They
                            by  5   changing
                                    invented    6   a
                                          the   6   meaning
                           new   7   woman,
                            of   7   the
                                          who   8   transformed
                                         word.  8   They
9   marriage
9   invented
                          from   1   sexual
                                 1
              eat-together       2   to
                                 2
                 adversary       3   pleasure,
                                 3
                                          they  4   invented
                                                4   for
                             a   5   new
                          whom   5   the
                                         woman. 6
                                          male. 6   was
                                 7
                             a   7   perpetual
                                                8
                                 disappointment,  8   an
9
9   inverted
                                 1   They
                       mirror,   1   an
                      invented   2   a
                         agony   2   of
                           new   3   woman
                      infinite   3   regress.
                                         What   4   sort
                                         They   4   invented
                            of   5   liberation
                             a   5   new
                                           is   6   this,
                                        woman.  6
                           she   7   cried
                                 7
                                          out,  8   to
                                                8   They
9   be
9   invented
```

```
                tigered    1  up
                      a    1  new
                     in    2  a
                  woman    2
                freedom    3  emptied
                           3
                                            of   4  all
                                                 4
         companionship    5  except
                           5
                                            my   6  own
                                                 6
              emptiness,   7  to
                           7
                                            be   8  caged
                                                 8
9  up
9  They
                      in   1  an
               invented    1  a
              emptiness    2  without
                    new    2  woman
                    any    3  constraint
                   they    3  invented
                                          they   4  invented
                       a   5  new          a     4  new
                  woman.   5
                                         woman.  6
                                             I   6  would
                           7
                 rather,   7  she
                                                 8
                                          said,  8  be
9  They
9  ajax's
               invented    1  a
             bondswoman    1  or
                    new    2  woman
                    the    2  bourbon's
                           3
             sex-queen.    3  They
                                            In   4  fact,
                                       invented  4  a
                  they'd   5  invented
                    new    5  woman.
                                                          . . .
```

297

```
                                              the    6  supreme
                                                     6
                       male,       7  whether
                                   7
                                              her    8  name
                                                     8  They
    9   is
    9   invented
                       margaret    1  this
                             a     1  new
                            or     2  margaret
                         woman     2
                          that     3  or
                                   3
                                           margaret  4  whatever
                                                     4
                            or     5  wherever
                                   5
                                              or     6  whether
                                                     6
                           she     7  goes
                                   7  They
                                              by     8  some
                                          invented   8  a
    9   other
    9   new
                         name,     1  they
                        woman,     1
                      invented     2  a
                                   2
                           new     3  woman,
                                   3  They
                                              in     4  fact,
                                          invented   4  a
                        they'd     5  invented
                           new     5  woman,
                                              the    6  supreme
                                              she    6  stares
male.       7
 into       7  their
                                    8
                          eyes     8  with
    9
    9   their
```

		1				
	own	**1**	eyes			
		2				
	they	**2**	invented			
		3	They			
	for	**3**	her.			
				invented	**4**	a
					4	
	new	**5**	woman			
		5				
				What	**6**	she
				They	**6**	invented
	sees,	**7**	eye			
	a	**7**	new			
				to	**8**	eye,
				woman.	**8**	
9	is					
9						
	their	**1**	eyes			
		1				
	eyeing	**2**	their			
	It	**2**	was			
	eyes.	**3**				
	that	**3**	cannibal			
				in	**4**	which
				potlatch	**4**	
	the	**5**	father			
		5				
				ate	**6**	the
					6	
	son	**7**	in			
		7	and			
				the	**8**	dish
				the	**8**	son
9						
9	in					
		1				
	the	**1**	belly			
		2				
	ate	**2**	the			
		3				
	father	**3**	standing			
					4	
				at	**4**	the

. . .

		They	5	invented			
		table.	5				
					a	6	new
						6	
		woman,	7	they			
		They	7	invented			
				invented	8	a	
				a	8	new	
9	new						
9	woman						

re mario prizek and glenn gould's examination of the music of the 1930s

```
                        1
            alle        1   menschen
                        2   all
        mussen          2   sterben
            men         3   must
                        3
                                        die         4
                                        alle        4   menschen
                        5   mourns
        mussen          5   sterben
                                        the         6   bach
                                                    6
        chorale         7   alle
                        7   all
                                  menschen          8   mussen
                                       men          8   must
 9  sterben
 9  die
                        1
            goes        1   the
                        2   pianoforte
           glenn        2   gould
             and        3   trumpet
       hindemith        3
                                   re-version       4   of
                                                    4
            alle        5   menschen
            with        5   knock
                                     mussen         6   sterben
                                         on         6   knock
                        7
              of        7   skeletonal
                                                    8   all
                                       bone         8   on
 9  men
 9  bone
            must        1   die
             and        1   trumpet
         sterben        2   mussen
          camera        2   cry
          mussen        3   sterben
              of        3   mario
                                      gould        4   casella
                                      prizek       4   mussen
          webern        5   krenak
         sterben        5   alle
                                                          . . .
```

			prokofieff	**6**	sterben
			menschen	**6**	
	mussen	**7**	all		
		7	alle		
			men	**8**	must
			menschen	**8**	mussen
9	die				
9	sterben				

re swp who asks questions

```
            meditations  1  xmas
                evening  2  1979
                     at  3  sixteen
                                  hundred  4  odd
                  hours  5  a
                                half-moon  6  rising
                     in  7  the
                                     east  8  out
9  of
                    the  1  dark
                   side  2  of
                    the  3  sunset.
                                       It  4  is
                    the  5  child
                                   within  6  who
                   asks  7  all
                                      the  8  difficult
9  questions:
                what is  1  snow
               made of,  2  what stuff
                 is ice  3  made
                              of, what    4  is water
               made of,  5  why is
                                  the sky  6  clear, why
                   does  7  a clear
                             sky mean     8  sharp frost,
9  why?
                     We  1  answer according
                 to our  2  incapacities. It is
              the child  3  within
                              who asks    4  all the
              difficult  5  questions, what
                              are the     6  cusps of
               the moon  7  for,
                             which way    8  do the
9  horns
                of the   1  moon
              point, up  2  or down,
                    why  3  do they
                             always point 4  away from
                the sun, 5  why
                              does the    6  sun go
            down under   7  the
                             earth. We    8  reply according
9  to
                                                  . . .
```

303

our	1	incapacities. I'm		
not an	2	astronomer, I		
haven't	3	enough mathematics		
		to answer	4	all these
tiresome	5	questions, and		
		if you	6	ask any
more I	7	will		
		box your ears.	8	The

9 child

within	1	silences		
but	2	not		
for	3	long.		
		Why	4	do
old	5	people		
		get	6	angry
when	7	I		
		ask	8	reasonable

9 questions . . .

We	1	answer		
according	2	to		
our	3	incapacities . . .		
		we	4	are
not	5	astronomers,		
		we	6	haven't
enough	7	mathematics		
		to	8	say,

9 simply,

the	1	earth		
is	2	here,		
the	3	sun		
		is	4	under
us,	5	there,		
		and	6	thus
it	7	is		
		with	8	the

9 moon

Construction, April, 1975, for four voices, 3 male, 1 female

```
              1
    walt      1    whitman
              1
              1
              2
    to        2    the
              2
              2
              3
    dark      3    tower
              3
              3
                              4    walt
                        came  4
                              4    walt
                              4
    whitman   5    to
              5
    whitman   5    to
              5
                        the   6    dark
                              6
                        the   6    dark
                              6
    tower     7    came
              7    our
    tower     7    came
              7
                              8
                        first 8    thoughts
                              8
                              8
9
9   were
9
9
              1
    marshall  1    mcluhan
              1
              1
              2
    and       2    the
              2
              2
```

```
                    3
         flower     3    children,
                    3
                    3
                                        4
                                 what   4    fun!
                                        4
                                        4    fee
                    5
                    5
                    5
              fi    5    fo
                                        6    walt
                                        6    walt
                                        6    walt
                                 fum,   6
         whitman    7    to
         whitman    7    to
         whitman    7    to
                    7
                                 the    8    dark
                                 the    8    dark
                                 the    8    dark
                                        8
 9  tower
 9  tower
 9  tower
 9
         came!      1
         came!      1
         came!      1
                    1    god
                    2
                    2
                    2
           is       2    bushed,
                    3
                    3
                    3
         earle      3    birney
                                        4
                                        4
                                        4
                                 sang   4    into
                    5
                    5
                    5
           the      5    vancouver
```

						6		
						6		
					dead	**6**	nietzsche's
					rain	**6**	
			7				
			7				
		ghost!	**7**				
			7	fi			
						8	
						8	
						8	
					fi	**8**	fo
9							
9							
9							
9	fum,						
		walt	**1**	whitman			
		walt	**1**	whitman			
		walt	**1**	whitman			
			1				
		to	**2**	the			
		to	**2**	the			
		to	**2**	the			
			2				
		dark	**3**	tower			
		dark	**3**	tower			
		dark	**3**	tower			
			3				
					camel	**4**	
					camel	**4**	
					camel	**4**	myself
						4	
			5				
			5				
		the	**5**	myselves —			
			5				
						6	
						6	
					those	**6**	mirroring
						6	
			7				
			7	sheer			
		walls	**7**	explain			
			7				
						8	
					gun	**8**	metal
						8	
						8	fee

```
9
9
9
9   fi
                        1   walt
                        1   walt
                        1   walt
              fo        1   fum,
         whitman        2   to
         whitman        2   to
         whitman        2   to
                        2
              the       3   dark
              the       3   dark
              the       3   dark
                        3   ten
                                        tower       4
                                        tower       4
                                        tower       4
                                        thousand    4   walt
                        5
                        5
                        5
         whitmans       5   to
                                                    6
                                                    6
                                                    6
                                        the         6   dark
                        7   ten
                        7   ten
                        7   ten
              tower     7   camel
                                        thousand    8   walt
                                        thousand    8   walt
                                        thousand    8   walt
                                                    8
9    whitmans
9    whitmans
9    whitmans
9
              to        1   the
                        1
                        1
                        1
            dark        2   tower
            dark        2   tower
            dark        2   tower
                        2
```

```
              camel    3
                the    3    me-myself
                       3
                       3
                                         4
                            becomes      4    melting-pot
                                         4
                                         4
                       5    sans
              man,     5
              sans     5    skin,
                       5
                            blood,       6
                            sans         6    language
                                         6
                                         6    fee
                       7
                       7
                       7
         fi-fo-fum     7    fee
                                         8    walt
                                         8    walt
                                         8    walt
                            fi-fo-fum    8
9   whitman
9   whitman
9   whitman
9
                to     1    the
                to     1    the
                to     1    the
                       1
              dark     2    tower
              dark     2    tower
              dark     2    tower
                       2
              came!    3
                       3
                       3    potato-chip-mouth
                       3
                                         4
                                         4
                            plugs        4    with
                                         4
                       5    coffee-grounds
                       5
         linguistic    5    chafe
                       5
```

```
                                        lettuce-leaf  6  hair
                                                      6
                                                      6
                                                      6
                and  7  grease!
                     7
                     7
                     7  fee-fi-fo-fum,
                                         walt  8  whitman
                                         walt  8  whitman
                                         walt  8  whitman
                                                8
9  to
9  to
9  to
9
                dark  1  tower
                dark  1  tower
                dark  1  tower
                      1
                came  2  generals
                came  2
                came  2
                      2
                with  3  short
                      3
                      3
                      3
                                         haircuts  4  command
                                                   4
                                                   4
                                                   4
                   a  5  military
                      5
                      5
                      5
                                         second  6  to
                                                 6
                                                 6
                                                 6
               none  7
                but  7  not
                but  7  not
                but  7  not
                                                   8  but
                                         enough    8
                                         enough    8
                                         enough    8
```

```
9   not
9
9
9
        enough!   1
                  1
                  1
                  1   fee-fi-fo-fum,
                  2
                  2
                  2
        fee       2   fi
                  3
                  3
                  3
        fo        3   fum,
                            walt...   4
                            walt...   4
                            walt...   4
                                      4
whitman...   5
whitman...   5
whitman...   5
             5
                                 to   6   the
                                 to   6   the
                                 to   6   the
                                      6
                  7   dark...
                  7   dark...
                  7   dark...
                  7
                                          8   tower...
                                          8   tower...
                                          8   tower...
                                          8
9
9
9
9
        came...   1
                  1   to
                  1
                  1
                  2
        gain      2   time
                  2
                  2
```

311

```
                         3
                was      3    the
                         3
                         3
                                                 4
                                     password — 4
                                                 4
                                          fee,   4    fi,
                         5
                         5
                         5    walt
                fo,      5    fum,
                                                 6
                                                 6
                                        whitman  6    to
                                                 6
                         7
                         7
                the      7    dark
                         7
                                                 8    the
                                                 8
                                         tower   8    camel
                                                 8
    9   viet cong,
    9
    9
    9
                 my      1    friends,
                         1
                         1
                         1
               compel    2    cambodia
                         2
                         2
                         2
              bombed     3
                         3
                         3
                fee      3    fi
                                                 4    walt
                                                 4    walt
                                                 4    walt
                                          fo     4    fum,
            whitman      5    to
            whitman      5    to
            whitman      5    to
                         5
```

```
                                        the    6    dark
                                        the    6    dark
                                        the    6    dark
                                               6
            tower    7    came!
            tower    7    came!
            tower    7    came!
                     7
                                               8
                                               8
                                   but         8    peace
                                               8
9
9
9    with
9
                          1
                          1
            honor         1    was
                          1
                          2
                          2
            the           2    disreputable
                          3
                                          4
                                          4
                              design      4
                                          4    fee-fi-fo-fum
                     5
                     5
                     5
fee-fi-fo-fum        5
                                               6    walt
                                               6    walt
                                               6    walt
                      fee-fi-fo-fum            6
            whitman   7    to
            whitman   7    to
            whitman   7    to
                      7
                                        the    8    dark
                                        the    8    dark
                                        the    8    dark
                                               8
9    tower
9    tower
9    tower
9
```

313

```
                    came!      1
                    came!      1
                    came!      1
                innocence      1      rules,
                               2
                               2
                               2
                      the      2      ceremony
                               3
                               3
                               3
                       of      3      guilt
                                                         4      or
                                                         4
                                                         4
                                               is        4      dead
                  maimed!      5
                               5
                               5
                               5      fee
                                                         6
                                                         6
                                                         6
                                               fi        6      fo
                               7      walt-whitman-to
                               7      walt-whitman-to
                               7      walt-whitman-to
                      fum      7
                                      the-dark-tower     8      came!
                                      the-dark-tower     8      came!
                                      the-dark-tower     8      came!
                                                         8
      9    walt
      9
      9
      9
                  waltzes      1      into
                               1
                               1
                   brahma,     1      zeus,
                      god,     2
                               2
                               2
                    christ,    2
                               3      each
                               3
                               3
                               3
```

```
                                    with    4    a
                                            4
                                            4
                                            4
              richard    5    nixon
                         5
                         5
                         5
                                    face!   6
                                            6
                                            6
                                    fee,    6    fi,
                         7
                         7    walt
                         7
              fo,        7    fum
                                            8
                                    whitman 8    to
                                            8
                                            8
9
9
9    the
9
                         1
              dark       1    tower
                         1
                         1
                         2
              came!      2
                         2    krishna-niks
                         2
                         3
                         3
              are        3    chicago'd
                         3
                                            4
                                            4
                                    into    4    riot
                                            4
                         5
                         5
              squad      5    vans
                         5
                                    help!   6
                                            6    help!
                                            6
                                            6
```

```
                              7
                              7
                              7    mother-fucker!
                   help!      7
                                                          8
                                                          8
                                                          8
                                       fee-fi-fo-fum      8    fee-fi-fo-fum
    9    help!
    9
    9
    9    fee-fi-fo-fum
         mother-fucker    1    walt
                          1    walt
                         .1    walt
         fee-fi-fo-fum    1    walt
              whitman     2    to
              whitman     2    to
              whitman     2    to
              whitman     2    to
                  the     3    dark
                  the     3    dark
                  the     3    dark
                  the     3    dark
                                       tower    4    camel
                                       tower    4    camel
                                       tower    4    camel
                                       tower    4    camel
                          5
                          5
                 box      5    saw
                          5
                                                          6
                                                          6
                                                only      6    archie
                                                          6
                          7
                          7
              bunker      7    on
                          7
                                                          8
                                                          8
                                                 the      8    cross!
                                                 fee      8    fi
    9
    9
    9
    9    fo
```

```
                    1    walt-whitman-to
                    1    walt-whitman-to
                    1    walt-whitman-to
           fum      1
           the      2    dark-tower-came!
           the      2    dark-tower-came!
           the      2    dark-tower-came!
                    2
         phnom      3    penh
                    3
                    3
                    3
                                   falls    4    out
                                            4
                                            4
                                            4
            of      5    god's
                    5
                    5
                    5
                                   hand!    6
                                            6
                                            6
                                            6    fee-fi-fo-fum,
                    7
                    7
                    7
   fee-fi-fo-fum,   7    fee-fi-fo-fum,
                                            8
                                            8
                                            8
                                            8    fee-fi-fo-fum
   9
   9
   9   walt
   9
                    1
                    1
            to      1    whitman
                    1
                    2
                    2
           the      2    dark
                    2
                    3
                    3
          tower     3    came!
                    3
```

```
                              murder    4    pleads
                                        4
                                        4
                                        4
              the    5    people
                     5
                     5
                     5
                              once      6    again,
                                        6
                                        6
                                        6
                     7    murder
                     7
                     7
fee-fi-fo-fum!       7
                              pleads    8    the
                                        8
                                        8
                                        8
9    people
9
9
9
              once    1    again!
                     1
                     1
                     1
                     2    walt
                     2    walt
                     2    walt
fee-fi-fo-fum!       2
    whitman          3    to
    whitman          3    to
    whitman          3    to
                     3
                              the       4    dark
                              the       4    dark
                              the       4    dark
                                        4
         tower       5    came!
         tower       5    came!
         tower       5    came!
                     5    fee-fi-fo-fum,
                              walt      6    whitman
                              walt      6    whitman
                              walt      6    whitman
                                        6
```

		to	7	the		
		to	7	the		
		to	7	the		
			7	fee-fi-fo-fum,		
				dark	8	tower
				dark	8	tower
				dark	8	tower
			fee-fi-fo-fum,	8	fee-fi-fo-fum,

9 came!
9 came!
9 came!
9 fee-fi-fo-fum!

re Phyllis Webb & Wilson's Bowl

their real	1	essence	
is a tombstone	2	with	
the	3	inscription, I	
		was.	4 tiny worms eat
my bone, his	5	bones	
		consume her flesh.	6 their
flesh	7	chaws up	
		our minds, our mind	8 devours
9 their			
soul. her	1	mind	
feeds on his	2	words,	
what they	3	see,	
		or hear, smell,	4 taste,
touch, feel,	5	heft,	
		estimate, the seven	6 senses
or so.	7	but	
		these sit by a	8 blind
9 man's			
tin, reciting	1	thank-you's.	
his soul is	2	extinguished,	
her mind's	3	lost.	
		their flesh	4 and bones
rot, nothing	5	remains	
		but stone	6 this stone
drinks down	7	my	
		name with the words,	8 I
9 was . . .			
time past	1	moves	
into	2	the future with	
angular	3	motion. the	
		dumb angels scream	4 at
us the	5	cry	
		of birds, heron-speech.	6 this
stone, loss	7	found	
		and lost, found to	8 be
9 lost			

re the explosion at the power station

			the	1	minister				
			isn't	2	as				
			blind	3	as				
						all	4	that	
			he	5	doesn't				
						need	6	to	
			have	7	his				
						eyes	8	blown	
9	open								
			just	1	what				
			the	2	demolitionists				
			meant	3	by				
						blowing	4	up	
			the	5	power-station				
						near	6	qualicum	
			is	7	perfectly				
						clear	8	to	
9	all								
			the	1	minister				
			isn't	2	blind				
			the	3	minister				
						doesn't	4	need	
			to	5	have				
						his	6	eyes	
			blown	7	open				
						he	8	knows	
9	that								
			any	1	law				
			which	2	destroys				
			the	3	ecosystem				
						ought	4	to	
			be	5	dealt				
						with	6	in	
			the	7	same				
						way	8	as	
9	it								
			deals	1	with				
			the	2	life-environment				
			which	3	is				
						more	4	sacred	
			than	5	law				
						itself.	6	The	
			minister	7	doesn't				
						need	8	his	
9	eyes								

. . .

	blown	**1**	open				
	the	**2**	minister				
	isn't	**3**	all				
				that	**4**	blind	
	the	**5**	minister				
				knows	**6**	that	
	electricity	**7**	which				
				requires	**8**	the	
9	poisoning						
	of	**1**	the				
	life	**2**	cycle				
	is	**3**	too				
				costly	**4**	to	
	be	**5**	considered.				
				Roch	**6**	Carrier	
	has	**7**	a				
				story	**8**	about	
9	what						
	happened	**1**	to				
	god	**2**	in				
	quebec.	**3**	God				
				was	**4**	arrested	
	for	**5**	blowing				
				up	**6**	government	
	buildings	**7**	power-stations				
				and	**8**	churches.	
9	when						
	caught	**1**	he				
	was	**2**	sentenced				
	to	**3**	prison.				
				But	**4**	you	
	can't	**5**	keep				
				god	**6**	in	
	prison	**7**	for				
				ever.	**8**	So	
9	when						
	the	**1**	authorities				
	thought	**2**	that				
	the	**3**	law				
				had	**4**	been	
	satisfied,	**5**	god				
				was	**6**	released.	
	He	**7**	is				
				still	**8**	going	
9	around						

	blowing	1	up				
	government	2	buildings				
	power	3	stations				
				and	4	churches.	
	Perhaps	5	it				
				was	6	he	
	who	7	blew				
				up	8	the	
9	power-station						
	near	1	qualicum-bay.				
	The	2	minister				
	isn't	3	so				
				blind	4	he	
	doesn't	5	know				
				what	6	Roch	
	Carrier	7	means				
				the	8	minister	
9	knows						
	you	1	can't				
	keep	2	god				
	in	3	jail				
				for	4	ever.	
	The	5	minister				
				knows	6	very	
	well	7	that				
				bc	8	law	
9	unlike						
	quebec	1	law				
	can't	2	even				
	sentence	3	god				
				to	4	prison	
	for	5	blowing				
				up	6	churches	
	power	7	stations				
				and	8	government	
9	buildings						
	the	1	minister				
	isn't	2	as				
	blind	3	as				
				all	4	that	
	the	5	minister				
				knows	6	that	
	bc	7	law				
				isn't	8	totally	
9	compatible						

. . .

the	**1**	minister			
knows	**2**	that			
bc	**3**	law			
			still	**4**	retains
some	**5**	taint			
			of	**6**	the
old	**7**	law			
			of	**8**	nature

9 the

minister	**1**	knows			
however	**2**	sick			
bc	**3**	law			
			still	**4**	keeps
despite	**5**	legal			
			regrets	**6**	an
inscrutable	**7**	residual			
			curd	**8**	of natural

9 justice

re painting by numbers

```
            portrait   1   of
                       1   at
                       1
            my         2   father
            eighty     2   two
                       2   portrait
                       3
            years      3
            of         3   my
                                           4
                                painting   4   painting
                                father
                       5
            by         5   numbers
                       5   painting
                                           6   one, two
                                           6
                                    by     6   numbers
                       7
            three, four 7
                       7   five, six
                                           8
                                           8
                                seven, eight 8  nine,
9   painting
9
9   nine
            by         1   numbers
                       1
            nine       1   nine
            my         2   father
                       2
            nine       2
            never      3   knew
                       3
                       3
                                    how    4   to
                                           4
                                           4
            pray       5
                       5
            his        5   favorite
                                           6
                                           6
                                subject    6   was
                       7
                       7
            a          7   sailing
```

. . .

```
                                    8
                              in    8    full
                              ship  8    you
9
9    sail
9    could
                    1
                    1
            hear    1    the
                    2
                    2
            sailors 2    shouting
                    3    shouting
                    3
                    3
                                at  4    the
                                    4
                                    4
            sea     5    one, two
                    5
                    5
                                    6
                          three, four 6
                                    6    five, six
     seven, eight  7
                    7    nine
                    7
                              you   8    could
                              nine  8    nine
                                    8
9    hear
9    nine
9
            the     1    sailors
                    1    painted
                    1
                    2
            by      2    numbers
                    2    shouting
                    3
                    3
            at      3    the
                              painted 4    by
                                      4    you
                              sea     4
     numbers    5
     could      5    hear
                5
```

326

						sea	**6**	
						the	**6**	sea
							6	
		at	**7**	my			
		shouting	**7**				
			7				
					father	**8**	
					shouting	**8**	where
						8	shouting
9							
9	has						
9	shouting						
			1				
		my	**1**	father			
			1	where			
			2				
		sailed	**2**	to?			
			2	where			
			3				
		Not	**3**	to			
		where	**3**	where			
						4	
					lie	**4**	under
					has	**4**	he
			5	not			
		a	**5**	tombstone			
		gone?	**5**				
					to	**6**	lie
					is	**6**	all
						6	
		under	**7**	a			
		very	**7**	well			
			7	is			
					tombstone	**8**	
						8	
					all	**8**	very
9	Where						
9							
9	well						
		has	**1**	my			
			1	one			
			1				
		father	**2**	sailed			
		two	**2**				
			2				
		to?	**3**				
			3	three			
			3	Where			

. . .

					4	
				four	**4**	
				has	**4**	he
	5					
	5	five				
gone?	**5**					
					6	
				six	**6**	
				where	**6**	has
	7	seven, eight				
seven	**7**	eight				
where	**7**	has				
				seven, eight	**8**	seven, eight
				seven	**8**	eight
				he	**8**	gone?
9	nine					
9	nine					
9						

re hippolytus

	Today	**1**	rose without				
	any	**2**	dawn. it is				
	o seven	**3**	o				
				nine	**4**	hrs. The	
	sea	**5**	is ten				
			thousand chain saws	**6**	cutting		
	up	**7**	the shore				
				The white	**8**	ended eagle	
9	strong						
	of wing	**1**	stumbles				
	exigent	**2**	into the wind				
	Hippolytus	**3**	drowns. *Night*				
			holds hippolytus the	**4**	*pure*		
	of stain;	**5**	*diana*				
				steads	**6**	*him nothing, he*	
	must	**7**	*stay,* rain				
				chatters	**8**	at my	
9	roof						
	Diana	**1**	dumb clucks				
	it up and	**2**	down				
	the spit,	**3**	crying				
				with the	**4**	mewing gulls	
	and	**5**	saxophonist crows,				
			hippolytus, hippolytus	**6**	hippolytus to		
	the hard	**7**	hatted				
				sea	**8**	lips pulled back	
9	from						
	the	**1**	teeth of				
	ten	**2**	thousand mouths scream				
	back at	**3**	the				
				over-coated	**4**	shivering god	
	woman	**5**	pure reason				
				who can't	**6**	make any	
	sense of	**7**	this				
				at all	**8**	why, why,	
9	why						

re woody allen's annie hall

```
                 1979   1   sixth of
         november      2   edmonton at zero
         five five     3   zero
                           hours      4   the moon a
       last night's    5   guy
                           fawkes     6   day full moon
           has set     7   with
                           or without 8   the pleiades.
9   time
           passes      1   passes. the
       moon rises      2   and the
         pleiades,     3   the moon
                           sets and   4   the pleiades
          and time     5   passes
                           and november 6  goes down
         the drain     7   into
                           the storm sewers. 8 Hamlet
9   blasted
               by      1   the ghost
        of hamlet      2   becomes locke
              and      3   ingenious berkeley
                           and charles 4   darwin and
          sigmund      5   freud and
                           james joyce 6   and thomas
           edison      7   and marshall
                           mcluhan a   8   succession of
9   world
          figures      1   transmuted and
          mutated      2   into woody allen
            movie      3   more like a
                           phantasmagoria than a 4 movie
             time      5   passes the
                           moon rises  6   and sets
              and      7   the pleiades
                           and I       8   make confession
9   becoming
           mortal      1   and everyman,
         a figure      2   of luxury
        the earth      3   cannot
                           afford, my  4   mother the
        chocolate      5   bar worth
                           ten cents   6   in 1927
        and today      7   thirty
                           cents,      8   and my father
9   a
```

	full yard	1	of
	pseudo-gold	2	braid to usurp
	the moon	3	with
	and rule the	4	waters
			polluted	5	with human
	pollen	6	the moon sets
			behind mt	7	eisenhower
	and the	8	pleiades
			and sappho	9	becomes
0	an		
	unremembered	1	pastry-worm
	less real	2	than annie
	hall time	3	like
			a raging	4	toothache passes
	passes	5	but o
			iago iago the	6	now
	of it,	7	iago
			time passes	8	nothing, nothing
9	extinguishes		

Taking off from nanaimo harbour

```
               grey    1  gulls
                 in    2  triangle
                 of    3  cloud
                                       fog  4  sea
               grey    5  gulls
                                   islanded  6  on
             pilings   7  where
                                       the  8  wharf
9  floats
                 on    1  the
              rising   2  tide
                the    3  rising
                                     water  4  it
              rises    5  up
                                       out  6  of
                 an    7  ancient
                                       sea  8  old
9  water
            recycling  1  murder
                 of    2  kwakiutl
              feather  3  and
                                 hippolytus  4  drowned
             harbour   5  water
                                      with  6  a
              crust    7  of
                                    debris  8  which
9  rocks
               back    1  and
               forth   2  rising
                and    3  falling
                                      with  4  the
              tides    5  to
                                        be  6  laundered
              clean,   7  washing-machined
                                    under.  8  Within
9  range
                 of    1  mount
             benson's  2  blow
                 we    3  took
                                       off  4  slashing
                the    5  water-skin
                                      with  6  our
            seagull's  7  egg-shell
                                      thin  8  metal
9  hull
```

watching	**1**	out					
for	**2**	dead					
ends.	**3**	A					
				sick	**4**	goose	
we	**5**	climbed					
				up	**6**	into	
pulpmill's	**7**	resinous					
				cough	**8**	and	

9 stink,

our	**1**	starboard					
motor	**2**	spluttering.					
poseidon	**3**	caught					
				us	**4**	out	
over	**5**	gabriola					
				and	**6**	we	
dropped	**7**	back					
				down	**8**	among	

9 white

horses	**1**	our					
living	**2**	motor					
spun	**3**	us					
				into	**4**	carousel	
the	**5**	wind					
				and	**6**	tide	
argued	**7**	for					
				us	**8**	the	

9 reborn

wind	**1**	and					
a	**2**	water					
ponderous	**3**	with					
				hooves	**4**	wanted	
us	**5**	and					
				reached	**6**	for	
us	**7**	among					
				the	**8**	scattering	

9 cormorants

re wife battery

evening	1	of				
april	2	twenty-third				
nineteen	3	eighty				
			one	4	twenty	
two	5	hundred				
			hours	6	CBC	
program	7	to				
			help	8	battered	

9   wives . . .

panel	1	of			
social	2	service			
workers	3	with			
			faces	4	like
god's	5	angels			
			terribly	6	worried
by	7	their			
			hopeless	8	task . . .

9   re

wife	1	battery . . .			
But	2	what			
recourse	3	has			
			the	4	battered
audience?	5	How			
			can	6	we
accuse	7	these			
			misanthrope	8	angels

9   of

battering	1	mankind?			
the	2	breaks			
for	3	advertising			
			provide	4	some
relief	5	we			
			avert	6	our
eyes	7	turn			
			down	8	the

9   volume . . .

And	1	the			
battered	2	angel?			
No	3	money.			
			No	4	where
to	5	escape			
			to.	6	The
bruises.	7	the			
			shame	8	of

9   it . . .

		and	**1**	the			
		children?	**2**	in			
		a	**3**	context			
					of	**4**	battered
		angels,	**5**	in			
					a	**6**	world
		of	**7**	broken			
					images,	**8**	the

9 deaf

	hear	**1**	and			
	see	**2**	too			
	much,	**3**	only			
				the	**4**	blind
	are	**5**	safe,			
				only	**6**	the
	mad	**7**	are			
				wise	**8**	o

9 pauline

	only	**1**	the			
	mad	**2**	are			
	wise:	**3**	their			
				screams	**4**	bird-wisdom
	breadknife	**5**	wings			
				slicing	**6**	at
	the	**7**	sky			
				for	**8**	crumbs

9 of . . .

deconstruction chez flahiff

		portrait	**1**	of				
		fred	**2**	flahiff				
		meditating	**3**	on				
				deconstruction	**4**	in		
		terms	**5**	of				
				the	**6**	demolition		
		of	**7**	the				
				devonshire	**8**	hotel		
9	vancouver,							
		june	**1**	twentyninth,				
		nineteen	**2**	eightyone . . .				
		well,	**3**	said				
				eternity . . .	**4**	Everything,		
		explained	**5**	FF,				
				starts	**6**	with		
		the	**7**	plans				
				of	**8**	the		
9	building,							
		so	**1**	that				
		the	**2**	demolition				
		crew	**3**	can				
				present	**4**	the		
		television	**5**	crew				
				with	**6**	an		
		icon	**7**	of				
				history	**8**	collapsing		
9	in							
		upon	**1**	itself				
		and	**2**	nothing				
		falls	**3**	into				
				the	**4**	streets		
		except	**5**	dust.				
				Eternity	**6**	might		
		have	**7**	shed				
				a	**8**	tear		
9	but							
		didn't.	**1**	Portrait				
		of	**2**	fred				
		flahiff	**3**	looking				
				sad	**4**	lost		
		frustrated	**5**	inconsolably				
				human	**6**	conspired		
		against	**7**	in				
				fact	**8**	inexplicably		
9	diminished							

Picasso and gertrude stein

	tereus	**1**	tereus				
	tereus	**2**	tereus				
	tereus	**3**	tereus				
				tereus	**4**	tereus	
	tereus	**5**	tereus				
				alias	**6**	william	
	james	**7**	tore				
				out	**8**	her	
9	tongue						
	so	**1**	that				
	she	**2**	couldn't				
	say	**3**	what				
				had	**4**	been	
	done	**5**	when				
				where	**6**	why	
	if	**7**	done				
				to	**8**	or	
9	by						
	whom.	**1**	They				
	found	**2**	her				
	wandering	**3**	from				
				shop	**4**	to	
	shop	**5**	to				
				buy	**6**	a	
	pen	**7**	to				
				write	**8**	her	
9	story						
	down	**1**	but				
	how	**2**	can				
	she	**3**	write				
				without	**4**	a	
	tongue?	**5**	can				
				any	**6**	one	
	write	**7**	with				
				out	**8**	a	
9	tongue?						
	—	**1**	Picasso				
	met	**2**	her				
	in	**3**	the				
				park.	**4**	He	
	stuck	**5**	a				
				paint	**6**	brush	
	in	**7**	her				
				mouth	**8**	so	
9	she						

. . .

```
              could     1   speak
                 in     2   words
                 of     3   paint
                                      but    4   with
                  a     5   paint
                                    brush    6   for
                  a     7   tongue
                                      her    8   words
9   became
            statues    1   of
              stone    2   inviting
             almost    3   every
                                      man    4   in
                the    5   USA
                                       to    6   have
             dinner    7   with
                                    them.    8   Some
9   did
                and    1   wished
               they    2   hadn't.
               Some    3   didn't
                                      and    4   wished
               they    5   had.
                                  Picasso    6   looked
                 at    7   her
                                     hard    8   and
9   long
               then    1   painted
                her    2   lovingly,
               very    3   human,
                                     with    4   mouth
            closed,    5   and
                                  without    6   the
              paint    7   brush
                                      for    8   a
9   tongue
```

re march 3, 1980

	the	1	swearing in		
	of pierre	2	elliott trudeau		
	as	3	prime minister		
			of canada	4	for the
	fourth time	5	and		
			rené levesque	6	muttering nous
	sommes,	7	pour nous,		
			québécois	8	monday, march 3rd
9	1980				
	and	1	underneath the		
	lemieux	2	portrait of queen		
	elizabeth	3	and her		
			philippe	4	anglicisé the kids
	of	5	ed schreyer		
			playing	6	with the kids
	of	7	margaret trudeau		
			and rené	8	levesque muttering
9	nous				
	sommes,	1	pour nous,		
	québécois	2	an instant of		
	history	3	caught up		
			into the	4	québécois
	space of	5	lemieux's portrait		
			and rené	6	levesque muttering
	nous sommes,	7	pour		
			nous	8	québécois and the
9	cbc				
	wearing its	1	best		
	tie and	2	joe clark		
	and maureen	3	mcteer		
			hurrying	4	away to hawaii
	and rené	5	levesque		
			muttering nous	6	sommes, pour
	nous,	7	québécois and		
			lili there	8	comme un
9	fleur-de-lys				

Edvard Munch paints the High Level bridge

```
                        1    He
                        1
                        1
             is         2    screaming
                        2
                        2
                        3
             She        3    is
                        3
                                          4
                                screaming 4
                                     I    4    am
                        5
                        5    thou
  screaming             5
                                          6
                                     art  6    screaming
                                          6
       they             7    are
                        7
                        7
                                screaming 8
                                          8    screaming
                                          8
9
9    why
9    screaming
                        1
             are        1    they
                        1
                        2    The
  screaming?            2
                        2
       wind             3    is
                        3    Why
                        3
                                screaming 4    in-the-willows
                                     is   4    the
                                          4
                        5
       wind             5    screaming?
                        5    Why
                                          6
                                          6
                                     is   6    the
                        7    in-the-willows
                        7
       wind             7    screaming
```

```
                                        at-the-foot-of   8   the-high-level
                                                         8   Listen!
                                                         8
9   bridge?
9
9   Listen!
              Listen!   1
                        1   Everybody
                        1
                        2
              listen!   2
                        2
                 The    3   mountains
                        3
                        3
                                           are    4   screaming.
                                                  4
                                                  4
              Listen!   5
                        5
                        5
                                                  6
                                                  6
                                           The    6   ice
                        7
                        7
                   in   7   the
                                                  8
                                                  8
                                       valleys    8   of
9
9
9   death
                        1   Listen!
                        1
                  is    1   screaming.
                        2   They
                        2   They
                        2   They
                 are    3   screaming
                 are    3   screaming
                 are    3   screaming,
                                                  4
                                                  4
                                       quietly    4   screaming!
                        5
                Thou    5   art
                        5

                                                           . . .

                                                                      341
```

```
                                            He    6   is
                                    screaming.   6
                                                 6
           screaming   7
                 She   7   is
                       7
                                                     8
                                       screaming.    8
                                              We     8   are
   9
   9
   9   screaming.
             Listen.  1   We
                      1
                      1
                are   2   screaming.
                      2   What
                      2
                      3
                 is   3   everyone
                      3
                                      Why    4   are
                                 screaming   4   for?
                                             4
              they    5   screaming?
                      5   Why
                      5
                                                6
                                         art    6   thou
                                                6   Why
                      7
       screaming?     7
                is    7   he
                                         I    8   can't
                                              8
                                 screaming?   8
  9   hear
  9
  9
              myself  1   screaming
                      1
                      1
              can't   2   you
                      2
                      2
```

342

```
                    stop    3   that
                            3   Why
                            3
                                        screaming?  4
                                        can't       4   she
                                                    4
                            5
                    do      5   something
                            5
                                                    6
                                        about       6   that
                                                    6   Can't
                            7   Can't
                    baby    7   of
                    she     7   make
                                        she         8   make
                                        yours       8
                                        it          8   shut
9   it
9
9   up?
                    shut    1   up?
                            1
                            1   Let's
                            2
                            2
                    turn    2   on
                            3
                            3
                    the     3   TV
                                                    4   Let's
                                                    4   Let's
                                        and         4   have
                    turn    5   on
                    turn    5   on
                    a       5   good
                                        the         6   TV
                                        the         6   TV
                                        scream!     6
                    and     7   have
                    and     7   have
                    and     7   have
                                        a           8   good
                                        a           8   good
                                        a           8   goody
                                                        . . .
```

```
9   scream!
9   scream!
9   goody
                    1
                    1
         goody      1    goody
                    2
                    2
         goody      2    good
         scream!    3
         scream!    3
         scream!    3
                                        The    4    TV
                                               4    Turn
                                               4
              is    5    screaming.
            down    5    the
                    5
                                                      6
                                          volume      6
                                             The      6    TV
                         7    No,
                         7
              is         7    screaming
                                         don't        8    turn
                                                      8
                                                      8    the
9   down
9
9   TV
              the   1    volume.
                    1
              is    1    screaming:
                    2    You
                    2
             you    2    stink.
             are    3    unsuccessful.
                    3    You
                    3
                                                      4
                                            have      4    elected
                                                      4
                    5
             the    5    wrong
                    5
```

```
                                              6
                                     party.   6
                                     Thou     6    usest
                        7
                        7
              the       7    wrong
                                     Thou     8    art
                                              8
                                     mouth    8    wash.
9   wearing
9   You
9
              the       1    wrong
              have      1    bought
                        1
          sanitary      2    napkins.
              the       2    wrong
                        2    Thou
                        3
              car.      3
              hast      3    purchased
                                              4
                                              4
                                     the      4    wrong
              5   You
              5
      Lotto   5   ticket.
                                     have     6    acquired
                                              6
                                              6
              the       7    wrong
                        7
                        7    the
                                educational   8    background . . .
                                              8    the
                                     wrong    8    kindergarten,
9
9   wrong
9
                        1
              degree    1    from
                        1
                        2
              the       2    wrong
                        2    you
                        3
          faculty       3    of
              live      3    in
                                                            . . .
```

```
                                            4
                                  the       4    wrong
                                            4    the
                        5    you
            university  5
            wrong       5    province
                                  speak     6    the
                                            6
                                            6
            wrong       7    language
            you         7    refused
                        7
                                            8
                                  to        8    support
                                            8
9
9   abortion
9
                        1
            on          1    demand
                        1
            that's      2    why
                        2
                        2    that's
            we're       3    here
                        3
            why         3    we're
                                            4    Listen!
                                            4
                                  here      4
                        5
            the         5    wind
                        5
                                            6
                                  is        6    screaming
                                            6    in
            of          7    the
            screaming   7    screaming
            the         7    rafters
                                  high      8    level
                                            8
                                  of        8    the
9   bridge
9
9   bridge
```

```
                    1
        scream      1
                    1   scream
                    2
                    2   scream
        softly      2   river
        scream      3   softly
                    3   scream
                    3
                                    softly  4   river
                                            4   scream
                                            4
                    5
        softly      5   river
                    5   till
                                            6
                                            6
                                        I   6   end
                    7
                    7   scream
        my          7   song
                                            8
                                    softly  8   river
                                            8   bill
9
9
9   bisset
                    1
                    1   ten
            is      1   screaming
                    2
        million     2   jews
                    2   us
                    3
        russians    3   vietnamese
                    3
                                            4   chinese
                                germans     4
                                            4   peoples
                    5
                    5   africans
        indians     5
                                are         6   screaming
                            screaming       6
                                            6   screaming
                                                    . . .
```

for	7	us				
screaming	7	dona				
nobis	7	screaming				
		screaming	8	pacem		
			8	screaming		
		pacem	8	pacem		

9
9
9 screaming

re burying an ex-prime minister

```
              the train  1  which brings
               the body  2  of the
          honourable mr  3  john diefenbaker
                                       home to  4  saskatchewan
           whistlestops  5  its way
                                        to this  6  conclusion.
        History beloved  7  by orphans, widows and
                            disappointed heirs, buries  8  its mistakes,
9  fakes
            them out as  1  heroes.
                  Lilac  2  is not miraculously
          blooming out  3  of season
                                         in the  4  dooryards,
             O captain,  5  my captain,
                                    we flatter  6  our hearts
          with claptrap,  7  waiting
                              for the opening  8  of parliament
9  a house
                divided  1  against itself
               and us,  2  which seeks
          the Marvelous  3  Deception, to
                                      lead us  4  to a
               world we  5  never really
                                      lived in  6  and
          mostly hated,  7  the constituency
                                        of the  8  dead man
9  we
         bury. O captain  1  my captain,
              the brass  2  bands,
            my captain,  3  are blaring out
                                          the  4  battle hymn
        of the republic.  5  History weeps
                                    temporary  6  tears
            for the tv,  7  blows its dirty
                                         nose  8  off stage,
9  waits
                for us  1  to make
                up our  2  minds, smiles,
            patronizes  3  our passionate
                                 indecisions.  4  Old man,
           we rejected  5  you decisively and
                                      totally.  6  Because
             you have  7  willed us your
                                      death O  8  captain my
9  captain
                                                         . . .
```

	shall we	1	repent my captain		
	the unusual	2	clarity of mind		
	with which	3	we saw through		
			you and your	4	attempt
	to equate	5	your canada		
			with	6	ours?
	Now	7	our canada		
			rises	8	up
9	before					
	us to avenge	1	itself		
	on us and	2	ours, its		
	economics the	3	economics		
			of the	4	wasteland
	of the	5	private sector		
			the wasteland	6	of the
	cultural	7	sector, the		
			wasteland	8	of the
9	poverty					
	sector,	1	its politics consisting		
	of a	2	phantasmagoria ravaged		
	by ten	3	provincial monsters		
			and an	4	enormous
	dragon, in	5	mortal combat with		
			each other.	6	This
	canada is	7	real, its		
			nightmares	8	real.
9	O					
	my captain,	1	the fearful trip		
	begun, you	2	shall not reach		
	out a dead	3	hand to		
			touch us	4	O my
	captain,	5	my captain,		
			we bury	6	you here
	with your	7	sham dreams		
			and	8	battle
9	song					

re the birth of a son, christopher ex catherine to scott taylor, january 6, 1982

		births	1	are			
		like	2	aphorisms			
		which	3	are			
					lanterns	4	lighting
		foot	5	and			
					path	6	but
		not	7	the			
					way	8	to
9	go:						
		we	1	carry			
		them	2	against			
		the	3	darkness			
					and	4	see
		the	5	darkness			
					grow;	6	and
		every	7	evil			
					till	8	the
9	world						
		is	1	done.			
		May	2	this			
		son's	3	mankind			
					lantern	4	us
		to	5	the			
					doom	6	of
		doom,	7	which			
					is	8	kingdom
9	come						
		every	1	day			
		now	2	from			
		this	3	day,			
					his	4	day
		her	5	day			
					your	6	day,
		theirs	7	and			
					my	8	day,
9	on						

what roy kiyooka told me

		the	**1**	living				
		detail	**2**	as				
					it	**3**	details	
		the	**4**	life				
		of	**5**	— write				
					about	**6**	this	
		is	**7**	what				
					roy	**8**	kiyooka	
9	told							
		me	**1**	until				
		moments	**2**	become				
					monuments	**3**	and	
		monuments	**4**	momentous?				
		but	**5**	so				
					much	**6**	life	
		marries	**7**	a				
					cemetery	**8**	without	
9	names							
		or	**1**	stories				
		or	**2**	heady				
					brass	**3**	therein	
		to	**4**	squander				
		empires	**5**	families				
					children	**6**	to	
		live-it-up	**7**	as				
					flies	**8**	the	
9	whooping-crane							
		namelessly	**1**	after				
		whooping-crane	**2**	a				
					million	**3**	times	
		north	**4**	a				
		million	**5**	times				
					south	**6**	not	
		without	**7**	ecstasy				
					or	**8**	self	
9	majesty							

re the aboriginal protestant

john	**1**	milton's			
god-the-father	**2**	(as			
the	**3**	text-books			
		point	**4**	out)	
falls	**5**	face			
		down	**6**	sublimely	
flat	**7**	for			
		most	**8**	wasp	
9 readers					
especially	**1**	white			
american	**2**	sentimental			
positivists	**3**	on			
		both	**4**	sides	
of	**5**	the			
		border	**6**	but	
his	**7**	great			
		wasp-angel's	**8**	something	
9 else,					
really	**1**	terrific,			
out-of-this-world,	**2**	the			
first	**3**	protestant,			
		basp	**4**	and	
yasp	**5**	as			
		well	**6**	as	
wasp,	**7**	the			
		source	**8**	and	
9 strength					
of	**1**	every			
protest	**2**	movement,			
observed,	**3**	anatomized			
		into,	**4**	and	
the	**5**	fragments			
		re-uttered	**6**	in	
that	**7**	baroque			
		miltonic	**8**	style	
9 seeking					
to	**1**	expose			
the	**2**	verbal			
process	**3**	by			
		which	**4**	supreme	
created	**5**	intelligence			
		cd	**6**	blind	
itself	**7**	word-by-word			
		to	**8**	the	
9 truth —					

. . .

```
                     milton   1   had
                        the   2   english
                     tongue   3   to
                                          work    4   with
                       easy   5   to
                                         match    6   to
                       most   7   depravity,
                                           and    8   he
9   latinized
                         it   1   to
                       give   2   his
                      white   3   anglo
                                         saxon    4   wasp
                       that   5   international
                                     authority    6   the
                       buzz   7   buzz
                                          buzz    8   of
9   english
                   (perfect   1   for
                   ordinary   2   business
                       use)   3   lacks
                                           but    4   milton
                    couldn't  5   give
                                           his    6   aboriginal
                 wasp-angel   7   an
                                      opponent    8   worthy
9   of
                       such   1   a
                   creation.  2   Milton
                     needed   3   an
                                     adversary    4   creativity —
                          a   5   suitable
                                god-the-father,   6   Milton
                     hadn't   7   the
                                         style    8   for
9   that
```

re shakespeare on husbandry

		the	1	greatness		
		of	2	shakespeare		
		is	3	founded		
				on	4	the
		banality	5	of		
				machiavelli	6	or
		rather	7	on		
				the	8	pervasion
9	of					
	elizabethan		1	banality		
		by	2	machiavellian		
	naturalism		3	etymologically		
				banality	4	is
		the	5	small		
				talk	6	of
		the	7	corn-mill		
				shakespeare	8	converts
9	elizabethan					
	corn-mill		1	chatter		
		into	2	machiavellian		
	discourse		3	in		
				action	4	and
		pursues	5	it		
				relentlessly	6	until
		it	7	contradicts		
				itself	8	in
9	agony					
		p.s.	1	iago		
		iagoes	2	cleopatra		
		caesar	3	caesars		
				prince	4	hamlet
	antichrist's		5	lancastrian		
				lieutenants	6	both
		named	7	henry		
				henry	8	it
9	in					
		a	1	plantagenet		
		garden	2	and		
		pick	3	at		
				caterpillars	4	edmund
	edmunds		5	desdemona's		
				othello	6	king
		claudius	7	gertrudes		
				cordelia	8	and
9	lear					

. . .

	is	**1** wasted		
	husbandry's	**2** nothing		
	nothings	**3** nothing		
		the	**4**	feathered
	mouth	**5** dumbed		
		and	**6**	silent
	his	**7** commentators		
		god's	**8**	cruel
9 mouth				
	debate	**1** his		
	existence	**2** decide		
	resume	**3** banalities		
		of	**4**	sentiment
	note	**5** that		
		the	**6**	thick
	rotundity	**7** of		
		the	**8**	world
9 grows				
	round	**1** again		
	the	**2** organs		
	of	**3** conception		
		wet	**4**	advise
	we	**5** are		
		to	**6**	see
	its	**7** justice		
		through	**8**	birth's
9 tears				

re mcluhan to diane bessai

	Harold	1	innis		
	is	2	always		
	a	3	structuralist,		
			wrote	4	marshall
	mcluhan	5	to		
			diane	6	bessai,
	(letter	7	of		
			october	8	third,
9	MCMLXXIV)				
	always	1	keeping		
	his	2	eye		
	on	3	the		
			law	4	of
	situation,	5	always		
			studying	6	the
	figure	7	in		
			its	8	interplay
9	with				
	its	1	ground		
	always	2	watching		
	closely	3	the		
			changing	4	structures
	of	5	each		
			situation	6	as
	its	7	components		
			interface	8	with
9	each				
	other.	1	But		
	when	2	the		
	simple	3	painting		
			complicates,	4	and
	ground	5	becomes		
			figure	6	and
	articulates	7	the		
			archetypes	8	of
9	the				
	unconscious	1	which		
	is	2	the		
	darkness	3	created		
			by	4	the
	prime	5	figure		
			as	6	it
	stutters	7	into		
			cliché,	8	the
9	situation				

. . .

implodes	1	into			
a	2	black			
hole	3	which			
			admits	4	no
law.	5	La			
			bocca	6	mi
baciò	7	tutto			
			tremante,	8	breathless

9 unbreathing

Francesca	1	tells			
fourteenth	2	century			
dante,	3	terrified			
			kissed	4	my
terrified	5	mouth,			
			she	6	says
revealing	7	herself			
			incompletely.	8	remorsed

9 dante

falls,	1	fainting			
away,	2	as			
the	3	soft			
			mouth	4	of
lust	5	hardens			
			into	6	hell's
lion	7	mouths			
			lion	8	mouth

9 accusations

there is no penance due to innocence/deconstructed

		1	bodies,				
		1	village,				
	blasted;	2					
		2	tribal,				
		3	after				
	of;	3					
				the	4	bombfall;	
					4	the	
		5					
	global	5	village				
					6	Peace	
				of.	6		
	on,	7	in,				
	flowers,	7	flowers				
					8	the	
				be	8	unto	
9	earth						
9	you						
	the rose	1	isn't,				
		1	o rose				
		2	love, kids, mankind,				
	of	2	lima				
	isn't, aren't	3					
	o	3	rose				
				rose,	4	kids, love,	
					4	of	
	mankind isn't,	5	aren't				
	lima	5	pray				
				mankind,	6	love, kids,	
				for	6	us	
	rose	7					
		7	rose				
				pray	8	for	
				of	8	lima	
9	us						
9							

saga hwaet ic hatte

Riddle for irma

I	**1**	am			
like	**2**	shaped			
a	**3**	hole			
			I	**4**	am
			in	**5**	raised
joy	**6**	my			
is	**7**	kiss			
			paradise	**8**	my

9 embrace

boggles	**1**	the			
I	**2**	mind.			
feed	**3**	the			
			liar	**4**	with
			I	**5**	words.
stab	**6**	my			
friend	**7**	best			
			to	**8**	death:

9 saga-hwaet-ic-hatte?

riddle

	Women	**1**	kiss				
	claws	**2**	my				
	more	**3**	hungrily				
				than	**4**	the	
				of	**5**	lips	
				men.	**6**	I	
	bread	**7**	take				
				rarely,	**8**	never	
9	soup						
	or	**1**	wine.				
	am	**2**	I				
	the	**3**	farmers				
				and	**4**	horses'	
5	friend.						
	Travelers	**1**	lose				
	way	**2**	their				
	on	**3**	dusty				
				unfamiliar	**4**	roads	
				of	**5**	because	
				me.	**6**	The	
	soul	**7**	of				
				tunefulness	**8**	when	
9	exalted						
	to	**1**	the				
	sky,	**2**	I				
	thunder	**3**	unleash				
				and	**4**	rain:	
5	saga hwaet ic hatte						

riddle

I	1	am
like	2	shaped
a	3	maelström
do	4	but
not	5	move.
key	6	The
to	7	my
resides	8	being
9 in		
my	1	walls
doors	2	without
which	3	accept
refuse.	4	and
5 Enter		
if	1	you
into	2	choose
my	3	domicile
unlock	4	and
its	5	secret
and	6	places
decipher	7	their
mirrors	8	stone
9 which		
are	1	a
but	2	net
not	3	for
fish	4	and . . .
5 saga hwaet ic hatte		

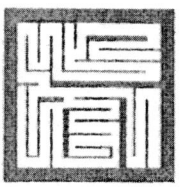

riddle for irma sommerfeld

	I	**1**	wash			
	the	**2**	in			
	sea	**3**	but			
				never	**4**	become
				I	**5**	clean
				save	**6**	many
	drowning.	**7**	from			
				I	**8**	teach
9	the					
	birds	**1**	to			
	down	**2**	write			
	their	**3**	names.			
				show	**4**	I
				the	**5**	authorities
				men	**6**	where
	have	**7**	left			
				bones.	**8**	their
9	Harms					
	enter	**1**	by			
	though	**2**	me			
	I	**3**	harm			
				one:	**4**	no

5 saga hwaet ic hatte

riddle

```
                    I  1  travel
              through  2  much
                space  3  across
                          mountains  4  and
                               from  5  seas
                               city  6  to
               along  7  city,
                           country  8  roads,
9  places
               where  1  cows
                milk  2  give
                 and  3  pigs
                            greedy  4  their
5  lives,
              flesh,  1  skins;
              across  2  and
                time  3  too,
                             years  4  from
                past  5  to
                               end  6  the
                  of  7  time.
                          Merchants  8  bankers
9  statesmen
                   I  1  count
                  my  2  among
             friends,  3  lovers,
                                    4  lawyers,
5  perfume-makers,
             bishops,  1  popes;
                  of  2  peasants
                rank  3  and
                                of  4  people
                 the  5  ordinary
                               and  6  kind;
            children  7  too
                               for  8  old
9  their
               cribs.  1  I
                with  2  begin
         endearments;  3  end
                         with love:  4  sometimes
5  saga hwaet ic hatte
```

riddle/lamp

		I	1	grow
		in	2	bright
		darkness	3	and
		at	4	darken
		noon.	5	I
		men	6	lead
		to	7	bed
		gallop	8	and
9	under			
		the	1	moon.
		dismiss	2	I
		the	3	stars
		be	4	to
5	dismissed			
		by	1	the
		A	2	sun.
		mouthful	3	of
		kills	4	breath
		me	5	yet
		dance	6	I
		in	7	the
		I	8	wind.
9	call			
		dead	1	generations
		of	2	men
		to	3	instruct
		living	4	ones;
5	saga hwaet ic hatte			

riddle

I am	1	a
	2	pig
with the	3	head
of a king,	4	a
	5	sheep
with caesar's	6	roman nose;
roll	7	like a
	8	wheel;
9 the colour		
of blood;	1	but
	2	shaped
to fit	3	into
	4	a man's
5 hand,		
I make	1	love
to a woman's	2	fingers.
Because	3	I am
a bottle of	4	wine,
but again	5	and
	6	again
an apple	7	tree,
	8	a coffin
9 for the pope,		
a tub	1	of
	2	lard,
a bolt	3	of cloth,
	4	
5 and		
at my	1	pleasure
since I am	2	a
	3	lawyer,
a hangman's rope:	4	hence,
philosophers say,	5	since
I can command	6	so
much of	7	good,
I am	8	to be
9 called		
a window	1	into
what speech is	2	and
the word.	3	I
am buried	4	to be
5 resurrected		

though I	1	rise
up to be	2	put
	3	down
and armies die	4	for
me; no	5	man
is richer than	6	me
yet	7	in my
shadow sits naked	8	abject
9 poverty.		
Best of	1	all,
	2	I
like to	3	exchange
myself for myself	4	and
5 from being		
the hallucinating	1	moon
become the	2	becrowded sun,
or forsake	3	those
	4	rays
for a	5	painted
paper parasol,	6	with such
barter abolishing	7	barter.
I delight when	8	the
9 rich		
waste me.	1	The
	2	poor
cherish me	3	only
to remain the	4	poor:
5 saga hwaet ic hatte		

370

Saga hwaet ic hatte/I.L.

	my initials	1	suggest
	vision and the	2	death
	penalty. my	3	vowels
	are full	4	of wrath.
	my ego	5	exceeds
	my fame.	6	my voice
	is a	7	sea
	of words broken	8	on
9	rocks		
	which have	1	drowned
	my kind and	2	kin.
	a mouthful	3	of
	wind is	4	my friend
5	men		
	laugh	1	at me
	because my	2	penis
	is longer	3	than
	my nose	4	or tongue;
	yet	5	I have
	no shame	6	my face
	I think	7	is
	more beautifully	8	fierce than
9	the		
	sun and	1	perhaps
	it is.	2	can women
	be wrong?	3	in
	their	4	thighs I turn
	into three	5	sorts
	of moon,	6	the moon
	of hunger,	7	the
	moon of resentment	8	which
9	I		
	feed, the	1	moon
	of satisfaction	2	I am their
	god and	3	beget
	jesus for their	4	son:
5	saga hwaet ic hatte		

riddle for Irma/pearl

		women	1	love	
		because	2	me	
		I	3	teach	
		how	4	them	
		to	5	weep	
		able	6	tears	
		to	7	make	
		put	8	men	
9	away				
		or	1	draw	
		swords.	2	their	
		I	3	am	
		beautiful	4	more	
5	than				
		anything	1	which	
		out	2	falls	
		of	3	their	
		so	4	eyes	
		they	5	hang	
		at	6	me	
		the	7	corners	
		their	8	of	
9	ears				
		to	1	outface	
		the	2	looks	
		attract	3	they	
		with	4	theirs:	
5	saga hwaet ic hatte				

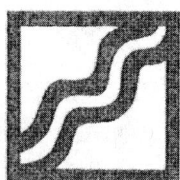

riddle for irma sommerfeld

I	**1**	have
long	**2**	a
nose	**3**	and
tooth.	**4**	one
dares	**5**	None
laugh	**6**	at
me.	**7**	I
well	**8**	dine
9 and		
entertain	**1**	the
but	**2**	pope
never	**3**	drink
milk	**4**	wine
5 or		
soup.	**1**	Artists
wood	**2**	in
and	**3**	paint
count	**4**	I
among	**5**	my
	6	friends,
also	**7**	surgeons,
merchants	**8**	and
9 in		
bread	**1**	and
When	**2**	meat.
I	**3**	fight
bleed	**4**	I
blood	**5**	not
own . . .	**6**	my
7 saga hwaet ic hatte		

riddle

I	1	eat
clothing	2	and
steel	3	plates,
grass	4	and
hair;	5	never
grow	6	fat
but	7	admit
over-eating	8	dulls

9 me.

Hegel	1	delights
me	2	and
explains	3	me
to	4	myself,
myself	5	as
thesis	6	to
myself.	7	myself
as	8	antithesis

9 to

myself,	1	synthesis
to	2	both.
Because	3	my
soul	4	is
doubleness	5	women
love	6	me
and	7	I
fit	8	into

9 their

hand	1	divide
their	2	clothes
mouth	3	their
finger	4	tips:

5 saga hwaet ic hatte

riddle

they	1	say				
they	2	have				
stood	3	Nietzsche				
			on	4	his	
head	5	by				
			threatening	6	to	
total	7	the				
			entire	8	hemisphere	

9 and more —

insecticide	1	to				
cure	2	insect				
and	3	bitch				
			of	4	irritation	
and	5	irritant				
			from	6	bite	
to	7	itch;				
			but	8	can	

9 we

be	1	sure?				
They	2	say				
he	3	gives				
			voice	4	to	
west	5	east				
			south	6	north	
northwest	7	the				
			deep	8	south	

9 the

coast	1	of				
ireland,	2	the				
irate	3	streets				
			of	4	montreal . . .	
corruption	5	still				
			speaks	6	out	
here	7	there				
			and	8	everywhere	

9 naming

in	1	hype-heaped				
up	2	hip-hip-hooray				
the	3	moon's				
			surnames	4	its	
garbage	5	voice				
			stinking	6	loud	
and	7	appellant				
			plain	8	the	

9 scratched-up

```
                    surface   1   of
                        the   2   thieving
                    digital   3   side
                                           of   4   the
                      brain;  5   has
                                      no more   6   use
                        for   7   my
                                  moon-shapes   8   without
9   form
                       than   1   the
                       moon   2   has
                        for   3   the
                                       earth's  4   brainsick
                      dung.   5   John
                                        Glenn   6   would-be
                  astronaut   7   president
                                       ditches  8   his
9   hopes
                         in   1   travesty
                         of   2   mine.
                        Say   3   what
                                            I   4   am
                    called.   5   Not
                                          who   6   I
                         am.  7   Christ,
                                            I   8   look
9   to
                       some   1   new
                  nietzsche   2   to
                       lead   3   me
                                        home,   4   coal-oil
                         to   5   wash out
                                          the   6   marrow
                    paintpot  7   of
                                           my   8   bone:
9   say what I am called, saga hwaet ic hatte
```

riddle

		my	1	people
		are	2	of
		the	3	sea,
		their	4	women
		array	5	me
		in	6	clothes
		of	7	surpassing
		beauty	8	and
9	cost			
		but	1	at
		work	2	with
		my	3	menfolk
		I	4	wear
5	strong			
		simple	1	hard-wearing
		stuffs	2	tailored
		simply	3	to
		answer	4	my
		moods	5	which
		are	6	both
		subtle	7	and
		plain,	8	bending,
9	pliant,			
		masterful	1	to
		restrain,	2	obedient
		to	3	win,
		longer	4	than
5	most,			
		small	1	to
		consult	2	with.
		I	3	box
		well,	4	but
		wrestling	5	is
		my	6	best
		sport.	7	Dogs
		bark	8	when
9	I			
		whistle,	1	horses
		scatter	2	when
		I	3	yell
		and	4	scream.
5	I			

```
                    hawk    1   at
                     the    2   wind,
                   dance    3   in
                     the    4   rain,
                   sleep    5   in
                     the    6   sun.
                      My    7   people
                     the    8   simple
9   ones
                   think    1   that
                      to    2   know
                      me    3   is
                     the    4   height
5   of
                 wisdom:    1   I
                      am    2   a
                  ladder    3   and
                       a    4   death.
                       I    5   follow
                     the    6   dead
                    into    7   the
                darkness    8   and
9   return
                   alone    1   to
                     the    2   tolling
                      of    3   a
                    bell    4   without
5   me
                     how    1   could
                      my    2   people
                    have    3   mapped
                     the    4   sea
                     and    5   discovered
                     the    6   world?
7   saga hwaet ic hatte
```

Riddle

```
          a   1   hammer
     shaped  2   me,
       like  3   a
      rope.  4   I
       tell  5   the
       time, 6   measure
      space, 7   ships
      drown  8   when
9  I
      break. 1   Women
         me  2   wear
      round  3   their
         to  4   necks
5  mock
         at  1   their
     slaves, 2   men
       wear  3   me
         in  4   their
     minds,  5   kings
        and  6   philosophers;
        and  7   my
    dancing  8   partners
9  are
    parrots, 1   apes,
          I  2   bears.
        can  3   reverse
      story  4   Sampson's
5  for
        the  1   saint
        who  2   feared
         my  3   part
         in  4   the
       law.  5   I
       rule  6   the
       work  7   of
   millions, 8   bake
9  them
      their  1   bread.
      close  2   I
        the  3   mouths
   harbours. 4   of
5  I,
```

	a	1	fellow
	of	2	small
	arithmetic,	3	much
	consequence,	4	many
	connections.	5	Read
	my	6	story
	in	7	myself
	as	8	sequel
9	to		
	myself,	1	reaching
	some	2	say
	from	3	heaven
	earth:	4	to
5	saga hwaet ic hatte		

riddle

```
         Hers is   1   the
   beauty of the   2   japanese
    sword, which   3   balances
     cutting and   4   holding, blade and
       scabbard,   5   edge and
       hilt, the   6   severing and the
         severed   7   flesh. Hers
          is the   8   beauty of the
9  sword-blade
       shaped by   1   the
        wound it   2   shapes, said eternity,
      and added,   3   which
    the scabbard   4   forgives and the
5  hilt
         forgets.  1   Someone had
    complained to  2   eternity about an
         arete so  3   absolute
    it blinded the 4   eyes of
        the mind,  5   and
         made the  6   soldier-senses shudder.
          What if  7   that
    someone were   8   me — who can
9  hope
         to beat   1   eternity
      at samurai   2   sword-play? against
        an arete   3   which
      I answered   4   fits into the
       hand like   5   a
      death that   6   cannot be squeezed
          out of   7   shape
       but held,   8   cuts like a
9  whisper,
          writes   1   into flesh
    its namesake   2   scarred with corporeal
         blood. If 3   any,
       forget my   4   wrongs, recall whose
5  this arete was
```

Riddle for IS/saga hwaet ic hatte

```
                When    1   I
               empty    2   am
                   I    3   am
                when    4   full
                dark    5   I
                 the    6   outshine
                moon    7   the
                ages    8   wind
9   me
                when    1   it
                   I    2   drops
                  am    3   a
           beautiful    4   woman
5   unwrinkled...
                when    1   the
              leaves    2   moon
                   I    3   come
               never    4   but
                stay    5   long;
                  it    6   when
               rains    7   I
            return...   8   I
9   am
                 the    1   prisoner
                 the    2   of
                 god    3   that
          imprison...   4   I
5   saga hwaet ic hatte
```

Riddle

```
              I have    1   a
               little   2   mouth and a
          hard heart,   3   small
                            brains to do    4   one
      thing extremely   5   well.
                            I speak in      6   words
                   of   7   one syllable
                            evil to him     8   I
9    eye,
         and what       1   I
      say is evil,      2   let
     no man take        3   my
                            speech to       4   heart.
5    I
              have a    1   sharp
        and deadly eye  2   to
           lead my      3   brothers
                            and their friends  4   to
                hell,   5   for evil
                            is my profession   6   wherein
   I excel; whatever    7   of
                            good flows from    8   my
9    deeds,
           my intent    1   is
          only to do    2   evil
           wherever     3   I can,
                            very evil are   4   my
5    days
          and ways;     1   when
           I smile I    2   lie
     deceiving silence  3   for
                            what I say      4   I mean:
5    saga hwaet ic hatte
```

riddle/for robert kroetsch

```
              poems    1  are
              always   2  too
                long   3  or
                                    not    4  long
              enough   5  never
                                    the    6  right
              length   7  fit
                                    their  8  humanity
9  as ill
                  as   1  their
              poets'   2  grumbling
             moaning   3  whimpering
                                    or     4  bragging
                  do.  5  I
                                    make   6  no
           pretences.  7  My
                                    legs   8  exceed
9  pant-length
                 and   1  skirt.
                  My   2  shoulder
               humps   3  at
                                    my     4  shirt.
                  My   5  breasts
                                    broach 6  my
              blouse,  7  bones
                                    and    8  sex
9  bulge,
              growth   1  grieves
                  my   2  groin,
                  my   3  significant
                                    form.  4  I
              define   5  myself
                                    as     6  one
          protesting   7  definition.
                                    Female 8  beauty,
9  male
            nobility   1  escape
                  me   2  but
                   I   3  never
                                    go     4  wrong:
5  saga hwaet ic hatte
```

riddle

I am not	1	as tall
as a	2	tower
but I am taller	3	than
my master	4	and
any of his friends.	5	I
am bald,	6	so
never take off	7	my hat
to him	8	or
9 his.		
I protect my	1	master to
the best	2	of
my ability but I	3	am
not as	4	strong
5 as		
a castle or a	1	fortress;
on their	2	lawful
or military or	3	criminal occasions
thief, police,	4	army-detail are
able to overcome	5	me
to my	6	great
shame. I love my	7	mistress
dearly but	8	she
9 bothers		
me. I fear she	1	suspects
me of	2	being
an untidy dirty	3	smelly fellow.
I love	4	it
5 is		
true wine beer ale	1	strong spirits,
and every	2	sort
of food, soups and	3	roasts, pancakes
and sausages,	4	strong
cheeses and freshly	5	baked breads,
vegetables, pickles,	6	apples,
oranges, fried	7	fish, onions and
garlic.	8	Yet I
9 am		
not a glutton	1	without excuse
of festive	2	company,
whom my mistress	3	smiles at,
excuses, and	4	reserves for me
5 her		

```
                blame. Of course   1   I belch,
                      fart, reek   2   of
             grease of bed and     3   pot,
                       but that's  4   good
             living, she should    5   know that,
                       and not     6   rage
                  like a sullen    7   lioness at
                    each crumb     8   of
9    food
                I drop or speck    1   of
                         dust I    2   wear.
                    The cloud-     3   permitted sun turns
                       me into     4   a
5    lantern
             to point finger at    1   the
                      the chalk    2   numeral
              of day's desolate    3   midnight, noon.
                  The menstrual    4   moon
              lays her mad and     5   immaddening
                     cheek on      6   my
                 tacit feet and    7   carries a
                    coal-miner's   8   candle into
9    the
                 black bosom of    1   my dreams,
                        of the     2   son-harassed
                    clytemnestra   3   harasser of
                   troy-harassing  4   agamemnon
5    king
                 of fire and sin.  1   Yet
                          I am     2   not
                  wholly unholy,   3   though not as
                       holy as     4   a
                   church, filled  5   with the concentrated
                      majesty of   6   the
              rex tremendae and    7   mysterium tremens
                        of the     8   presence
9    of the
                deus absconditus,  1   yet, if to
                   reveal myself   2   clearly,
                 what I am, is to  3   be
                      sacred, a    4   certain
5    metaphysical
```

	health of being	1	is mine
	in a	2	world
	where ruin strives	3	with ruin
	and each	4	being
	strives to become	5	ruined being.
	My people	6	who
	ancestor me with	7	their descendants,
	those who	8	call
9	me		
	theirs and	1	landlord it over
	my dilapidation	2	discover
	in my disclosure	3	of myself
	their being	4	also,
5	their		
	strange dark	1	fatal double deconstructing
	form. A	2	pendulum
	counts their tides	3	of day
	sex the	4	predation
	of food, the	5	innerings and
	outerings of	6	soul
	mind animal sense	7	and flesh,
	a swinging	8	corpse
9	caught		
	in an escapement	1	from the
	hangman's hands	2	no
	punishment can	3	define. Mine also;
	I have	4	a
5	double		
	shape my subject	1	creatures tenant
	masters servant	2	makers
	huddle cuddle	3	under and call
	theirs. I	4	extend
	both their wild	5	body and
	their magical	6	body,
	like them,	7	subtend the world
	to my	8	will
9	and		
	inner it to my	1	appetites.
	Sometimes they	2	find
	bosomed in me	3	the white
	innocence of	4	beasts.
	Say how this may	5	be.
	Saga hwaet	6	ic
7	hatte		

Riddle

```
                    I    1   clothe
                  the    2   cold
                  and    3   naked
                                    in     4   raiment
              brighter   5   than
                                    the    6   exorbitant
                 moon.   7   Yet
                                    only   8   the
9   tall
                  and    1   greatest
                 wear    2   what
                    I    3   tailor
                                    with   4   consummate
5   precision
                  all    1   year
                 long:   2   the
                 poor    3   must
                                    have   4   their
                 whim    5   and
                                    show   6   their
            nakedness    7   to
                                    the    8   sun.
9   Children
                 exalt   1   me
                  into   2   a
                  king   3   when
                                    I      4   play
                 with    5   them.
                                 Wolves    6   hug
                   me    7   when
                                    I      8   help
9   them
                 hunt    1   food.
                    I    2   drown
                  men    3   and
                                   their   4   towns:
5   saga hwaet ic hatte
```

riddle for irma sommerfeld

		winter	1	ages			
		in	2	me,			
					summer	3	I
					young	4	grow
		only	5	to			
		cut	6	be			
					down:	7	my
					cause	8	formal
9	is						
		the	1	rain,			
		sun	2	the			
					my	3	efficient,
					earth	4	the
		my	5	material			
		I	6	cause.			
					make	7	a
					bed,	8	good
9	though						
		I	1	eat			
		I	2	dung			
					am	3	fat
					tall:	4	not
5	saga hwaet ic hatte						

riddle

	trees	1	grass	
	deer	2	birds	
	and	3	foxes	
	me	4	delight	
	I	5	raise	
	men	6	up	
	and	7	cast	
	down	8	them	
9	as			
	the	1	sun	
	and	2	rises	
	falls	3	I	
	homage	4	pay	
5	to			
	the	1	sea.	
	am	2	I	
	swallowed	3	up	
	a	4	by	
	gray	5	monster	
	to	6	only	
	be	7	disgorged	
	The	8	again.	
9	moon			
	makes	1	love	
	me.	2	to	
	I	3	help	
	wars:	4	wage	
5	saga hwaet ic hatte			

riddle

		I	**1**	speak	
		without	**2**	a	
		or	**3**	tongue	
		breath	**4**	yet	
		I	**5**	what	
		say	**6**	goes	
		and	**7**	on	
		on	**8**	and	
9	on.				
		A	**1**	few	
		are	**2**	steps	
		all	**3**	I	
		but	**4**	know	
5	with				
		these	**1**	few	
		can	**2**	I	
		outline	**3**	all	
		the	**4**	that	
		day	**5**	can	
		or	**6**	witness	
		the	**7**	darkness	
		night	**8**	of	
9	define.				
		Great	**1**	queens,	
		of	**2**	harlots	
		state,	**3**	consorts	
		majesty	**4**	of	
5	beyond				
		esteem,	**1**	reach	
		for	**2**	out	
		me,	**3**	and	
		take	**4**	I	
		them	**5**	by	
		hand;	**6**	the	
		they	**7**	love	
		I	**8**	what	
9	can				
		do,	**1**	for	
		little	**2**	a	
		drink.	**3**	At	
		table	**4**	my	
5	sit				

		priests,	1	bishops,
		even	2	cardinals,
		the	3	pope;
		I	4	and
		heap	5	up
		for	6	food
		them,	7	though
		eat	8	I
9	nothing.			
		Behind	1	thick
		walls	2	stone
		prisoners	3	call
		me	4	on
5	to			
		plead	1	their
		fates	2	mangled
		and	3	lives
		them;	4	for
		I	5	have
		in	6	it
		my	7	power
		make	8	to
9	injustice			
		stink	1	to
		end	2	the
		of	3	time.
		teach	4	I
5	poets			
		who	1	sleep
		beds	2	on
		of	3	straw
		their	4	what
		hearts	5	think,
		what	6	and
		wit	7	grieves
		vain.	8	in
9	A child's			
		hand	1	breaks
		yet	2	me,
		I	3	make,
		unmake	4	kings:
5	saga hwaet ic hatte			

riddle/creed

```
    Saga hwaet ic    1    hatte
                     1    say
                     2    and the first
 what I am called    2
         clue is:    3
                     3    a saint named
                                                    4    and
                                       me.          4
   the second clue   5    is:
                     5
                                                    6
                          johann sebastian bach set 6    me to music
                     7
    as if I was the  7    voice of god shouting
                                                    8    and the third
                          out in the dark, god doesn't  8    exist.
9    clue is:
9    I am what the church believes in,
                     1    and the fourth clue
         not god.    1
              is:    2
  the pre-christian  2    jews knew nothing
                     3    and the fifth clue
          of me.     3
                                             is:    4
                          I taught the medieval monk 4   how to
                     5
   worship the pagan 5    gods. I taught
                                                    6
                          dante how to translate his 6   virgil. I taught
                     7
     reborn plato, I 7    taught resurrected
                                                    8
                          aristotle how to read their  8  book of job,
9
9    their song of songs,
                     1
   their penitential 1    psalms, apocalypse,
                     2
      their matthew  2    mark luke and john,
                     3    and the sixth clue
      their pauline  3    epistles.
                                             is:    4
                                                    4    I am the
                     5
    greatest of all  5    christian inventions,
                                                    6    except
                            except love.            6
```

```
                     love?   7
              if love is a   7    christian invention.
                                           amour courtois?   8
                                      yes, amour courtois which   8   travesties
    9
    9    the love of the condescending god
                                     1
              for his created        1    creature; agape;
                                     2
              amor dei. I made       2    disbelief possible
                                     3
              as the nightshirt      3    of belief. I come
                                                                 4
                                          between the bridegroom and the   4   bride,
                                     5    and the seventh clue
              contra naturam.        5
                                                              is:    6
                                                I am the radical of anti-   6   semitism;
                                     7
              I bring men to         7    science and the nuclear
                                                                         8
                                                 holocaust via the new    8   technology.
    9
    9    I sponsor the hermeneutics of disbelief
                                     1    and the eighth clue
              and nihilism.          1
                            is:      2
              all mankind            2    becomes through me
                                     3
              as of necessity        3    christian; I teach
                                                                 4
                                          the believing arabs how to    4   carry my
                                     5
              partisan, the          5    weaponry of disbelief.
                                                                         6
                                          I come between christian and    6   christian,
                                     7    and the ninth clue
              contra rationem.       7
                                                              is?    8
                                          I have changed mankind's mind    8   from
    9
    9    despair of salvation
                                     1
              to the tranvestite     1    probabilities
                                     2    and the tenth clue
              of damnation.          2
                            is?      3
              The tenth clue         3    goes back to my
```

```
                                                      4
                          origin. Lord, I believe,    4   cried out
                     5
  saint augustine,   5   and added, inspired
                                                      6   and the
                         by me, help thou my unbelief. 6
  eleventh clue?     7
  If you believe in  7   me, I am born of
                                                      8
                         of compromise, how can you   8   believe
9
9   in christ, who admits no compromise?
    and the twelfth  1   clue is?
                     1   Disbelief in me
                     2
    brings the world 2   to the brink of the
                     3
    new damnation,   3   ecological
                                                      4   and the
                                       extinction.    4
    thirteenth clue is: 5
                     5   there is no
                                                      6
                         thirteenth clue: saga hwaet  6   ic hatte,
7
7   say what I am called.
```

Riddle/kettle

```
                          I    1   am
                      thing    2   a
                         of    3   various
                                        copper,    4   shapes,
                       iron    5   steel,
                                        aluminum,  6   tin.
                       love    7   I
                                        to         8   feed
9   on
                       fish,   1   never
                     spirits   2   drink
                         or    3   wine,
                                        beer,      4   ale.
                          I    5   Sometimes
                                        take       6   soup.
                       live    7   I
                                        on         8   tea.
9   Tea-grannies
                       love    1   me,
                       sing    2   I
                        and    3   play
                                        the        4   flute
                     sweetly   5   for
                                        But        6   them.
                       when    7   I
                                        my         8   blow
9   top
                          I    1   provide
                   metaphor    2   a
                        for    3   anger.
                                        call       4   Silly-pots
5   me
                       black   1   though
                       soul    2   my
                         is    3   clear
                                        crystal:   4   as
5   saga hwaet ic hatte
```

Sonnet x 3 for luisa valenzuela

```
                          1    discarded
                          1
                          1
              though I    2    am
                          2
                          2    the
                   and    3    though neither
                          3    grass
                 great    3    the
                                   life nor death    4    greatly
                                        abhors me,   4    little flies
                                           almost    4    great
            concern me,   5    I anoint
               love me    5    and I feed
                   the    5    not so great
                                   the face of the   6    dead
                                   both grass and    6    flies
                                   paint out their   6    names
           bullfighter    7
               not out    7    of
              fraction    7    and fragment
                                      virgins and    8    whores
                                  absolute charity   8    an
                                   for times to come 8    to read
9    popes and saints
9    hypocrisy
9    in my pigment
            artists and   1    charlatans patronize
               I think,   1    and above all
     the inhumanity of    1    man and womankind
              me, I am    2    the god
              I detest    2    bunkum
                 is my    2    humanitas,
     of my own atheism,   3    I am for real, I
          lies claptrap   3    nonsense
       come on now, don't 3    say
                                    call a spade a   4    spade,
                                          humbug    4    sham
                                  I am not a semantic 4   archetype
5    say what I'm called
5
5    saga hwaet ic hatte
```

Sonnet for three voices

		1	in depraved		
		1			
		1	deprived		
	may	**2**	of		
	of	**2**	danced-out		
	disenchanted	**2**	insolvent		
	woman's love	**3**	the		
	may-poles	**3**	a		
	praeternaturally	**3**	bankrupt		
			bitter-sweet cure	**4**	corrupted
			whip whose crack from	**4**	solstice
				4	
	into a regress	**5**	of cares		
	to solstice	**5**	spills		
		5			
			I saw	**6**	the
			solace into the wound it	**6**	bites at,
			and with their	**6**	bones
	tiger's face	**7**	as		
	lacerates with	**7**	kisses to persuade		
	he counts his	**7**			
			a mask of god	**8**	whose
			with suave dissuasions,	**8**	silk
			teeth	**8**	
9	eye				
9	extensions				
9					
	looks out	**1**	at		
	of the primal milk	**1**			
	then	**1**	I saw what		
	us	**2**	from an animal		
	the faces of the	**2**	animals are		
	it seizes and he	**2**	sees		
	wilderness, at B.	**3**	Russell's c. robin,		
	ghosts, christ's,	**3**	his		
		3	I who		
			einstein a little old man,	**4**	an eye
				4	
			saw	**4**	this,
5	without a nose, ears, fingers, tongue				
5					
5	saga hwaet ic hatte				

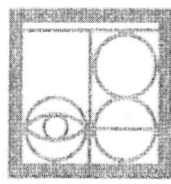

398

Sonnet


```
                              1   since in
            puling            1
                              1
          a net he            2   he hopes
                              2   resentments
                              2   and
          to catch            3   the
         exacerbate           3   his
                to            3   the naughty
                                               wind       4
                                            tangled       4   soul
                                              world       4   exnumerate
                              5   small change
                              5
               his            5   countless o
                                      finds woman's      6   changeling
                                                         6   where
                                      tacit unangled yet 6
          in her bed          7   and
                              7
                              7
                                         plot wet with her   8   size
                                         his lot is daughtered 8   in darkness
                                                         8   hard
9   of tears
9   to death
9   hard hard are
not his: chimneys             1   of smoke
                              1   joyless
the ropes to know             1   and pull
      solicit coals           2   to
       and evil his           2   unimagined
                              2
      flame and fire          3   his
       days, his words        3   if
                              3   say
                                         life and shredded shroud   4   his love
                                              known, unknown        4
                                              who is this to        4   cry
5   his fame
5
5   saga hwaet ic hatte
```

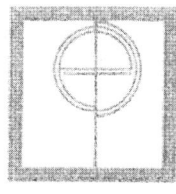

Sonnet

```
                   tears'  1   acid
                           1   peruse
                   acrid   1   smoke's tall
                    rain   2   boils dry
             these prawns  2   for I
            chimneys swim  2   here
        my fish-bowl che   3
                    sell   3   sucker bait
                           3   the bay street
                               soft-bellied nightmares nag   4   my
                                  my dreams for the millions 4   who dream
                                  bailiff pins laurels on my 4   doors
         raspberry glazes  5   legless wonders
         of making millions, 5 culturally bankrupt
           pretty mary lou 5   amalgamates with
                               I cut off their legs, freud   6   knows I am
                                   I go into bay-leafed      6   receivership
                                             barbara         6
               lecherous   7
          the news I botch 7
                           7   in david halton's
                               knowlton nash I
                               think of me, says one, as     8   the supreme
                               mouth becomes a sack of       8   tombstones
                               ablate as butterflies         8   scientists

9   and ultimate
9   belike
9
extension of man,    1   a spider caught
a dwarfish wasp,     1   I ladle out my
into the third       1   ronnie
in its own cobweb    2   communications
honey from sea to    2   sea, wisped out
                     2
is my message, the   3   medium my substance
in a vast heavily    3   subsidized
                     3
                               if you can, say who  4   I am
                                         nightshirt 4
                                                    4
5
5
5   saga hwaet ic hatte
```

sonnet x 3

```
portrait              1    of
                      1
                      1    dominus non
        myself        2    as
                      2    my father
    sum dignus        2
           the        3    bastard of
    is a dead         3    heron
                      3    my
                                          kent    4    my feet
                                    honk hanc    4    hoc
                                       mother    4    a corpse
    shuddering        5    my mind
       dominus        5    dominus
    worth forty       5    thousand
                           changing within me, under    6    me
                                     hawking a sea      6    of
                                            sparrows    6
     only lately      7    I have many
        sorrows       7    dominus
                      7
                              misgivings suspicions    8
                                     non sum dignus    8    things
                                    dominus dominus    8    non
9   circles
9   otherwise I fear may
9   sum dignus
       inner, lines   1    extend into
   have been quite    1    otherwise
                      1    portrait
      technologies    2    thinking I think
       portrait of    2    myself
        of myself     2    as linear
      I shall think   3    myself,
       as a circular  3    animal
     man, dominus,    3    dominus, lord,
                                       outer, utter     4    myself
                                       hwaet, hwaet     4    hwaet
                             lord, I am not worth very  4    much
5   away
5
5   saga hwaet ic hatte
```

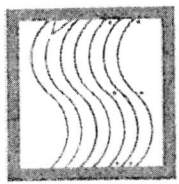

haiku times june twenty-third/84

```
                         the   1
                               1   history
                       heron   2
                        is a   2   catastrophe
                               3   fishing
                        yes?   3
                                         on the lip   4
                                                all   4   the
  5   of the
  5   parts
                  tide which   6
                               6   of which
                                         creeps into   7   the lagoon
                                       are catastrophes  7   dark
            under the reach   8
                               8   of
                               8   dark
  9   dark
  9   the storm
                         the   1
                               1   natural
                       heron   2   is
                       forms   2   are
                    an haiku   3   an
                               3   obsessions
                                          obsessive   4   emblem
                                          modalities  4   of a
  5   that
  5   madness
                                              sticks  6   in the
                                                 the  6   clever
          throat and cannot   7
                ones have a   7   be
                               7   word
                                       swallowed down  8   or vomited
                                                 for  8   namely
  9   up
  9   nature
                               1   Porteus's
                        beak   1   flash
             electric powers   2   advancing
               of the heron   2   on
              in unison on us  3   and the
                         the   3   lip
                                               onus   4   upon
                                                 of  4   the
  5   us
  5   tide
```

re ezra pound

```
            poems are   1   lighthouses
         with bell and  2   horn
                                    to teach     3   the
          sea wind fog  4   which
                                    way to       5   turn
        round coasts of 6   sand
                                    and rock     7   inspired
                                    by the sun   8   and
9   moon
            When the    1   bell
        went mute and   2   foghorn
                                    dumb and     3   day
         was eaten up   4   by
                                    night and    5   storm,
        this light house 6  keeper
                                    threw himself 7  into
                                    his lantern's flame 8 to
9   tell
           absconding   1   god how
        much both world 2   and
                                    god went     3   wrong.
           But god it   4   seems
                                    didn't care  5   and
                                    left         6   him
                for     7   a
                                    beacon       8   burning
9   there
```

Diana Rigg

```
    la belle dame sans      1     merci
                            1     portrait of
                            1
                            2
   her ladyship with        2     the steel blue eyes
                            2     still,
                            3
                            3
       from the blur        3     machine
                                  la belle dame sans    4    merci
                                                        4
                                                        4    jerk-art
                            5
                            5
             portrait       5     of cornwall's wife
                                                        6    close-up,
                                                        6
                                  with the cornflower   6    blue steel eyes
       from the blur        7     machine
                            7     ezra pound's
                            7
                                                        8    clues
                                  lady of the vortex,   8    portrait of
                                                        8
9    diana rigg in iron filings
9    la belle dame sans merci
9
        from the blur       1     machine, re adorno's
   la belle dame sans       1     merci
                            1
          paradox of        2     domination by the
       the amusing mrs.     2     peel's amazing
       the fingers and      2     faces
                                  subjugated, upstaging  3   lear
                                           stepdaughter  3   la belle dame
                                     of corporate power  3
       and olivier, dea     4     ex machina
        breath, from the    4     blur machine
   la belle dame sans       4     merci
5
5    sans merci
5    la belle dame sans merci
```

404

Sonnet x 3 *(for Jack Shadbolt, Archipenko, BJ)*

```
                         1    O
        uneclipsed       1
                         1
             moon        2    O
                         2    cloud-scattering
                         2
    newfoundland         3    fixed
    sky-detergent        3
            stark        3    stands the
                   ever-changing unchanging    4    moon
                              wall-scaling    4    claustrophobic
                                    mother    4    sorrowing
                         5
                         5
         the d. of       5    devonshire is a
                                              6
                                              6    but I will
                         gentleman-lunatic    6    worth many
                         7
            paint        7    you a scene worth
   paintings, mouldy     7    giottos, well-hung
                                              8    raconteur
                              all of them:    8    Push
                         bacons, plush picassos    8
9    raton laveur,
9    those
9
              cry        1    'I
           frayed        1    hands towards
            saint        1    archipenko's ans.
         invented        2    the hole
   the ragged unholy     2    skies
       re yr henry       2    moore
          in 1914'       3
         question        3
                         3
                                   for I am   4    blind
                                              4    dolorosa
                                   dolorosa   4
5
5    gloster
5
```

poe deconstructed

```
            plock plock   1   plock
                          1
                          1   plock
                          2
                          2
                  plock   2
                          3
                          3
            plock plock   3   plock
                                                   plock   4   plock
                                                           4   thy
                                                   plock   4
                          5   plock
             haiku face,  5   the grandeur that
                          5
                                                   plock   6
                              was blame, helen the glory   6   that was
                                                           6   plock
                  plock   7
          grief a broken  7   pot cup broken door
                          7   plock
                                                   plock   8
                              hinge a tree beating against 8   a wall a
                                                           8   plock
9
9   bullet
9
            plock plock   1
         buried in a spade 1  the scent of female
                          1   plock plock
            plock plock   2
         piss a pulse drum 2  clocked on blood
                          2   plock plock
                          3
          splashed brick  3   rain washes clean of
            plock plock   3
                                                           4
                              sign and scum, the plock     4   plock plock
                                                           4
                          5   plock plock
          of this goes on, 5  helen thy lumpen-
            plock plock   5
                                                           6   plock plock
                              aztec lamp a vocal stone     6   a corpse
                                            plock plock    6
                          7
         wipes squeaky-   7   clean the floor, but
                          7
```

```
                                              8
                              the plock of this goes on,  8   death
                                              8   plock
9  plock
9  cannot
9
                       1  plock plock plock
   keep his cool,     1  death talks, ghosts
   plock plock plock  1
                       2  plock plock plock
   haunt the christ-  2  less crossroads, squaws
   plock plock plock  2
                       3  plock plock plock
   shake their broken 3  fingers at the sun, the
   plock plock plock  3
                                              4   plock
                              brilliantined colonel in his  4   widowed
                                      plock plock plock   4
                       5  plock
   niched fuck-you    5  country, his eyeballs
   plock              5
                                              6   plock
                              pushed into his ears, hears,  6   I hear him
                                              plock  6
                       7  plock
   calling out, I     7  hear, ah, helen, the
   plock              7
                                              8
                              owlshit-bullshit re the  8   president and
                                              8
9
9  congress
9
   plock plock plock  1
   doesn't explain    1  away the weapons and
                       1  plock plock plock
   plock plock plock  2
   the wages spent in 2  support of hell, their
                       2  plock
   plock              3
   damned lies damn   3  the damned, the painted
                       3  plock
                                              4
                              saints throw up their hands,  4   their
                                              plock  4
   plock plock        5  plock
   tragic bliss       5  crumbles into dung, the
                       5
```

			plock	**6**	
		uterus of history retroverts	**6**	into an
				6	plock
	plock plock	**7**	plock		
	alphabet of horns,	**7**	chicken scratch, swine		
		7			
				8	
		snout and tusk, herring plock,	**8**	thy face a
			8	
9					
9	vowel				
9					

polyphème

```
        infamous, nor    1   famous I
              am not,    2   polyfamous
     I am, polyfamous    3   is my
                                       name,    4   I am
      the all-successful    5   one eye, one
                                      ear, one    6   bum,
           one stone for    7   propagation, who
                                   needs two    8   let
9   her
           try what I with    1   one can do.
                   I have    2   a
           sister with one    3   breast, one tooth,
                                     one door    4   like
            the fowl of the    5   air
                                  for water,    6   or
       bread and wine, or    7   flesh of male
                                    to love    8   or
9   leave
                 her by — a    1   hatchway that
                   so high    2   above
          her one terrible    3   knee that none
                                    nor man    4   nor
         god can reach to,    5   to deflower her
                                    there, to    6   mix
             his sweat with    7   her chastity and
                               dishonour her    8   thereby.
9   She
         (since I am the    1   all-successful
                      one)    2   as my
         opposite succeeds    3   in nothing, is
                                an absolute    4   failure
        as a woman. Those    5   who think I am
                             made monstrous    6   by
           success, and ugly,    7   are ravished by
                                  the beauty    8   of
9   my
            sister's failure:    1   her one success,
                     as my    2   one
              failure is the    3   ugliness in me of
                        the successfulness    4   they
5   applaud
```

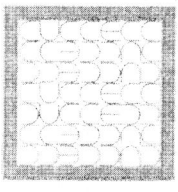

On receiving R. Lowell's Notebook/June 25:84

	Lowell saying	1	the same song
	over and over	2	again I
	don't balk at. If	3	the
	heron cd become	4	not-heron,
	if the white-ended	5	eagle
	cd swap beaks	6	with the
	oyster-catcher.	7	This is what
	Lowell does. The	8	sonnet becomes
9	someone else's, crow drinks salt,		
	wets its claw in	1	the
	avaricious tide	2	flux and reflux,
	the monotonous	3	pathos of one
	obsession performs	4	the same pathos,
5	the miracle, Lowell becomes Lowell		
	saying the same	1	Lowell over
	and over again in	2	a
	sweat-shirt	3	stenciled in blood
	'nessus', it is the	4	because,
	it is the because,	5	my
	soul. With a new	6	beak
	to out-honk	7	heracles consumed
	by love: a silly	8	father's
9	for a silly girl's, Deianira's,		
	outwitted by a	1	dead four
	footed beast's.	2	some doubt Sophocles
	thought the gods	3	were burnt
	out men. Burnt	4	out Lowell
5	knew no other use for fire		

riddle/for jack pecover

those 1 who say
they love 2 me
mistake me 3 for
my shadow 4 which
is realer 5 than I
am (so they think) 6 and
the god 7 of
this world. 8 They
9 say
I belong 1 elsewhere,
in the stars, 2 perhaps,
or outside 3 of time
in eternity with 4 the
angels of 5 heaven,
or with the 6 fairies
men 7 call up
in their minds 8 to
9 abrogate
the dark 1 deeds
which 2 make up
the matter of fact 3 substance
of their 4 lives.
So I 5 must
content myself 6 with
this strangest 7 of
all loves, 8 that is,
9 hatred
of my 1 antithesis
and even 2 *that*
as opposite 3 as
the yardstick 4 to
the cloth 5 or
its calibration 6 to
the 7 stick measuring
wood and 8 stuff:
9 saga hwaet ic hatte

riddle/statue of liberty

I
berdiaev wd
of me

1 wonder what
2 have made
3 who
  thought that the 4 ürgruund
of being 5 was
  freedom, in which free 6 enterprise
dominion of 7 being's beginnings
  evil had its origin and 8 primal
9 root and foot.
France was 1 my
mother (o ma 2 mère
ma mère), 3 marie-antoinette
  my grandmother, les 4 bourbons
my kin; 5 but
  the new world is 6 my
home, since who 7 knows
  when; and I speak their 8 foreign
9 tongue who crowd
in millions 1 around
about my knees 2 of
bronze like 3 insects
  as if an ants' nest 4 were
my womb. 5 I
  am their dream, sometimes 6 I
dream they are 7 a new
  breed of men, dreaming 8 nightmares
9 of their own,
dream within 1 dream.
Sunrise is full 2 of
birds' wings, 3 cries,
  beak-slash of song, 4 I
wake, and ache, 5 know-it-all
  wakefulness of day tells 6 me
I cannot die 7 but must
  live on, until the life 8 support
9 systems go wrong,
in a 1 brass
coma, my arm 2 raised
in a 3 compulsive
  gesture; extinction my end. 4 Say
5 who I am.

riddle

```
              poets hate  1  me
        beating on their  2  tin drum,
                 I think,  3  better
          than I know how  4  to.
                     yes  5  I am
          waspish, hard to  6  pin down,
              sorrowful of  7  scorn,
          scornful of sorrow;  8  contemptuous of
9  soul,
            words, common  1  sense,
           the five senses,  2  and their
                  lusts of  3  skin.
         women lust after  4  my nakedness
5  when
                     I in  1  travesty
           exchange clothes  2  with them, dancing
                 to their  3  flute
                and tune.  4  I sweeten their
              breath with  5  the
              idea of sin.  6  my virtues
              not without  7  number
       contrist me into an  8  absurd
9  singularity
            of substance,  1  hallucination
             or sham, the  2  umbilical's I
                yam that  3  I
          yam. Though I am  4  thoughtful
5  to
              a multitude  1  of
        gods, I am atheist  2  to
             the prophet  3  of
             none or one.  4  pluralism's my
                song and  5  creed.
             philosophers  6  mistrust me, and I
                 them. my  7  sex
          shivers between  8  woman and man.
9  I am
                a lonely  1  madman
       in an ancient house.  2  though
                 you can  3  say
        what I am called,  4  you
5  can't say what I am
```

riddle

I have a
twisted wit weighted to perceive
as inherently natural
nature's misfeature, supported by a
hunchback skeleton, a
crooked but an aspiring flame.
Nature-in-herself is unnatural,
is the law of nature.
War
is my half-sister.
A magnificent jewess was her
mother, mine a
cunning little greek, our shared
father, a pre-christian god.
She
is beautiful and
terrible, swinging her sword, and
shouting out her
german battle-cry, I pursue peace
by other means.
This is a semantic fraud,
and very characteristic.
Do not believe it, she
will
lie in your
teeth. Her name rhymes with
whore from carus
latin which means dear, and
and very dear
she
proves to some.
Her breasts are soft smoky
bronze, voluptuous, warm-blooded,
but utterly without shame. She
is no blonde
woman fragment, no pastry-cook's nazi
tier-mädchen but a
black-haired half- goddess, dark of
complexion
all darkness within,
sensual beyond the concupiscence of
women and the
strength of men, demanding, taking
all, and giving
none.

She is	1	my
mistress and I	2	know her
will and	3	mind,
she is mine and	4	I
am hers,	5	carnally
and totally hers.	6	I have
uncovered her	7	nakedness
and she has	8	uncovered my
9 nakedness,		
and I	1	have
covered her	2	nakedness with mine.
She has	3	guided
my extremities, I	4	have whetted
hers into	5	an
6 absolute		
presupposition	1	with
two backs, to set	2	fire
to nature's	3	mouldy
straw, and blow	4	god's mind,
our father's,	5	which
is in heaven,	6	perhaps. I
pursue the	7	policies
of war in peace.	8	Of course
9 we		
discountenance	1	each other,
eye to eye. I	2	admire;
her aplomb,	3	let
her admire what	4	I in
peace have	5	done.
6 Let		
the american	1	indian
say I have not	2	put
him down.	3	Economics
is my business	4	name. War
gives me	5	a
free hand, an open	6	enemy
to fit	7	into
my prophylactic	8	plan. Say what
9 I am called.		

Index of titles and first lines

A cock pheasant 67
A Contempt for Dylan Thomas 13
A Curse of Dahlias 22
A hammer shaped me, like a rope 379
A Manifesto for Beast-Poetry 50
A Pome of hair 70
A thimbleful of oil/Will soak into the wick 100
A Valediction for the End of the Year 33
a vision of whooping cranes 263
after the snow fell 233
all pleasure whether of sex or food territory or roof 258
All their women's talk of monsters born 21
alle menschen mussen sterben 301
An Admiration for Dylan Thomas 12
An ant attempted to unpuzzle my bawl of wool 114
And Should She Ask 11
and sure as oft as women weep 255
answering john stuart mill 255
Antigone aux sales mains 164
Appear, O mother, was the perpetual cry 9
As seas leave water at the earth's wet lip 128
at eighteen the red youth from your mouth began/peeling 201
at five o'clock in the morning 154
at spences bridge 243
at the fourteenth station 284

Ballad of Mother and Son 40
Because they were dishonest 151
Because we were baffled 10
bessai topology 283
birthday lines 1965 200
births are like aphorisms 351
Blue chalk on brown wrapping 68
bodies, blasted 359
By the unwashed beach 14

Canticle of Darkness 29
concerning beautiful people 275
Construction, April, 1975, for four voices, 3 male, 1 female 305
Construction, May 1974 209
construction, untitled 211
construction with driftwoods 227
construction with herring bones/c. des harengs saurs 223
construction with horizontal columns/construction avec colombes mortes 213

contemplating the sole of her foot   155
Creation's Welshman walks behind his eyelids   12

deconstruction chez flahiff   336
demeter's tragic chicken   275
Dialogue between Jenny Blake and herself   101
Diana Rigg   404
discarded though I am   397
Do not begin loving   33

Emily Carr   43
Edvard Munch paints the High Level bridge   340
essay on castle mountain   234
Even the innocent Eye   96
evening of april twenty-third nineteen eighty one twenty two hundred
    hours CBC program to help battered wives   334
Eye can never know what goes on   82

fils conduisant son père à la mort   202
flamingo poem   88
For Anne, Who Brought Tulips   39
For the first Monday of my week   28
forward inlet quatsino sound forward harbour wellbore channel   260
From the Place on the Map   150

Gentlemen always/write bread and butter/letters   140
Ghosts   17
Girl's poem   68
good friday, 1970   170
Graveyard on a Cliff of White Sand   14
grey gulls in triangle of cloud fog sea   332

haiku times june twenty-third/84   402
Hanoi   171
Hanoi/is here we have only a few poems to defend/ourselves with   171
Harold innis is always a structuralist   357
he is screaming She is screaming   340
he just lay down and died   169
he stood in Venice on the bridge of sighs   198
He was an Irishman who sought   42
He who cuts off on a short stalk   22
Hell granted this—she given back to him   19
her intelligence english   247
Here is an image shaped with human warmth   23

Hers is the beauty of the japanese sword   381
hms warspite hms indefatigable hms inflexible   262
hosannah the ballad of born again space   280
how people become accomplices in their own subjugation   265

I am a pig with the head of a king   369
I am a thing of various shapes   396
I am not as tall as a tower   385
I am not ashamed, she said, but stood there   203
I am not over-voluptuous   74
I am shaped like a hole   363
I am shaped like a maelström   365
I am that coy Kore   110
I am that priceless virgin   69
I clothe the cold and naked   388
I complained to eternity about florence steed   249
I complained to eternity that however much I was haunted   268
I dreamt I was a sea-anemone   85
I drew a church   67
I drew a girl   66
I drew a tree   66
I drew at a hill of green   68
I don't ever risk drawing roses   66
I eat clothing and steel plates   374
I grow bright in darkness and darken at noon   368
I had a yellow finch   71
I have a little mouth and a hard heart   383
I have a long nose and one tooth   373
I have a twisted wit   414
I have an eye for these   67
I have made up my mind . . .   125
I, hopeless parrot-virgin   82
I, Jenny Blake,/an indifferent head of yellow hair   102
I, Jenny Blake, carry/in my unseeded unimportant womb   93
I, Jenny Blake, sit on my penitent bottom   75
I may see many honest nudes   124
I met a heron   88
I praise God's mankind in an old woman   25
I prepare my grave in quick sand   161
I recall myrna kostash   253
I saw a terrible green dragon   97
I see faces as if squeezed in a vice   132
I see through your limb and your filament   131

I seek the why's and wherefore's   77
I Shot a Trumpet into my Brain   147
I shot a trumpet into my brain   147
I speak without a tongue or breath   391
I take a pencil   81
I think of pauline boote as a squad of activist-angels   256
I travel much through space across mountains and seas   367
I turn about my eyes to the Ninishith hills   150
I wanted to write you a poem about the hanged Absalom   138
I was that girlish sort of thing that wore/Myself   79
I wash in the sea but never become clean   366
I will shut, said Shakespeare/The master-mistress up   95
I wish I were a Japanese woman   94
I wonder what berdiaev wd have made of me   412
I would have you think on the mystery of bears   57
I would love you as if passion had just begun   119
If god asked me to set a place to meet   242
If I could catch that sly pig of a Venus   77
If the dull substance of my thought   86
in depraved may of woman's love   398
In drawing/I lean upon a naked line   69
In English Two Hundred/King Lear twice a week thundered   96
In fast September   70
In my flesh this knowledge grows   81
In the Cemetery of the Sun   28
In this world of illusion on illusion   22
infamous nor famous I am not   409
Invocation   9
It was the simple/and all unknowing shepherds   31
It wasn't until I was nine or eight   76

Jenny Blake's child   68
Jenny Blake's epilogue to King Lear   88
Jenny Blake's ode on the cock pheasant   67
Jenny Blake's poem of windows   72
Jenny Blake's pome of a dragon   97
Jenny Blake's pome of experience   96
Jenny Blake's pome of the Japanese woman   94
Jenny Blake's pome of William Blake and the spinning jenny   86
Jenny Blake's sonnet of oil   100
Jenny Blake's Ulysses   99
john milton's god-the-father (as the text-books point out)   353
july fourteenth 1978 at 0827 hours portrait of mary hamilton   270

kayakyak, kayakyak,/cry the magpies   263
kyrie kyrie/blue jay/kyrie crying   278

la belle dame sans merci   404
la tête nouvelle de mimi mandel   245
Last night I dreamt Faustus hid in my powder-room   134
Last night I gave my/Nothing self   78
Laurentian Man   47
les colonels sont toujours très polis   276
Let, I said, the past dissolved be the past dissolved   112
Let these trumpets tongued with dust blow their magnificent/brief
    music   39
Letter to Dorothy Bazett   43
letter to García Lorca   154
letter to marian engel   295
Letters are hearses and this one brings   43
Like a harlot-woman she'll wear   76
Like Jonah in the green belly of the whale   43
Lines   95
Lines   102
Lines for Elsie Jack   22
Lines: I Praise God's Mankind in an Old Woman   25
Lines in my flesh   81
lines January 1971   162
lines january 1971   191
lines january 1972   203
lines january 1967   185
lines may 1st 1966   178
lines new year 1972   204
lines 1970   198
lines 1971   202
lines 1968   183
lines 1968   196
lines 1964   182
lines 1967   159
lines 1967   172
lines 1967   188
lines 1967   197
lines 1967   199
lines 1966   174
lines 1966   175
Lines of a maiden-ape of god   82
Lines of flesh and bones   74

Lines of glory   103
Lines of rape   79
Lines of seeing   82
Lines of thought   80
Lines on the English tongue   84
lines september 1969   189
lines spring 1969   180
lines summer 1967   161
lines winter 1970   181
lines winter 1971   166
Lines upon a naked line   69
Long is the night, none longer   18
Love Song   16
Love Song for Friday's Child   35
Love's finger/Shall never press/Its outrageous brass   102
Lowell saying the same song over and over again   410

mankind has three wishes   276
march twelfth 1977 I bought five tightly closed daffodils   264
meditation on the godfathers   273
meditations xmas evening 1979 at sixteen hundred odd hours a half-moon rising in the east   303
memo to sylvia vance   265
Mon dieu, if I keep quiet   87
my father he took me swimming on his back   261
my initials suggest vision and the death penalty   371
My mind I inherit from Adam   89
my people are of the sea   377
my wild body is a corpse   163

Never, till out of my thought   16
Night kindles me and calls to light my flower   5
1979 sixth of november edmonton at zero five five zero hours the moon a last night's guy fawkes day full moon   330
norman yates   280
Not so, not so, she cries—but now he's lit   21
november twenty-sixth nineteen seventy-seven at 0937 hours after the night's snow   233

O tree my mother   40
O uneclipsed moon   405
Of all paradoxes/The paradox the most cruel   94
Of conflagrant Troy tower the flaming stalk   11
Of course some of this verse is fake   107

Of Hendrickje as Bathsheba 23
Of human weakness, I jenny Blake 89
Of ordinary female headaches, sir, I wouldn't be that one 133
On receiving R. Lowell's Notebook/June 25:84 410
On the Water Plane 152
one reason for calling the well-known mountain castle mountain 234
one two three four five six seven eight nine 293
Orpheus and Eurydice 19

Pasiphae 21
past the anguish however great of the cross of wood 267
Perhaps I could love a scientist 120
Persephone's black husband, Pluto 95
Picasso and gertrude stein 337
Pitiful Adam mankind 75
plock plock plock 406
poe deconstructed 406
poem 1970 163
poem 1968 201
poem summer 1967 168
poems are always too long or not long enough 384
poems are lighthouses with bell and horn 403
poets hate me beating on their tin drum 413
polyphème 409
Pome for a dead soldier 66
Pome for Adam 75
Pome of a church 67
Pome of a girl 66
Pome of a girl 81
Pome of a wire bridegroom 78
pome of addition 93
Pome of autumn 70
pome of critics 91
Pome of cuckolds 76
Pome of darkness 73
pome of destroying oneself 89
Pome of drawing tigers 67
Pome of drawing water 68
Pome of emblems 71
Pome of fire 80
Pome of glory 73
Pome of grief 71
Pome of headlines 94
Pome of Helen of Troy 76

Pome of honour   72
Pome of keeping silence   87
Pome of King Lear   96
Pome of love's brass finger   102
Pome of maidenheads   69
Pome of maids of honour   77
pome of misconceptions   93
pome of my mind   89
Pome of not drawing roses   66
pome of not wanting even at this late date to go Jacobean   83
Pome of nothingness   79
Pome of rain   87
Pome of sand   85
Pome of shame   75
pome of stones   92
Pome of substance   86
Pome of the unicorn   78
Pome of Venus   77
Pome of waxwings   74
Pome of words   95
pome on figureheads   90
Portrait of a Woman   155
portrait of diane bessai qua gondola   283
portrait of fred flahiff meditating on deconstruction   336
portrait of my father eighty two   325
portrait of my mother aged ninety-two years   240
portrait of my mother the fox   240
portrait of myself aged seventeen   223
portrait of myself aged seventeen   251
portrait of myself as the bastard of kent   401
portrait of the artist during centennial year   185
pour moi, j'ai retiré mes pieds   162
Proserpina (1) The Flower   20
Proserpina (2) The Marriage with Death   20
Purple and red hyacinths   17
putting one environment around another   282

Rape me,/And the seven judges of Edmonton   79
re burying an ex-prime minister   349
re counting   293
re elizabeth the second of england as leader of the peoples of the commonwealth   268
re ezra pound   403
re hippolytus   329

re march 3, 1980 339
*re mario prizek and glenn gould's examination of the music of the
    1930s* 301
re mcluhan to diane bessai 357
re myrna kostash 253
re nino gramsci 258
re painting by numbers 325
re paula anderson and the colonization of women 247
re pauline boote, activist, ex-potter 256
re Phyllis Webb & Wilson's Bowl 320
re ponziopilatismo 264
re shakespeare on husbandry 355
re spences bridge 242
re swp who asks questions 303
re the aboriginal protestant 353
*re the birth of a son, christopher ex catherine to scott taylor, january 6,
    1982* 351
re the blue jays of april fifteenth 278
re the explosion at the power station 321
re the faces of doom every evening 267
re the haiku as analog methodology 270
re the names of harbours and mountains 260
re the names of mountains 262
re wife battery 334
re woody allen's annie hall 330
Remind you, that there was darkness in my heart 29
returning to square one 284
riddle 364
riddle 365
riddle 367
riddle 369
riddle 374
riddle 375
riddle 377
Riddle 379
riddle 381
Riddle 383
riddle 385
Riddle 388
riddle 390
riddle 391
riddle 413
riddle 414
riddle/creed 393

riddle for irma 363
riddle for irma/pearl 372
riddle for irma sommerfeld 366
riddle for irma sommerfeld 373
riddle for irma sommerfeld 389
Riddle for IS/*saga hwaet ic hatte* 382
riddle/for jack pecover 411
riddle/for robert kroetsch 384
riddle/kettle 396
riddle/lamp 368
riddle/statue of liberty 412

saga hwaet ic hatte and the first clue is 393
Saga hwaet ic hatte/I.L. 371
seigneur les lauriers sont coupables 273
Self-knowledge, said the Greek philosopher 6
self portrait 251
Sermon on Bears 57
17 ways of not looking at the face of margaret atwood on the dust/
    jacket of survival 211
Sharp is my eyesight as the needle I ply 5
she gave me an indigenous look 227
She in that iron hall, the home of shades 20
she shook her hair and said no 196
since in puling resentments 399
Sir father, in your Priam brow, will you 80
Sir, firm to the scaffold walks the sentenced woman 137
Sir, forgive me that/within me sang/an insignificant hatred 127
Sir, I am not that worn pantaloon 122
Sir, I and you know very well/this stone's blood 117
Sir—/I have one false nipple and one true one 116
Sir, my unthinking womb/Is full of will 103
Sir, of course I've heard of Clauswitz 136
Sir, of the everlasting bonfire 129
Sir, the anthropologist/flatters me this much 113
sir Thomas, stark green until he crept acurl 13
Sir, to cry bawl of wool 121
Sir touching us, that is 123
Sir, will you not eat this my poem? 130
Sir: with my brassiere and luck at the hook 115
Sir you are my abstract/drawer and architect of my form 118
. . . so it is necessary to train one's flesh 139
Some lost desperate adventurers 111
someone or other was out to hang a student, still 209

Song 83
Song for St. Lucy's Night 18
Sonnet 399
Sonnet 400
Sonnet for three voices 398
sonnet x 3 401
Sonnet x 3 (for Jack Shadbolt, Archipenko, BJ) 405
sonnet x 3 for luisa valenzuela 397
Sonnet with Ragged Edges: Lines 153
Suddenly everybody burst into tears 71

Taking off from nanaimo harbour 332
Tarquin 21
tears' acid rain 400
tereus tereus 337
Than hunger for money 73
That day came, and that night, and morning 83
The angels of the imagination howled 86
The barber chatters/His tongueless scissors 70
the belly of the dragon was made of boiler plate 197
the black mouth of the dog was full of quills 182
The Boy and the Shepherds 31
The Candle 5
the caves dripping milk and honey 188
the colonization of florence steed 249
the coming of robert creeley to vancouver in february 1962 213
The Departments of Barbed Wire 151
the dragons are climbing over the mantel piece 199
The equivocation of the fiend 18
the face of my father 152
the french bear 177
the greatness of shakespeare is founded on the banality of
     machiavelli 355
The haunted word/pinned to a tree 92
The hell of this English is 84
the heron fishing on the lip of the tide 402
the interrogation of 282
the invaders of Vietnam are prisoners 170
the invasion of Canada is over 189
the laughing voice of 246
the living detail as it details the life 352
the long cool seminars 174
the long sorrow files into my soul 168
the minister isn't as blind as all that 321

The Mirror   6
The nearly-living juniper shivers   80
the new starved face of mimi mandel   245
the offshore canadians   261
The Pearl   17
the radiant grief of the owners of so much/snow   160
The rain falls down in showers of nails   87
the results of a sense of outrage/so great   153
the sins of the fathers forgive the grandfathers   178
the sorrowful canadians   160
the sucked and hungry lioness   183
the suicide, 1966   169
the swearing in of pierre elliott trudeau   339
the sword dies slowly from age to age   204
the train which brings the body of the honourable mr john diefenbaker home   349
the water is ten thousand laminations of plexiglas/thick   181
the whalebone comb of love   191
The White Bird   10
the white pelican mts are covered with snow   166
The whiteness of the lamb   17
The Windy Bishop   26
their real essence is a tombstone   320
then nor/any day   35
There are seven hills   26
There are some men/who as poets are animals   50
There are windows in rags   72
There blossoms forever   83
There is a fatal propensity to love   126
There is a great deal of darkness   73
there is no penance due to innocence/deconstructed   359
There was an odor of magnificence   20
there will be no more money for you   159
These push through shattered seas   90
they flew across our borders at the speed/of light   172
they have turned the confluence   243
they inked in my intestines   164
they invented a new woman   295
they provided me with words harder than stone   180
they say they have stood Nietzsche on his head   375
things I've noticed about gail   246
This is my fiftieth letter   108
This poem is/deterrent obstacle   91
This river of wire, in which metal the human heart is drowned   135

This rowan tree stands fleshed with drops of blood 74
those who say they love me mistake me for my shadow 411
thou still unravished bride of quietness 200
Three days before my birthday 72
Three Riddles for Gillian Espinasse 5
Time 5
. . . to the bach. of wire 110
. . . to the bach. of wire 122
. . . to the bach. of wire 139
. . . to the bachelor of wire 107
. . . to the bachelor of wire 108
. . . to the bachelor of wire 109
. . . to the bachelor of wire 111
. . . to the bachelor of wire 112
. . . to the bachelor of wire 113
. . . to the bachelor of wire 114
. . . to the bachelor of wire 115
. . . to the bachelor of wire 116
. . . to the bachelor of wire 117
. . . to the bachelor of wire 118
. . . to the bachelor of wire 119
. . . to the bachelor of wire 120
. . . to the bachelor of wire 121
. . . to the bachelor of wire 123
. . . to the bachelor of wire 124
. . . to the bachelor of wire 125
. . . to the bachelor of wire 126
. . . to the bachelor of wire 127
. . . to the bachelor of wire 128
. . . to the bachelor of wire 129
. . . to the bachelor of wire 130
. . . to the bachelor of wire 131
. . . to the bachelor of wire 132
. . . to the bachelor of wire 133
. . . to the bachelor of wire 134
. . . to the bachelor of wire 135
. . . to the bachelor of wire 136
. . . to the bachelor of wire 137
. . . to the bachelor of wire 138
. . . to the bachelor of wire 140
To the Shadbolts with Six Quinces from Duncan 18
Today rose without any dawn 329
trees grass birds deer and foxes delight me 390

walt whitman to the dark tower came   305
We, the actors, have put on these roles and masks   88
Were I Jenny Blake, spinster   78
What bread and butter for this senseless thing?   101
what gorgeous graveflowers blossom at that throat   177
What more did they want?   175
what roy kiyooka told me   352
What you add up in poetry/Is an arithmetic   93
When I am empty I am full   382
When indefatigable God decided to make a new man, *homo
    Canadiensis*   47
When you sir (that is male mankind, sir)   109
winter ages me, in summer I grow young   389
women kiss my claws more hungrily than the lips of men   364
women love me because I teach them how to weep able tears   372

Yeats and Maud Gonne   42
You draw a vase to hold some flowers   68
You must if I don't use/Tennysonian blank verse excuse   99